JESUS *and the* POLITICS *of* ROMAN PALESTINE

CENTER AND LIBRARY FOR THE BIBLE AND SOCIAL JUSTICE SERIES

Laurel Dykstra and Ched Myers, editors
Liberating Biblical Study
Scholarship, Art, and Action in Honor of the Center and Library for the Bible
and Social Justice

Norman K. Gottwald
Social Justice and the Hebrew Bible
3 volumes

Elaine Enns and Ched Myers
Healing Haunted Histories
A Settler Discipleship of Decolonization

Richard A. Horsley
Jesus and the Politics of Roman Palestine

JESUS *and the*
POLITICS *of*
ROMAN
PALESTINE

Richard A. Horsley

CASCADE *Books* • Eugene, Oregon

JESUS AND THE POLITICS OF ROMAN PALESTINE
Revised with a New Preface

Center and Library for the Bible and Social Justice Series

Original hardback edition (2014) published by the University of South Carolina Press, Columbia, South Carolina 29208.

Cascade Books
An Imprint of Wipf and Stock Publishers
199 W. 8th Ave., Suite 3
Eugene, OR 97401

www.wipfandstock.com

PAPERBACK ISBN: 978-1-6667-0742-7

Cataloging-in-Publication Data:

Names: Horsley, Richard A., author.
Title: Jesus and the politics of Roman Palestine : revised with a new preface / Richard A. Horsley.
Description: Eugene, OR : Cascade Books, 2021. | Center and Library for the Bible and Social Justice Series. | Includes bibliographical references and index.
    Original hardback publication, 2014.
Identifiers: ISBN 978-1-6667-0742-7 (paperback).
Subjects: Jesus Christ—Historicity. | Palestine—History, to 135 AD. | Biblical healing.
Classification: BT303.2 H675 2021 (print).

Contents

Abbreviations

1QapGen	Genesis Apocryphon from Qumran
1QpHab	Commentary on Habakkuk from Qumran
1QS	Community Rule from Qumran
4Q159	Ordinances manuscript a from Qumran
4Q169	Commentary on Nahum from Qumran
4Q448	Apocryphal Psalm and Prayer from Qumran
4Q491	War Scroll manuscript a from Qumran (1QM)
4QFlor	Florilegium from Qumran
4QSam^b	Samuel manuscript b (4Q52) from Qumran
Ann.	Tacitus, *Annales*
Ant.	Josephus, *Antiquities of the Jews*
b.	Babylonian Talmud (Babli) tractates
Bell. Gall.	Julius Caesar, *Bellum gallicum*
Carm.	Horace, *Carmina*
CD	Damascus Document from the Cairo Genizah
Decl.	Quintilian, *Declamationes*
Ep.	Pliny, *Epistulae*
Ep.	Seneca, *Epistulae*
Ep. Barn.	Epistle of Barnabas
Geogr.	Strabo, *Geographica*
Ḥag.	Ḥagigah tractate
Hist.	Polybius, *History*
Jub.	Jubilees
KJV	King James Version of the Bible
m.	Mishnah tractates
Leg. Man.	Cicero, *Pro Legia manilia*
Life	Josephus, *The Life*
Mith.	Appian, *Mithradatic Wars*
NJB	New Jerusalem Bible

NRSV	New Revised Standard Version
Pes.	Pesaḥim tractate
Pomp.	Plutarch, *Pompeius*
Prov. cons.	Cicero, *De Provinciis Consularibus*
Q	Sayings Source Q
Sabb.	Sabbath tractate
T. Mos.	Testament of Moses
Verr.	Cicero, *In Verrem*
War	Josephus, *The Jewish War*
War Scroll	War Scroll from Qumran (1QM)
Yoma	Yoma tractate

Preface

The core chapters of this book are expansions of the 2010 Hall Lectures at the University of South Carolina and associated institutions. The overall theme of the Lectures was "Jesus and Empire." The three lectures were titled:

I. Jesus and the Politics of Roman Palestine

II. Jesus's Healing and Exorcism

III. Jesus and the New World (Dis)Order

Insofar as the Hall Lectures were delivered in different venues to somewhat different audiences, each lecture had to be semi-independent, without presupposing what was said in the other lectures. Yet they were interrelated, the first lecture setting the context for the second and third, and the second leading to the third. The revision and expansion of the Lectures here makes them more interdependent, particularly insofar as Lecture I (= chapter 2) lays out the historical context of Lectures II and III (chapters 4 and 5), as well as the other chapters.

Chapter 1 was written specifically for this volume. Insofar as new research in several related areas is challenging the standard assumptions of historical Jesus studies and the standard approach has come to a procedural dead-end, it is necessary to explore new possibilities that take the recent research into account. This chapter expands on some of the necessarily cursory explanations of my procedure in each of the Hall Lectures and adds important considerations that were too complex to deal with as preliminaries in the lectures.

Chapter 3 explores Roman imperial violence and Jesus's response to it, which were important aspects of the politics of Roman Palestine but required more focused discussion. Violence and Jesus's response are also issues debated long before serious attention was given to the political economic dynamics in the Roman imperial world. Recent books on Jesus, however, have almost avoided the subject. More critical and candid recent treatment of the brutal

Roman military practices by Roman historians, on the other hand, suggests that imperial violence may have been more of a factor in the context in which Jesus worked than previously recognized.

Chapter 6 explores Jesus's conflict with the scribes and Pharisees. Scribal "retainers" including the Pharisees continued to play an active role in the politics of Roman Palestine under the rule of Herod the Great and the high priestly aristocracy, contrary to the recently influential hypothesis that they had withdrawn from politics to emphasize piety. Recent books on the historical Jesus have almost avoided the conflict between Jesus and the Pharisees that is so prominent in the Gospel sources. This expansion of the Hall Lectures offers an opportunity for a provisional treatment that takes into account recent research on scribal roles and practices in second-temple Judea. The examination in this chapter is a provisional step toward a more critical, comprehensive, and wide-ranging investigation of the Pharisees and the Gospels' portrayal of Jesus's conflict with them.

Since crucifixion played a key role in the politics of Roman Palestine, it seemed not only appropriate but important to discuss the Roman crucifixion of Jesus, which is often not dealt with in books on the historical Jesus. Chapter 7 thus considers the crucifixion of Jesus in the historical context laid out in chapter 2 and in connection with Jesus's mission of renewal of the people in opposition to the rulers in chapters 3–6.

The sequence of the chapters hopefully provides a coherence of presentation. As with any historical investigation, it is important to begin, in chapter 1, with a critical examination of assumptions, procedures, and established discourse, and especially a critical consideration of the historical sources, the Gospels. Chapter 2 offers a broad survey of the politics of Roman Palestine and where and how Jesus was evidently engaged and implicated. This chapter thus lays out the broad historical context and considers the overall agenda of Jesus's mission. The ensuing chapters focus on more particular aspects of the context and particular aspects of Jesus's mission. Chapter 3 examines the imperial violence that in key ways determined the conditions of both the politics of Palestine and Jesus response. Chapter 4 attempts to find a less limiting way to understand the aspect of Jesus's mission most directly affected by the politics of Roman Palestine and especially the imperial violence, his healing of illness and exorcism of spirit-possession. Chapter 5 argues that Jesus's "teaching" coheres around his (Mosaic) covenantal renewal of disintegrating village communities, renewal emphasizing the economic cooperation and mutual assistance that was central to traditional Israelite covenantal teaching (torah). Chapter 6 examines the political-economic-religious position and role of scribes and Pharisees in the Judean temple-state and then attempts to discern the basis and substance of their conflict with Jesus that is so prominent in the Gospel sources. Chapter 7, finally, locates Jesus's crucifixion in the historical context outlined in chapter 2 and presents it as the "breakthrough" event that energized the movement Jesus had catalyzed and resulted in his becoming a historically significant figure.

Toward a More Comprehensive Understanding of Jesus-in-Interaction in Historical Context

Readers will find the assumptions, approach, analysis, and discourse in this volume to be different in many ways from what has been standard in investigation of the historical Jesus. For this I should deliver an apology, in the double sense that I indicate the interrelated ways that I am "out of step" in presenting "revisionist" history and that I attempt to explain what I am doing and why.

Coming from undergraduate study of history into New Testament studies and other divisions of theology in divinity school (in the 1960s) required considerable "reorientation." New Testament studies was a field of ostensibly historical study in which the sources were read and studied piecemeal, verse by verse, with emphasis on "word-study." Peoples, the state, movements, historical actors, events, and even what texts articulated were (and still are) dissolved into "-isms," such as "Judaism," "Hellenism," or "apocalypticism." The political-economic-religious divisions, dynamics, and diversity attested in ancient texts became invisible as they were dissolved into composite theological constructs and schemes. Focused on a scriptural attestation of doctrines, such as "christology" or "soteriology," New Testament scholars neglected the overall narratives of the Gospels and their contingent historical contexts as irrelevant for the ideas or prooftexts they were abstracting from texts or for the separate "pericopes," the scripture lessons for which they provided theological exegesis.

Jesus Christ had been understood in Christian theology as the unique revealer as well as the incarnation of God. Focus on the "historical Jesus" began in attempts to discern the human Jesus underneath the resurrected and exalted Lord and second person of the trinity. This meant going underneath the Gospels themselves, which were products of resurrection faith. Under the influence of Enlightenment reason that reduced reality to what is apprehendable by reason, the overall Gospel narratives that included resurrection and angels and miracles were dismissed as unreliable for knowing what Jesus the person had said and done. Given the Christian theological emphasis on teaching, reinforced by outsiders' suspicion of Christianity and the Gospels being irrational, the only defensible material in the Gospels as seemingly rational were Jesus's teachings. And insofar as the reading habits of scholars had been decisively shaped by the KJV and Lutherbibel translations of the Gospels codified and formatted into separate verses, Jesus's teachings appeared to have consisted of separate sayings. It was important to isolate the sayings as precious nuggets of what Jesus had taught. This focus on Jesus as an individual teacher of sayings to individual disciples who remembered them was still the focus in the surge of Jesus-books in the 1990s. Jesus-studies built largely on standard previous criticisms, especially form-criticism of text-fragments of which they believed the Gospels were mere collections. "Jesus scholars" worked mainly at refining the criteria by which the "authenticity" of the separate sayings of Jesus were evaluated.

The subfield of Jesus-studies, however, remained within the broader Christian theological scheme of Christian origins, the master-narrative of New Testament studies: Jesus was the unique revealer figure at the center of the origin of (early) Christianity as a more universal and spiritual religion from more parochial religion of ("late," or now rather early) Judaism. By the end of the nineteenth century a dichotomy emerged between the Jesus of liberal theology and the apocalyptic Jesus popularized by Albert Schweitzer, but in both Jesus was mainly a teacher who uttered sayings to disciples. Later, after his (supposed) resurrection, the disciples organized a religious community or movement (the "church") that quickly became predominantly Gentile. Jesus-studies still works within this broad scheme, including the most controlling synthetic constructs of the field, (early) Judaism and (early) Christianity. The sub-field of Jesus-studies accepts and perpetuates the modern western assumptions that Jesus was a religious figure dealing with ("Jewish") religious matters, such as "the Torah/ Law" and "the temple" and "synagogues" and "religious leaders." And Jesus-studies continues to work within other standard synthetic constructs of New Testament studies, such as "apocalypticism" and "miracles."[1]

Such assumptions and synthetic theological constructs, however, hide and prevent our recognition of the *political-economic divisions and dynamics (conflicts), diversity,* and complexities of the historical context of Jesus attested in the principal sources for the period. Accordingly, in my earlier investigations and critical analyses of the sources, I attempted to discern and describe those complexities. In the ancient world there was no separation between religion and the political-economic structure and relations. The Jerusalem temple headed by the high priests was not only a religious, but also the central political-economic institution of Judean society. The sources do not attest ("common" or "formative") Judaism, but *a temple-state subject to a sequence of empires*, somewhat analogous to the *colonial situation* of many African and Asian peoples in modern times. Roman imperial conquest and rule of Judea and Galilee was the general context of Jesus's mission. *The fundamental political-economic-religious division* was between the Romans and their client high priestly and Herodian rulers, on the one hand, and the Galilean and Judean people, on the other.

The Judean and Galilean people, moreover, formed *protests* and mounted *resistance* and even *revolts* against the Romans and their client high priestly and Herodian rulers. The wealthy Judean priest Flavius Josephus provides sharply hostile accounts of these popular protests and *movements* in his extensive histories, several of which *took distinctively Israelite forms* patterned after the formative stories of liberation from earlier rulers led by the figures of Moses or the young David. The occurrence of several such distinctively Israelite movements at the time of Jesus, moreover, suggests that a *popular Israelite tradition* similar to but also different from the more official Judean tradition embodied in written texts of "the law and the prophets" laid up in the temple. These would be analogous to what sociologists and anthropologists distinguish as the "little" and the "great" traditions of other agrarian societies. The Gospel stories of Jesus's mission fit into just this historical context of structural division, dynamics, and diversity of movements. As portrayed in the Gospels, Jesus even *resembles the popular prophets* who led movements that emerged immediately after his mission. The Gospel texts, moreover, are not simply collections of separate sayings and miracle stories and pronouncement stories but exhibit *sets of sayings* that have *certain traditional patterns*. The teachings of Jesus were not isolated sayings calling individuals to abandon families and villages to become "wandering charismatics" but sets of sayings calling for *community renewal* in mutual cancellation of debts and local cooperation and solidarity. Jesus was not teaching individuals but *catalyzing a movement* of renewal of the people in their village communities.

In this volume I draw on these interrelated aspects of my earlier alternative construction of the historical context and of Jesus's mission (and refer to them for further analyses, procedures, and discussion).[2] Some Jesus scholars picked up on the diversity of popular movements, although only a very few recognized the semi-separate reality of the Israelite popular tradition that had "in-formed" them.[3] Jesus studies, like New Testament studies more generally, however, resists recognizing the fundamental political-economic division and conflict in the historical context and in the Gospel stories. The subfield of Jesus-studies generally, moreover, remains individualistic with its focus on isolated sayings and shows few if any signs of recognizing patterns in Jesus-traditions, much less of imagining that Jesus himself was advocating community coopera- tion and catalyzing a movement.

My earlier critical investigation and critical construction of the historical context and how Jesus's mission responds to it led to the realization that further steps of investigation and rethinking are necessary if we are to move toward a more appropriate and comprehensive approach to the historical Jesus in his- torical context. It had become evident that the synthetic construct of Judaism was also preventing recognition of the *regional differences between Galileans and Judeans.* While not always consistent, the historian Josephus usually re- fers to people of Israelite heritage by region, "Galileans" in Galilee in the north, "Judeans" in Judea, "Samaritans" in between. Extensive investigation using ar- chaeological and rabbinic sources as well as Josephus' histories and the Gospels made clear that Galileans had lived under imperial jurisdiction separate from Judea and Samaria, until the Hasmonean high priests took over Galilee in 104 BCE and required the Galileans to live under "the laws of the Judeans." After only a century under Jerusalem rule, however, the Romans put Galilee under Herod Antipas, so that Galileans were no longer under Jerusalem control. Critical investigation found that Galileans, while presumably Israelites as were Judeans, may not have been closely engaged with the temple and "the Law" as previously claimed.[4]

It had also become evident that the *focus on isolated sayings* of Jesus as a "data-base" was leading into a cul-de-sac, that it was simply *indefensible* as the basis for reconstruction of an historical figure in historical context. Since the delivery of the Hall Lectures some voices from a younger generation of Jesus scholars are confirming my sense that application of criteria for the authentic- ity of separate Jesus sayings is indefensible as historical method, although the focus on individual sayings continues.[5] Sayings separated from a communica- tions context are susceptible of being used for domesticated and anachronistic constructions of Jesus as a "talking head" that have little to do with the complex and conflictual historical context and the mission of Jesus as portrayed in the Gospels. The only guides to the communication context are the Gospels in which sayings were components of the speeches of Jesus and the stories and longer narratives about his interactive mission. It seemed necessary to "back up" to the *Gospel stories and speeches* as *the sources.* Ironically Jesus-studies had been ignoring developments in the closely related subfield of Gospel studies that had begun well before the resurgence of interest in the historical Jesus in the 1990s. Gospel scholars realized that the Gospels were not mere collections of sayings and miracle stories and pronouncement stories but sustained narratives with plots and subplots of interrelated episodes and speeches.

In order to understand the broader Gospel stories, however, Gospel scholars applied various new literary approaches such as narrative criticism and reader-response theory, thus treating the Gospel stories like contemporary fiction that literary critics insisted could be understood mainly from the internal story-world. In order to use the Gospel stories with speeches as historical sources it was necessary first to understand them as historical stories in their historical context. Most of Jesus's teaching in the Gospels, moreover, took the form of shorter or longer speeches on key issues for the lives of the addressees, not separate sayings.[6]

The discovery that the Gospels were sustained stories was an example of how the field of New Testament studies had diversified (and splintered!) into various "criticisms" and areas of specialization (a process that only intensified in the next thirty years). Every largely separate "silo" of research and/or interpretation developed its own distinctive orientation, discourse, and agenda. This meant that specialists in one or two "criticisms" and specialties did not, and perhaps could not stay abreast of developments in other specialties. Scholars focused on Jesus-studies continued to discuss and debate among themselves and did not attend to what Gospel scholars were "discovering," or to the ever more extensive investigations into the divisions, dynamics, and diverse particulars of the historical context.

Attempting to understand the Gospel stories and speeches as ancient people's texts brought me into discovery of how different communication and communication media in the ancient world were from the print-culture that produced biblical studies and its assumptions, concepts, procedures, and anachronistic impositions. And this led to prolonged involvement in the largely separate lines of rapidly developing new research into ancient communications media, first in other fields and then in biblical studies itself, and the challenges these closely related lines of research pose to biblical studies in general and to Jesus studies in particular.[7]

The last third of chapter 1 provides an all-too brief summary of most of these lines of research and their implications as of the time of the delivery of the Hall Lectures in 2010. Only a small (but growing) number of colleagues in biblical studies had been involved in one or another of these lines of research and their implications for understanding texts later included in the Hebrew Bible or the New Testament. But there was now a solid base of research on the limits of literacy and the dominance of oral communication, even among the literate elite. Also a wider appreciation of oral performance was developing, although more of the present possibilities than of ancient practices.

In retrospect on the summary of recent research in chapter 1 I did not adequately draw out how revisionist text criticism of the Gospel texts undermines Jesus-studies (and New Testament studies in general) that is so deeply rooted in the assumptions of modern print-culture. It has been assumed that the Gospels texts were composed in writing and provided stability of wording to Jesus-sayings that had previously been unstable in their oral transmission. As noted, recent revisionist text criticism is finding that the wording of particular sayings in early Gospel manuscripts (and other witnesses), particularly those of special importance to communities of Jesus-loyalists, displays considerable variation. Given the extensive research and documentation that oral communications was dominant and that texts were orally performed, even if and after they were written down, the explanation is that the varying manuscripts and other witnesses were (like) transcripts of continuing oral performance. Studies of long, complex orally-performed texts such as sagas and epic poems in other fields, however, indicate that while particular performances exhibit considerable variation in component lines and stanzas, the overall stories are fairly consistent from performance to performance. If the Gospel stories were analogous, then it seems highly likely that the overall stories were more stable than the wording of particular sayings and episodes, hence are more reliable than individual sayings as sources for Jesus in interaction in context.

These largely separate but related lines of recent research into ancient communications media are decisively challenging the print-cultural assumptions in which Jesus-studies and New Testament studies in general are based. The extensive evidence that oral communication was dominant in antiquity and that even the literate scribes learned and cultivated texts by recitation (relying on the texts that had become "inscribed" in their memory) force the conclusion that among ordinary people who had not been trained to read and write texts were orally performed. As noted just above, the obvious way to explain the variations in early manuscripts of the Gospels is that they reflect the ongoing oral performance in communities of Jesus-loyalists, further undermining the previously dominant print-culture assumptions. While Jesus scholars were focused on further refining the criteria for "authenticity" of Jesus's sayings, at least a few New Testament scholars, recognizing the extremely limited literacy, began investigating how texts such as the Gospel of Mark and the speeches parallel in Matthew and Luke ("Q") may have been performed orally.[8] The introduction of studies of "social memory" already well underway in other fields

into New Testament studies strongly reinforced the exploration of oral performance of texts, leading to recognition that there was no clear demarcation
and difference between oral Jesus-tradition and composed Gospel stories orally
performed.[9]

Since training in New Testament studies has not included attention to
oral performance or oral-derived texts such as the Gospels, reaching outside
the field to theory and studies of oral performance, especially of long complex
texts, will help us understand the Gospel sources as texts-in-performance and
discern how they impacted their audiences in context. A few others and I are
convinced that the widely-based and interdisciplinary theory of John Miles
Foley is particularly helpful for our attempt to appreciate more fully the Gospel
texts in oral performance in their historical contexts as they resonated with
communities of Jesus's loyalists by referencing Israelite tradition.[10]

The surge of Jesus-books in the 1990s tended to give little attention to
Jesus's exorcism and healing and to Jesus's controversies with the scribes and
Pharisees. Having recognized that the Judean and Galilean people had suffered
repeated violence, it seemed likely that Jesus's exorcism and healing could be
understood as responses to the people's plight. Having recognized from sources
such as Josephus' histories that scribes and Pharisees served as advisors of the
ruling high priestly aristocracy and custodians of the elite scribal tradition that
legitimated the temple-state it appeared that we could move beyond the previously standard Christian theological tradition that had construed the Pharisees
as the spokesmen and leaders of legalistic Judaism obsessed with casuistry and
purity codes. These recognitions of key aspects of the historical context seemed
to make possible and necessary some serious rethinking of both Jesus's healing and exorcism and his conflict with the scribes and Pharisees. These had
been on my agenda of research and reflection since the 1980s.[11] Fortunately it
was not possible to explore them more thoroughly before recognizing that the
whole Gospel stories with speeches, and not individual sayings and "miracle
stories" and "controversy stories," are the sources for Jesus-in-interaction in historical context and the recognition that oral communication was dominant in
antiquity. In contrast with the focus of standard Jesus-studies on his teaching
in the form of individual saying, the Gospel stories with speeches give nearly as
much attention to his healings and exorcism and to his conflict with the scribes
and Pharisees as they do to his teachings.

Healings and exorcisms had been lumped into the general modern category of miracle and even that of magic. Because to modern rationalistic and
scientific minds they appeared to involve divine or supernatural causation they

had become embarrassing to theologians and biblical scholars. It was necessary to focus on healings and exorcisms freed from those categories. Meanwhile the translation committee(s) of the Gospels had ironically narrowed Jesus's "healing" of "illnesses" to "curing" of "diseases," following the newly dominant biomedicine in the Western healthcare industry. It was necessary also to learn from the relatively new field of medical anthropology about the psycho-social dimension of sickness and healing that modern medicine had almost excluded and especially from critical medical anthropology that discerned clearly the political-economic factors in sickness and healing. The contours of a far more comprehensive approach to Jesus's exorcism and healing was beginning to emerge. The Hall Lectures offered an opportunity to sketch out a summary (in chapter 4) of the broader and complex program of research and interpretation on which I am still engaged and hope to bring to completion soon.

Among the many matters of the Judean temple that had been hidden by the synthetic construct of Judaism was the social position and role of the scribes and Pharisees. Research on the position, practice, and learning of educated scribes in ancient imperial regimes invited critical examination of learned scribes' social-political-religious role and oral-written cultivation of scribal tradition and texts in late second temple times.[12] That in turn informed a critical reading of Josephus' accounts of the role of the Pharisees in the temple-state under the Hasmonean high priests and the priestly aristocracy under Roman rule. That research and the recognition that Jesus and his movement were deeply rooted in Israelite popular tradition made possible the provisional sketch in chapter 6 of role and agenda of the Pharisees and the conflict between Jesus and the Pharisees portrayed in the Gospels and their speeches. This project of research, critical analysis of sources, and critical interpretation continues as well.

Ongoing Investigation and Exploration

The Hall Lectures and related investigations into key aspects of Jesus's mission were my first attempt both to build on the more comprehensive and precise historical knowledge of the historical context laid out in previous publications and to take into account the implications of the lines of new research in related areas in further investigation of the historical Jesus. Because the new lines of research are recent and still developing and the investigation into Israelite popular tradition only beginning and the application of theory of oral performance not that far along, much of the discussion in the chapters below is necessarily provisional. Much further investigation and critical reflection will be necessary to figure out the implications.

As should be evident from the summary of the related lines of research into ancient communications media, their implication is that *the Gospel texts were probably not composed in writing but in continuing oral performance in communities of (non-literate) ordinary people.* Those of us deeply involved in coming to grips with these new researches were hesitant to push this implication, thinking it strategic to call for recognition of oral performance in a way that stopped short of a direct challenge to the prevailing print-cultural assumption that long complex texts such as the Gospels could only have been composed in writing. Shortly after the completion of the chapters of this book, however, a few of us became bolder in drawing out this implication of what we were learning about ancient communications media. I was emboldened in my previous suggestions about the composition of the Gospel of Mark by the well-conceived and executed step-by-step argument by Antoinette Clark Wire, and I attempted to build on her work.[13]

Nearly all of the previous explorations of Gospel texts as orally performed were focused on the Gospel of Mark and the Jesus-speeches paralleled in Matthew and Luke (commonly referred to as Q). These enabled us to recognize how the fairly clearly plotted Markan story and the series of "Q" speeches focused on particular topics could have been composed in repeated oral performance. But it still seemed difficult to imagine how even more complex texts than the Markan story could have been composed based on memory of the component episodes and speeches. Investigation of composition of how more complex later texts drew on memory of already defined earlier texts- and traditions-in-memory in scribal circles suggested that ordinary people would have been capable of analogous composition processes. The Gospel of Matthew, for example, is more clearly composed in easily remembered sections of narrative-plus-speech steps than the shorter Markan story.

That communication among ordinary people was almost exclusively oral and they probably had little contact with written texts produced by the scribal elite means that they would have been embedded in Israelite popular tradition (as distinguished from the elite, scribal tradition embodied in written texts on which most biblical study has focused). Since the Gospel texts were almost certainly orally performed and would have resonated with the listening communities by referencing the Israelite popular tradition in which they were embedded, it is important to know as much as possible about that popular tradition in order to know how to use these oral-derived texts as sources. Although written texts later included in the Hebrew Bible and other extant written Judean texts do not offer direct evidence for popular traditions, they do provide indirect evidence insofar as the scribes who produced them adapted earlier popular traditions and customs into the texts they produced. Previous critical analysis of the origin and layers of development of these texts by biblical scholars would indicate the possibilities of finding indirect evidence for popular culture. Knowing more of the Israelite popular tradition or social memory (the well-cooked "hidden transcript") of villagers would help our understanding of whole Gospel stories and of most all episodes and speeches in the Gospels, such as covenant renewal speeches and conflicts with the Pharisees.

Fuller and deeper understanding of all the lines of recent research summarized in chapter 1 and their implications will be essential to further critical and comprehensive understanding of the historical Jesus-in-interaction in historical context. This will also help us understand the ways in which the Gospel sources give us access to Jesus-in-interaction. The interaction of Jesus himself with people happened in terms of the popular Israelite tradition/social memory in which both Jesus and the people were embedded. The development of Jesus speeches and episodes and the larger Gospel stories continued in communities of Jesus loyalists embedded in Israelite popular tradition. It seems unlikely that it will be possible to distinguish the earliest stage of Jesus's interactions from the development of particular episodes and speeches based on them. There is also no clear mark of distinction between a supposedly earlier phase of development of "oral tradition" of episodes and speeches performed in communities and a supposedly subsequent phase of the composition of the larger Gospel stories, which would also have happened in composition in repeated oral performances. This means that the historical Jesus became embedded in the developing Jesus-tradition and communities of Jesus loyalists. The clear implications are that the historical Jesus is now embedded in the Gospel stories and speeches. As stated in the final paragraph of chapter 1, for access *we must go through the Gospel stories and speeches and cannot go underneath them.*

I am currently involved in further exploration of the implications of the new lines of research and work on oral performance of long, complex, oral-derived texts in order to reach a more comprehensive approach to the historical Jesus-in-interaction that takes the interrelated lines of new research into account. And an integral part of this agenda is a deeper understanding of how to use sophisticated interdisciplinary theory of oral performance. I am hopeful that others, most likely those of a younger generation, will join me.

1. Getting the Whole Story

Persistent tension seems to be inherent in study of the historical Jesus, a tension between the Gospel sources' portrayal of Jesus and the pictures of Jesus presented by scholarly interpreters. Three conflicts with the Gospels are particularly prominent in the main lines of interpretation by American scholars in the recent "growth industry" of Jesus books.

The feature of the Gospels' presentation of Jesus of which we are most confident is that he was crucified by order of the Roman governor, Pontius Pilate. Insofar as crucifixion was the form of execution that the Romans used for political agitators in the provinces, Jesus must have been executed because he was at least thought to be a rebel against the Roman imperial order. That is, he was executed as a political actor.

The Gospels also portray Jesus as proclaiming the presence of God's (direct) rule, as well as healing illnesses in villages and village assemblies (*synagogai*) and sending his disciples into village communities to expand this program. Followed by ever-larger crowds, he marches up to Jerusalem, where he confronts the high priestly rulers of Judea.

The Gospels further present Jesus as delivering many speeches, both long and short, to the crowds and/or to his disciples. The longest and most famous of these, of course, is the "Sermon on the Mount," a renewal and intensification of the Mosaic covenantal commandments as a sort of charter for community life.

Despite their dramatically different (even diametrically opposite) reconstructions of Jesus, the main lines of recent interpretation of Jesus seemingly ignore or dismiss these aspects of the Gospels' portrayals. The liberal interpreters in "the Jesus Seminar," rejecting Albert Schweitzer's "end of the world" Jesus, dismissed the judgmental or "apocalyptic" sayings in the Gospels as later formulations by his followers and constructed Jesus as a Cynic-like wisdom teacher.[1] In reaction, other interpreters reasserted Schweitzer's view of a century earlier that Jesus was proclaiming an apocalyptic scenario of the end of the world.[2] Also in reaction to the liberals' wisdom teacher, more theologically conservative interpreters focused on aspects of Jesus that correspond to the later creedal statements of faith.[3]

Despite the sharp differences among them, however, all of these lines of interpretation share the same three key differences from the Gospel portrayals. First, they all present Jesus as a religious figure, with little or no engagement with politics. It is impossible to discern why the Romans would have crucified either a teacher of a carefree individual lifestyle or a fanatical preacher of the end of the world. Second, the liberals' wisdom teacher, the neo-Schweitzerians' isolated figure proclaiming the end of the world, and the crucified-and-risen savior are all strikingly individualistic. None of these Jesuses engages in social interaction, much less organizes a movement. Third, both the liberal scholars and the neo-Schweitzerians (and to an extent the more traditional theologians) simply assume that they should start with and focus on the individual sayings of Jesus isolated from their literary context. They all evidently assume that Jesus uttered individual sayings one at a time.

Moving beyond the Confines of Modern Western Assumptions and Constructions

That these three sharply divergent lines of Jesus interpretation all share the same significant differences from the Gospel sources suggests that they have much to do with the New Testament studies in which they are rooted. It does not take much critical distance to recognize that these three scholarly differences from the Gospel sources—the separation of religion from politics, the individualism, and the focus on separate sayings—are also deeply rooted in Western culture more broadly and that these features of Western culture are all the more intense in American culture. The separation of religion from politics, individualism, and the focus on separate sayings of Jesus, however, are inappropriate for the Gospels and for the people and society that the Gospels portray.

Beyond the Separation between Religion and Political-Economic Life

Investigation and interpretation of the historical Jesus has developed largely within the field of New Testament studies, which has traditionally been a branch of theology in Western universities. Jesus is classified and understood as a religious figure, whether in academic and ecclesial circles or in the culture at large.

The assumption that religion is separate from politics and economics, moreover, is deeply rooted in Western culture. That separation is reinforced in the United States and many other Western societies by the institutionalized separation of "church" (and/or other "religions") and state. Not surprisingly, therefore, most books on the historical Jesus pay little or no attention to the politics of the historical context, much less to Jesus's engagement with political and economic matters.[4]

This limitation to religion has become built into the theological field of New Testament studies, in which study of the historical Jesus has dutifully remained. The field has long since developed its own discourse, with distinctive concepts, by which it abstracts the religious dimension of life from more complex historical realities. New Testament studies and theology, of course, have not been alone in separating the text and figures they interpret from the harsh realities of politics and economics. In the twentieth century the newly established fields of literary studies often focused narrowly on the aesthetic dimensions of poetry and fiction. Interpreters of English novels, for example, would simply not notice that the families of the major characters were living on wealth generated from industries or from colonial enterprises.[5] In recent decades, however, literary studies have (re)discovered the political-economic dimensions of literature. It seems timely that New Testament studies as well recognize the political-economic realities with which religion was embedded in the ancient world.

Insofar as religion was inseparable from political-economic life in Roman Palestine, where Jesus lived, a Jesus who was only religious cannot have been historical. Religion as a separate sphere is simply not attested in our sources for the time of Jesus, nor is such a separation evident in the Gospel sources for Jesus. The Lord's Prayer, for example, is inseparably political and economic as well as religious: Jesus teaches people to pray for the direct rule (kingdom) of God and for sufficient bread and for the cancellation of debts. Perhaps a more telling example is Jesus's exhortation to "render to Caesar the things that are Caesar's and to God the things that are God's," which has often been understood in accordance with the modern Western separation of politics and religion. Caesar, however, was not only the emperor but a "son of god," the divine (inseparably political-economic-religious) "Lord" and "Savior" of the world. His power over the empire worked more through the images, shrines, statues, temples, and festivals, in which his presence pervaded public space, than through bureaucracy and army.[6] This happened even in Palestine, where Herod the Great built whole new cities as well as temples in honor of Augustus and erected a golden Roman eagle above the gate of the temple. Indeed, for ancient

Judeans and Galileans, rendering to Caesar was a violation of the first two commandments of the Mosaic covenant (discussed in chapter 2). Investigation of Jesus as a historical figure in historical context thus requires comprehensive critical consideration of political-economic-religious life in ancient Palestine under Roman rule and how Jesus was involved.

This comprehensive historical investigation would appear to require some critical "deconstruction" of the standard synthetic Christian theological constructs that block recognition of the historical realities our principal historical sources portray. Particularly problematic are two closely interrelated modern scholarly constructs deeply embedded in the discourse of New Testament studies: "(early) Christianity" and "(early) Judaism." Like the parallel modern Western constructs "Buddhism" and "Hinduism," "Christianity" and "Judaism" select and synthesize certain religious features abstracted from historical sources, often according to Christian theological interests.[7]

"Christianity" is usually understood as the "religion" that resulted from the mission of Jesus (via the mission of Paul and other apostles). The name "Christian(s)," however, does not appear until nearly two generations after Jesus's crucifixion. Just as it would be anachronistic to speak of the "United States" in the history of North America until 1776, so it is anachronistic to refer to "Christianity" as a definable religion until the third or, better, fourth century. Most of the texts that were later included in the "New Testament" were not "(early) Christian." The Gospels of Mark, Matthew, and evidently John as well all understand not only Jesus but the communities of his followers as still belonging to the people of Israel. The communities or movements of those followers and their concerns, moreover, were not confined narrowly to "religion."

The construct "Judaism" is similarly anachronistic. The sources for life in Palestine under Hellenistic and Roman rule, whether the books of Sirach and Daniel or the Psalms of Solomon or the histories of the Judean historian Josephus, portray a complex and divided society and its political-economic-religious structure and dynamics. While some scholars still emphasize a "common Judaism,"[8] prominent Jewish scholars have been emphasizing the diversity of "Judaisms" that cannot be comprehended by the modern construct "Judaism" or the closely related construct of four Jewish "sects" ("sectarian Judaism").[9] Conceptualization in terms of diversity, however, still avoids recognition of the political-economic-religious structures and conflictual dynamics attested in our principal textual sources such as the histories of Flavius Josephus. The temple, for example, was indeed the central sanctuary where the priests conducted sacrifices and offerings to God. More comprehensively, however, it was the political-economic-religious institution headed by the high priests installed by the Romans to control the people of Judea and to collect the tribute to Caesar (to be discussed in chapter 2).

To take yet another, very general example, the books that were later included in the Hebrew Bible and the God they portray are concerned with all aspects of life, political-economic as well as religious. The Gospel sources, moreover, portray Jesus as concerned with issues that are inseparably political-economic-religious. Investigation of the *historical* Jesus therefore requires consideration of the political-economic-religious realities portrayed in our sources.

Beyond Individualism to Interaction

Another major obstacle that blocks access to the *historical* Jesus is the individualism that dominates modern Western religion and culture, particularly American culture and Christianity. This is strikingly manifested in how the construction of Jesus as an advocate of "itinerant radicalism" for individuals who were to abandon their families was uncritically taken over by American interpreters (despite criticism of the underlying assumptions and approach).[10] The liberals' Jesus is an individual teacher who uttered individual sayings that apparently were heard only by individuals, who remembered them and then transmitted them to other individuals. Finding the actual phrase "kingdom of God" only in the treatises of the Hellenistic Jewish theologian Philo of Alexandria somehow justifies dismissing (Palestinian) Israelite covenantal and prophetic traditions and rabbinic (Targumic) sources in which God was the true, transcendent ruler (king) of Israel and ultimately of all history as possible background of Jesus's central concept. Like the mystic Philo, Jesus was speaking about the kingdom that comes to the individual.[11] The occurrence of the actual phrase "kingdom of God" trumps even Jesus's declaration that "the kingdom of God is *among* you" (or *in the midst of* the people; Luke 17:21).[12]

Even scholars who consider comparative material in which relations between leaders and followers are constitutive of historical movements nevertheless construct an individualistic Jesus. Among the liberal interpreters, for example, Crossan gives extensive coverage to popular prophets and popular messiahs as leaders of movements in Jesus's historical context. Yet in order to develop his governing paradigm of Jesus as teaching an unmediated relation of the individual and God, he projects Jesus as an individual sage teaching a kingdom of God for the "child"-like individual.[13] Among the neo-Schweitzerians, Allison makes a list of nineteen common features of "millenarianism" compiled from many different societies and historical circumstances, in a "Detached

Note."[14] The particular cases from which he abstracts the features, however, were mostly movements of resistance to modern European or American colonial invasion produced by the response of large numbers of followers to a leader or leaders. These collective responses to the impact of imperial expansion catalyzed by a "charismatic" leader, however, do not lead Allison (or others) to an investigation of Jesus as anything beyond an isolated individual preacher of the themes of the apocalyptic scenario.[15]

One suspects that the individualistic construction of Jesus is also determined by both traditional Christological concerns and the closely related standard theological scheme of Christian origins. Jesus Christ is both *the revealer* whose words are the vehicles of the revelation of God and *the redeemer* who in self-sacrifice died on the cross for people's sins. Despite the doctrine of the incarnation, little attention is given to how Jesus was engaged in contingent social relations and conflicts. According to the standard scheme of Christian origins (from Judaism), moreover, Jesus was an individual revealer who delivered teachings to individual disciples who *after* his death and resurrection formed communities that eventually became the church. In this scheme, Jesus himself did not catalyze a movement during his "ministry." But there is no reason why Jesus cannot have been *the revealer* and *redeemer* while also being engaged in interaction and conflict with other people in the concrete circumstances and particular social (political-economic-religious) forms of first-century Roman Palestine. Indeed, this more complex relational Jesus would presumably be more consistent with the doctrine of incarnation. The Gospels, moreover, portray Jesus in regular interaction with disciples and followers and in conflict with the Pharisees and the high priests, while only rarely teaching one individual.

The predominantly individualistic Jesus is also unengaged with, even disengaged from human interaction in the most fundamental social forms of Galilean and Judean society, families and village communities. Indeed, recent critical liberal scholarship often has Jesus advocating the abandonment of family in order to pursue an itinerant lifestyle. Again this involves ignoring or rejecting the Gospel portrayals, which represent Jesus as engaged with families and working in villages. But it is difficult to imagine a *historical* figure who was not embedded in and engaged with the human contingencies of fundamental social forms as well as engaged in social interaction and conflict with others in society. Investigation of the *historical* Jesus in *historical* context thus requires moving beyond the limits of modern Western individualism and developing a fully *relational* and *contextual* approach.

It may be helpful to consider how historians approach and deal with other historical figures, such as Abraham Lincoln or Martin Luther King. Leaders generally become historically significant figures because they provide leadership of people in situations of historical crisis. To deal adequately with the complexity of relational leadership in context, it is thus necessary to consider the historical crisis in which the person provided leadership, the cultural tradition out of which the leader and the followers responded to the crisis, how the leader adapted an office or role(s) given in the society or cultural tradition, and the process by which the leader catalyzed a movement that "made history" such that the person became a significant historical figure.[16] Analysis and discussion in the following chapters attempt to consider all of these factors.

Beyond Individual Sayings to Communication and Stories

Closely related to the problematic individualism of Jesus interpretation is the focus on the individual sayings of Jesus. The standard critical approach to "the historical Jesus" has worked on the assumption that the sources for (re)construction of the historical Jesus are the individual sayings contained in the Gospels.[17] Viewing the Gospels as post-Easter statements of "Christian" faith and as mere containers of sayings and stories strung end to end, scholars purposely isolate individual sayings from their literary context in the Gospels. They then evaluate them for their "authenticity" according to a set of criteria, such as "multiple attestation" and their dissimilarity to materials of contemporary "Judaism" and/or subsequent "early Christianity." They also classify and group them according to form and/or subject and attempt to discern their meaning as separate sayings. The varying number of sayings deemed authentic, suitably classified, make up the "data" for the reconstruction mainly of the teachings of Jesus.

A powerful impetus for the crystallization of the focus on the individual *sayings* of Jesus came from the Enlightenment, which gave rise to interest in "the historical Jesus" in the first place. The Enlightenment's emphasis on Reason sharpened critical biblical scholars' sense of what seemed to be the "supernatural" or "irrational" worldview evident in the Gospel narratives, which stood in stark contrast to the modern scientific understanding of reality. The Enlightenment's reduction of reality to fit the canons of Reason and Nature left theologians, including New Testament scholars, embarrassed about the Gospels, with all their "miracle stories," as historical sources. The only reliable materials that could meet modern scientific criteria for historical evidence were the teachings of Jesus, which they had come to assume consisted of individual sayings.

The focus on the individual sayings of Jesus received confirmation and momentum from the "discovery" and delineation of the Source (*Quelle* in German, usually shortened to Q) that scholars posited to explain the close verbal parallels between the teachings of Jesus in Matthew and in Luke but are not in Mark. On the assumption that Jesus's teachings took the form of individual sayings, this was taken as a mere "collection" of individual sayings and designated "the Synoptic Sayings Source." The discovery in the early twentieth century of the Gospel of Thomas, which had the form of a seemingly random collection of individual or double sayings or parables, strongly reinforced the standard assumption about the form of the teachings on which the (re)construction of the historical Jesus was focused. Further refining the "form-critical" approach started by Bultmann and Dibelius but concentrating primarily on the form and neglecting the function, the self-selecting regular gathering of liberal scholars in the Jesus Seminar proceeded precisely by focusing on the separate sayings of Jesus. With less critical rigor, perhaps, many other interpreters of Jesus also continued to focus on the isolated individual sayings of Jesus as the "data" for reconstructing his teachings.

Treating the separate individual sayings as the sources (data) for reconstruction of Jesus is seriously problematic as historical method. In this context it must suffice to summarize only a few of the most basic interrelated reasons.

First, no one can *communicate* in isolated individual sayings—indeed, it is difficult to imagine anyone who speaks only in isolated utterances. In order to have become a historically significant figure Jesus would have to have communicated with other people who responded to his speech and actions in social interactions in the circumstances in which they lived. If we were attempting to understand the historical Abraham Lincoln or the historical Martin Luther King, we would not extract individual statements from their speeches. Lincoln and King communicated with people both in a particular social-political context and in a larger historical context. "I have a dream" has become a brief "sound bite." But individual and collective memory is still close enough to the 1960s that it cues us into a broad and deep social memory at the center of which King was the best-known leader of and inseparable from the civil rights movement and the historical crisis in US history to which he and the movement responded.

Second, the meaning of a saying depends on its meaning-context, from which it cannot be intelligibly isolated. By extracting the sayings of Jesus from their literary context, Jesus scholars dispense with the only indication available for what that meaning-context may have been. The analogy drawn recently that scholars are "excavating" the Gospel sources for Jesus such as Q or even "excavating Jesus" may be more telling than they realize. This suggests that the sayings are precious artifacts that must be excavated from the piles of dirt and debris in which they have become buried. Then, like museum curators of a generation or two ago, interpreters of Jesus arrange those decontextualized artifacts by type ("apocalyptic" or "sapiential") and/or topic (children, meals, kingdom, wisdom), like fragments of lamps, vases, and pots in museum cases. Individual sayings of Jesus may be precious artifacts to the scholars who sort them out and categorize them. As isolated artifacts, however, they do not have or convey meaning, and they beg the question of context. The result is Jesus as a dehistoricized "talking head," devoid of life circumstances.

With their various "databases" of atomized Jesus sayings isolated from any mfeaning-context, the Jesus scholars then supply the meaning-context themselves, often from the constructs of New Testament studies. It has become standard among critical liberal scholars, for example, to isolate Jesus's admonition on what (not) to take for a/the journey from its immediate context in the "mission discourses" in both Mark 6:8–13 and Q/Luke 10:2–16. But what can this isolated saying about staff, sandals, bag, and so on mean in itself? Evidently nothing. So liberal interpreters recontextualize the saying in the modern scholarly construct of an itinerant vagabond lifestyle that Jesus was supposedly advocating to his individual disciples.[18]

The now century-old scholarly construct of a scenario of "Jewish apocalypticism" is the context still supplied by many interpreters to the sayings of Jesus and/or those of John the Baptist. The neo-Schweitzerian Allison lists whole sets of Jesus sayings isolated from literary context as illustrations ("prooftexts") of key themes of this apocalyptic scenario.[19] Similarly, Crossan interprets the (isolated) saying of John that the "coming one will baptize with Spirit and fire" as a reference to the "imminent apocalyptic intervention by God" as the "apocalyptic avenger" bringing "the fire storm" of eschatological judgment.[20] These isolated sayings, however, do not attest any such "apocalyptic" scenario, nor do Judean texts classified as "apocalyptic" attest such a scenario. While repentance and renewal in anticipation of God's coming in judgment and restoration are common themes in Israelite prophetic tradition, God as the fiery avenger acting on Israelites/Judeans is not found in "apocalyptic" texts.[21]

A third major reason that the focus on separate sayings of Jesus is problematic is that there is no basis in the Gospel sources themselves for isolating individual sayings. One of the first and most basic responsibilities of historians is to critically assess the character of their sources. Literary and rhetorical analysis of the sources is necessary to discern how they may be used for investigation of historical events, actors, and circumstances. Historians would not separate individual statements or short anecdotes from a source, categorize them by key words or apparent subject matter, and then seek the meaning of each statement by itself or assess the likelihood that particular anecdotes provide reliable attestation of actual historical incidents. It may be unfair to hold Jesus scholars to the standards of regular historians, since they have been trained in interpretation of sacred texts, not in the methods of historical investigation. Jesus scholars recognize the "rhetorical" perspective of the Gospels. But precisely because the Gospels express the Easter faith of the "early Christians," these scholars attempted to cut through or move underneath them by focusing on individual sayings (and stories) as their sources (or "data"), thus treating the Gospels as mere containers or collections. Work in other subfields of New Testament studies and related fields, however, is making this view of the Gospels untenable.

Taking the Gospels Whole as the Sources for the Historical Jesus

Even before the recent surge of interest in the historical Jesus, interpreters of the Gospels were (re)discovering their literary integrity as whole stories about Jesus's interaction with followers and opponents. Scholars recognized that the Gospels are sustained narratives in which earlier episodes and events set up subsequent episodes and events. The episodes are inseparable components of the whole story and are unintelligible apart from it.

In the excitement of discovery Gospel interpreters simply borrowed from criticism of modern narrative fiction. They read the Gospels in the same way that literary critics read modern novels or short stories, looking for (implied) authors, narrators, and (implied) readers and expecting suspenseful plots and character development. Like other ancient stories, however, the Gospels are different from modern novellas in significant ways. Their plots are not linear, and they are not full of suspense. Gospel stories have clear indications of how they will come out. The characters in the Gospels are types, even stereotypes or collectives, playing important roles but not undergoing "character development." The Gospel stories are simply not comparable to modern fiction. They purport to be historical stories and to narrate historical events; indeed, they include claims that the events they narrate are the fulfillment of history. To be understood, they therefore must be read in historical context.[22]

As the first step in approaching the historical Jesus, it is necessary to take the Gospel stories whole, to gain a clear sense of their overall portrayal of Jesus's mission in interaction with followers and opponents in the historical setting.[23] After getting clarity on the sources' portrayals of Jesus-in-interaction we can then compare the portrayals in different Gospel sources and assess the portrayals in the historical context as known from other sources.[24]

Mark

The Gospel of Mark is still, by a fairly wide consensus, thought to have been the first Gospel composed. Mark's Gospel was previously thought to revolve around "the messianic secret": only gradually in the story, after Jesus orders demons and others not to reveal who he is, does it become clear that he is "the Messiah." It became clear to many scholars of the previous generation that there was no standard Jewish expectation of "the Messiah" that Jesus supposedly fulfilled. If there is such a secret in Mark, moreover, the story never gets around to disclosing it. After Peter declares that Jesus is "the Messiah" in Caesarea Philippi and then objects when Jesus informs the disciples that "the son of man" must suffer and be killed, Jesus rebukes him: "get behind me Satan." It is unclear whether Mark's Jesus is simply rejecting Peter's understanding of the role or rejecting the role altogether. Certainly Mark's story does not portray Jesus as an anointed king; indeed, the idea of Jesus as (a) messiah is conspicuous by its absence from Mark, in contrast to the Gospels of Matthew and John.

The Gospel of Mark has often been understood as a story about discipleship. And, indeed, for many devoted Christians it has become a story about the difficulties of being a faithful disciple of Jesus. Yet the disciples' increasing misunderstanding of Jesus's mission after their call and commissioning and their eventual betrayal, denial, and abandonment is not the main plot in Mark's story.

The dominant conflict in Mark's story, especially when it is read in historical context, is between Jesus (and sometimes his followers) and the Jerusalem high priests and their scribal-Pharisaic representatives. The conflict climaxes in Jesus's sustained confrontation with the high priests, scribes, and elders in the temple, in response to which they arrest him and hand him over to the Roman governor Pontius Pilate for crucifixion as a rebel leader, "the king of the Judeans." But the conflict is explicit from the outset, as Jesus, in his first action (an exorcism in Capernaum) and in his climactic confrontation in Jerusalem, teaches and acts with authority, in contrast with the scribal and high priestly authorities. Early in the story, the Pharisees, who come down from Jerusalem to challenge Jesus's and his disciples' actions, plot with the Herodians to destroy Jesus. And the high priests finally implement a plot to capture him surreptitiously, after he boldly confronts and condemns them in the temple.

The substance of the conflict in nearly everything Jesus says and does, to state it succinctly, is his renewal of (the people of) Israel in opposition to the rulers of Israel. To appreciate this portrayal in Mark's Gospel, it is necessary to recognize the repeated references and allusions to Israelite history and tradition in one episode of the story after another. The story begins with John, the prophetic messenger in the wilderness, preparing the way of the Lord and proclaiming a baptism of repentance, in a new exodus and renewal of the Mosaic covenant. After his own baptism, Jesus, like Elijah, is tested for forty days in the wilderness and recruits protégés, as Elijah had Elisha. Jesus calls twelve disciples as representative of the people of Israel in its twelve tribes, who extend his own mission of proclaiming the presence of the kingdom of God and manifesting God's direct rule in the exorcism of demons in the village communities of Galilee and beyond. In the structure and substance of the second main narrative step of the story, Jesus performs two sequences of acts of power, sea crossings and feedings in the wilderness, as had Moses, and exorcisms and healings, reminiscent of Elijah. As if the audience of the story had not already recognized that Jesus has assumed the prophetic role as the new Moses, the founding prophet of Israel, and the new Elijah, the great prophet of renewal, both figures appear transfigured with Jesus on the mountain. Shortly after Jesus condemns the scribes and Pharisees for making void the basic covenantal commandment of God, just as he is about to head up to Jerusalem, he delivers new commandment-like pronouncements in a series of dialogues in which he cites most of the commandments.

Jesus's exorcisms and healings, however, are so threatening to the rulers that their Pharisaic (and Herodian) representatives not only challenge him but also plot to destroy him. Yet he boldly marches up to Jerusalem at the Passover celebration of the people's formative exodus and liberation from bondage, continuing his chosen prophetic role. There Jesus carries out an obstructive prophetic demonstration against the temple, tells a prophetic parable that condemns the high priests for their oppression of the people, declares that the people do not owe tribute to Caesar, and castigates the scribes for devouring widows' livelihood (encouraging them to give to the temple the minimal resources they have to live on). As he is about to be arrested, Jesus celebrates the Passover meal as a ceremony of covenant renewal (the blood of the cup being an allusion to the blood that bound God and the people in the original covenant ceremony on Sinai). In sum, the Gospel of Mark portrays Jesus as a prophet like Moses and Elijah, carrying out a renewal of Israel in opposition to the rulers of Israel.

Matthew and Luke

The Gospels of Matthew and Luke, as has long been recognized, repeat most of the episodes in Mark in much the same sequence, and their writers are thus usually thought to have independently known and followed Mark. Matthew's and Luke's stories, however, are longer and more complex, as they include a good deal of Jesus's teachings (much of which they have in common) and other Jesus traditions, such as legends of Jesus's birth. Again in these longer Gospels, the dominant conflict is between Jesus (and his followers) and the high priests and their representatives, the Pharisees. Jesus's conflict with the Pharisees is more intense in Matthew. The Gospel of Matthew positions Jesus and his mission explicitly as the fulfillment of prophecy and the fulfillment of the history of Israel in the "formula quotations" and genealogy at the beginning and places Jesus in the context of international history in the legend of the Magi and Herod's massacre of the innocents. The Gospel of Luke sets Jesus and his mission in the even wider contexts of the Roman Empire and world history, in the birth narrative and genealogy, respectively.

Parallel to Mark and probably following Mark, the Gospels of Matthew and Luke thus also portray Jesus as catalyzing a renewal of Israel in opposition to the rulers and their representatives. In the role mainly of a prophet like Moses and Elijah, Jesus (along with his disciples) is revitalizing a poor, hungry, and indebted people as they proclaim the kingdom of God and manifest God's rule in healings and exorcisms in the villages of Galilee. Again in the longer Gospels, after marching up to Jerusalem, Jesus confronts and condemns the high priests and other "authorities" in Jerusalem, leading them to capture him surreptitiously and hand him over to the Roman governor for crucifixion as a rebel leader. The principal difference at the climax of the story is that Matthew and Luke both shift more of the blame for Jesus's execution to the Jerusalem rulers.

The Q Speeches

The main difference between the longer Gospels and the Gospel of Mark is the extensive teachings of Jesus that the former incorporate into the basic story of the renewal of Israel. In Luke the principle of insertion or organization is unclear, with many of the teachings appearing in a long middle section of the story. The Gospel of Matthew presents Jesus's teachings systematically organized into five well-marked speeches of Jesus: renewal of covenantal community, the commissioning of the disciples for mission, a series of parables, instructions on community discipline, and descriptions of what to expect in the future. Although each Gospel has some of its own Jesus traditions, most of these teachings of Jesus (that are not derived from Mark) are strikingly parallel, often identical in sections on the same issues and mostly following the same order. This is why scholars have long since hypothesized that Matthew and Luke must be following the same source, known as Q (*Quelle* in German), to which they both had access (references to Q material is usually given according to its appearance in Luke). While some scholars find other hypotheses to account for the relations among the three "Synoptic" Gospels, there is fairly wide consensus that Matthew and Luke both used a source of Jesus's teachings.

As we become more aware of just how limited literacy was in the ancient world (discussed later in this chapter), it may seem increasingly questionable that this source of Jesus's teachings was circulated in writing, making it unlikely that the precise wording of the teachings can be critically established. Yet our increasingly critical understanding of how oral tradition operated may enable us to appreciate how a (still developing) body of Jesus's teachings could have been cultivated (and regularly recited) in the earliest communities of his followers. It is in any case clear that both Matthew and Luke presupposed a body of Jesus's teachings that had taken recognizable form in the first few decades after Jesus's mission. Through the Gospels of Matthew and Luke, therefore, we have access to another source for Jesus that is contemporary with the earliest Gospel, that of Mark, but with a very different form and (mostly) different Jesus traditions.

Because interpretation of Jesus was oriented to separate sayings and Q was *the* prime source for Jesus's teachings, Q was understood as a mere collection of sayings, as "the Synoptic *Sayings* Source." This was reinforced by the discovery of the Gospel of Thomas, which does have the form of separate individual or double sayings or parables. Ironically, even though these teachings of Jesus appeared in Matthew and Luke in parallel *speeches* or "discourses" of Jesus, such as the Lord's Prayer and the "mission discourse"—and these appeared as coherent paragraphs (with subtitles) in standard translations such as the (New) Revised Standard Version and (New) Jerusalem Bible—scholars continued to focus on separate sayings.

Only recently, in the development of "composition criticism" of Q, have some North American scholars recognized that the teachings of Jesus in Q have the form not of a mere collection of sayings but of a series of Jesus's speeches on key concerns of communities of a Jesus movement.[25] The series of Q speeches is thus quite different in form from the Gospel of Thomas in which, keying from its own stated hermeneutic in the first logion, sayings are separated for spiritual contemplation by devout individuals. Among the Jesus speeches most clearly discernible through the parallels in Matthew and Luke are those on covenant renewal (Q/Luke 6:20–49), on the respective historic roles of John and Jesus (Q/Luke 7:18–22, 24–28, 31–35), on mission (Q/Luke 10:2–16), on prayer (Q/Luke 11:2–4, 9–13), on the charge of having Beelzebul (Q/Luke 11:14–20), on bold confession in court (Q/Luke 12:2–9), and on seeking first the kingdom in the face of destitution (Q/Luke 12:22–31). The theme that runs like a thread through these speeches, holding them together in a series, is "the kingdom of God," which appears at a key point in most speeches (e.g., Q/Luke 6:20; 7:28; 10:9, 11; 11:20; 12:31).

Although the Q series of speeches does not "portray" Jesus in the same way that the Gospel narratives do, we can discern what the speeches represent him as saying and doing. While it would be going too far to claim that Q has a "plot," the first several speeches do seem to follow an intelligible sequence of topics. It begins, evidently, with John the Baptist's speech in which he asserts that the coming one will baptize in Spirit and fire (Q/Luke 3:7–9, 16–17). In his first and longest speech (Q/Luke 6:20–49) Jesus then pronounces a renewal of the Mosaic covenant, recognizable from its adaptation of the components of the Mosaic covenant form, beginning with a new declaration of deliverance and offering the kingdom of God to the poor and hungry (Q/Luke 6:20–49). Then Jesus replies to the Baptist's disciples' question whether he is the coming one by referring to how he is fulfilling the longings of the people in his healing and proclamation of the good news and linking the Baptist and himself in the coming of the kingdom (Q/Luke 7:18–35). Jesus then sends his envoys two by two to village communities to extend his own mission of preaching the kingdom and expelling demons (Q/Luke 9:57–63; 10:2–16). The series of speeches also appears to have a coherent ending in the speech on the suddenness of judgment as a sanction on all the preceding speeches (Q/Luke 17:23–37) and on Jesus's final charge to his twelve disciples to lead the deliverance (*not* "judgment" in the negative sense) of the people of Israel, symbolized by the twelve tribes (Q/Luke 22:28–30). The whole series is held together by the theme of the presence of the kingdom of God, as noted.

The Q series of speeches, moreover, portrays a Jesus on a mission of the renewal of Israel. Throughout, Jesus (along with John) speaks and acts as a prophet, like Moses in the renewal of the covenant and like Elijah in the sending of envoys and healings. In several of the speeches, moreover, he represents both John and himself as the final prophets in the long line of Israelite prophets, many of whom were killed by the rulers for their warnings.[26] Baptizing with Spirit and fire is clearly an agenda of renewal of the people, as is his own standard list of his acts of healing and proclamation, in fulfillment of longings previously articulated in prophetic oracles (e.g., Isa 35:5–6; 42:6–7; 61:1). Central in his program is the enactment in performative speech of the renewal of the covenant community. And the commissioning of envoys expands the program of renewal into wider circles of village communities. The petitions for sufficient food and (mutual) cancellation of debts in the prayer for the coming of the kingdom of God indicate just how concretely economic the renewal is understood to be. The "punchline" of the Beelzebul speech declares that his exorcisms "by the finger of God" constitute, in effect, a new exodus.

Jesus's renewal of the people of Israel, moreover, is in opposition to the Jerusalem rulers and their Pharisaic and scribal representatives. His prophetic woes against the Pharisees, rhetorically mocking their obsession with purity issues, condemn them mainly for their exploitation of people through their scribal role. And, in the traditional form of a prophetic lament, he pronounces God's condemnation of the ruling house of Jerusalem for having killed the prophets sent to warn them. While the Jerusalem elite, who presumed on their lineage from Abraham, Isaac, and Jacob, find themselves cast out, the restored people from east and west, north and south, will gather in the banquet of the kingdom of God (Q/Luke 13:28–29), which is now happening as the renewal of the people in its ideal twelve tribes. Thus, in a series of speeches, a presentation very different from the sequence of episodes narrated in Mark but one that has many overlaps with it in both subjects and issues, Q presents a very similar and parallel overall portrayal of Jesus as a prophet pursuing the renewal of Israel in opposition to the rulers.

John

The Gospel of John has been generally dismissed as a source for the historical Jesus because it has been viewed as a "spiritual" Gospel, heavily theological and with long dialogues and monologues. More than the other Gospels, and certainly with more tragic historical effects in Christian anti-Judaism, John's story of Jesus and his mission has been distorted by being (mis)read as a "Christian" text that portrays Jesus in opposition to "the Jews" and "Judaism." So it is crucial at the outset to recognize that *hoi ioudaioi* in John, contrary to many standard translations (such as the NRSV), should not be translated as "the Jews." The Gospel of John, like the writings of the near-contemporary Judean historian Josephus, refers to the people of Israelite heritage in Roman

Palestine according to the region (and historical jurisdiction) in which they live: *hoi ioudaioi* in Judea, *hoi samareitai* in Samaria, and *hoi galilaioi* in Galilee. Many Judeans in John's story come to "trust in" or become "loyal to" Jesus ("believe in" is an inadequate translation).[27] But the Gospel frequently uses "the Judeans" in reference to the high priests and Pharisees, the rulers of the Judeans in Jerusalem. The dominant conflict in John's story is between Jesus (and those Galileans, Samaritans, and especially Judeans who trust in him) and (the rulers of) the Judeans based in the temple in Jerusalem. In a conflict more sustained than in the other Gospels, John's story has Jesus repeatedly go up to Jerusalem for one of "the festivals of the Judeans," at which he confronts and/or is confronted by the high priests and Pharisees, aka "the Judeans."

John's story portrays Jesus, who is a Galilean, working in all areas of Israelite heritage, and not only Galileans but also Samaritans, people in the trans-Jordan, and especially large numbers of Judeans come to "trust in" or "become loyal to" Jesus. He is thus clearly leading a renewal movement of the people of Israel, whether through his performance of signs or explanations of how he embodies the most prominent (symbolic) realities of Israelite tradition. While so much of the Gospel is devoted to Jesus's own dialogues and monologues, it also offers many indications that Jesus was building the infrastructure of a movement, with "disciples" as both an inner circle who advise and assist (John 2:11–12; 3:22; 6:3, 12–13, 66–70; 11:7–12, 54) and a larger circle of Jesus loyalists (John 4:1; 6:60–66; 8:31; 9:27–28; 15:8).

Indeed, from its outset and throughout, the Gospel of John presents Jesus and his mission as both enacting and declaring the fulfillment of Israelite tradition. John the Baptist accepts the role of the voice in the wilderness announcing the new exodus prophesied by Isaiah (1:23). Jesus is the new Moses, as in the discussion of the manna and the bread of life. Jesus is the renewer and guarantor of the inclusiveness of people in God's promise to Abraham, countering the use of the ancestor for special (elite) claims of lineage.

The most prominent of the Israelite expectations that Jesus fulfils is the role of an anointed one, as confirmed by Jesus to the Samaritan woman (John 4:25–26). Both Andrew and Simon at the beginning and the crowds at his dramatic entry into Jerusalem acclaim him as the "king of Israel." But he is also "the/a prophet," as evident particularly in his feeding of the multitude on the mountain (new Moses) and his healings (John 6:14; 7:40–41; 9:17). In nearly all of his "signs" and other actions, such as healings and charges against the Jerusalem rulers, Jesus is acting as a prophet rather than as a/the messiah. But John indicates in the narrative that (some of) the people wanted to take him

and make him king and that they recognized that he was a prophet, while the
Judean elite scoffed at the impossibility, according to official views, of either an
anointed one or a prophet coming from Galilee (John 6:15; 7:41, 50–52). Even
though the Gospel often portrays Jesus as a lone revealer in making declarations of how he embodies life (the "I am ..." statements), his "works" in the roles
of prophet and messiah are presented relationally in the story in the response
from the people affected. His "works" are always for the life, the renewal of the
people of Israel.

The signs that John presents as Jesus's key acts are both concrete and symbolic acts of renewal of the people. This is clearest in the feeding "on the mountain" that Jesus does "on the other side of the Sea of Galilee" as an alternative
to the official celebration of the Passover festival "of the Judeans" in Jerusalem.
The renewal of Israel is also embodied in Jesus's healings in Jerusalem on the
Sabbath and is most dramatically symbolic in his calling Lazarus to new life.

Almost from the beginning of the story, the Gospel of John presents
Jesus as generating the renewal of the people (in all of the areas of Israelite
heritage) in direct opposition to the high priests and Pharisees, (the rulers of)
"the Judeans" based in the temple. Again and again through the story, Jesus
travels up to Jerusalem for "the Passover festival of the Judeans" and other "festivals of the Judeans," where he mounts a forcible demonstration in the temple,
performs healings on the Sabbath that evoke attacks by the high priests and
Pharisees, and stages a provocative entry into the city in which a large crowd
(of Judeans) acclaim him as the king of Israel. With his movement building
in a crescendo, this last confrontation forces the hand of the Judean rulers in
Jerusalem and reveals their dependence on and subservience to the Romans.
The high priests and Pharisees recognize that, as the movement challenges the
Roman imperial order in Palestine, the Romans will take punitive military ac-
tion. As the high priest Caiaphas says with acute political realism, "it is better
to have one man die for the people than to have the whole people destroyed"
(John 11:47–50). More pointedly than any of the other Gospels, the Gospel of
John in its "passion narrative" clearly portrays the fundamental conflict between
Jesus, the prophet and messiah engaged in the renewal of the people of Israel,
and the rulers of Israel, as the high priests reveal their own subservience to
Roman rule ("we have no king but Caesar"; 19:15) and the Roman governor
has Jesus crucified as a rebel he takes to be posing as "the king of the Judeans."

Once we recognize that the (whole) Gospel stories are the principal
historical sources for investigation of the historical Jesus(-in-interaction-in-
context), we can probe their respective portrayals of Jesus and his mission. As

should become evident in the following chapters, these historical stories have a good deal of historical verisimilitude in their representation of the fundamental divide and conflicts in Roman Palestine. It is striking that, in their different ways, all of the Gospel sources portray Jesus-in-interaction as engaged in more or less the same basic agenda of renewal of Israel in opposition to the rulers. But the Gospels are plotted stories and speeches, and we should not imagine that Jesus's actions and teachings happened more or less as presented by one or another of them. It is necessary to critically analyze and assess their portrayals in the historical context as known from other sources. In that context we can then compare the respective Gospels' portrayals of particular actions and aspects of Jesus mission, keeping in mind that the portrayals and actions are embedded in the movements that formed in response to Jesus and produced the Gospels' portrayals. We can then critically "triangulate" from two or more Gospel portrayals to the action and/or speech of Jesus that lies "behind" and would account for the development of the different Gospel portrayals.

This approach is admittedly exploratory and provisional. With extensive further investigation it can become much more comprehensive and refined. To make the investigation manageable at this point, the following chapters work mainly from the Gospel of Mark and the Q series of speeches known from the parallel material in Matthew and Luke. These two sources are generally thought to be the earliest, closest to the time of Jesus. And they offer two very different kinds of presentation, a narrative sequence of episodes in Mark and a series of speeches in Q.

Hearing the Whole (Gospel) Story in Context

During and since the revival of interest in the historical Jesus in the 1980s, research has been carried out, largely separately, in a number of subfields of New Testament studies and related facets of ancient culture, that challenges what have been standard assumptions and procedures. The results of research in text criticism of the Hebrew Bible, in text criticism of the Gospels, on orality and literacy in antiquity, on ancient scribal practice, and on oral performance are all posing challenges to some of the most basic assumptions of biblical studies, a field developed for the interpretation of sacred texts on the basis of modern print culture.[28] Precisely because of the increasing specialization and splintering of scholarship, however, specialists in one area do not keep up with research on other subjects that are often closely related to their own. Just as interpreters of the historical Jesus have not attended to the implications of recent literary criticism of the Gospels, so also they have been slow to recognize the implications of these other lines of research for use of the Gospels as historical sources.

In what has long been standard study of Gospel texts (in the original Greek), we have assumed that specialists in text criticism had established the "best" or the "earliest" text, which is printed in standard editions for our use. Similarly, for the books of "the law and the prophets," we have assumed that text critics had established the best or earliest, if not original, text. In the study of early "Judaism" and early "Christianity," moreover, it has been widely assumed that, as "the people of the book," Jews were literate and read their scriptures, which were easily available, and that the Gospels and letters of Paul "circulated" and were read by early Christians. Another basic assumption is that "Mark" and the other evangelists "wrote" their Gospels (i.e., composed them in writing) and that Matthew and Luke had written copies of Mark and Q before them as they "wrote" their Gospels.

Multiple Versions of Authoritative Texts

As a result of recent research it is now becoming evident that the "biblical" texts established by text critics are the products of modern scholarship and that "early" or the "best" texts may be figments of the modern scholarly print-cultural imagination. The Dead Sea Scrolls included manuscripts of books later included in the Hebrew Bible that were more than a thousand years older than the medieval manuscripts previously known. Close study of those Dead Sea manuscripts has concluded that multiple versions of these texts coexisted in the Qumran community (and apparently in Jerusalem as well) and that the multiple textual traditions were all "unstable" and still developing.[29] The same process that scholars have concluded was involved in the composition of these (composite) texts evidently continued throughout the second-temple period.

Somewhat similarly, New Testament text critics are concluding that early manuscript and fragmentary papyrological evidence suggests considerable variation in the text of the Gospels. According to David Parker, "the further back we go, the greater seems to be the degree of variation."[30] Significantly, the variation is greater for the most frequently cited statements of Jesus, such as on marriage and divorce, than for other teachings. This suggests that the considerable differences across early manuscripts is not simply the result of the way copyists copied (already written) copies. Rather, it seems related to the importance of the particular teaching of Jesus to people's lives, particularly on key matters. Eldon Epp suggests that the diversity in early manuscripts attests the social contextualizations of the Gospel texts.[31] On this basis he also argues that textual *authority* was pluriform, thereby rejecting the previous print-cultural assumptions of text critics who took textual "variants" in early manuscripts as evidence of "tampering with the text" or "misquoting Jesus."[32] Not until the fourth century do manuscripts show evidence of some standardization of the text of the Gospels, which is evidently related to the establishment of Christianity in the Roman Empire.[33]

The Predominantly Oral Communication and the Functions of Written Texts

Other recent research, which should help explain what recent text criticism is finding, indicates that literacy was severely limited in antiquity. Well-documented studies have demonstrated that at its greatest extent in the Roman Empire, literacy was confined to between 10 and 15 percent of the urban population, with literacy in Roman Palestine limited mainly to the scribal elite.[34] Life for the vast majority of people in ancient societies did not require literacy. Among ordinary people transactions of all kinds took place via oral communication, usually face to face. Even "legal" agreements such as loans were conducted orally, governed by time-honored custom and ritual. The people trusted personal witnesses and testimony far more than written documents, which could be altered and used against them. More important than the rate of literacy in antiquity were the functions of writing, which was used mainly by the political and cultural elite, often as an instrument of power over the people. Yet even elite "literary" culture was largely oral, with poetry of various forms performed at festivals, plays performed in theaters, and speeches delivered by orators before imperial audiences.

It may come as a surprise to moderns accustomed to the ubiquity of writing in print culture to realize that in antiquity not all writing was intended to be read or even consulted. In societies where writing was rare, it had a mysterious aura or numinous quality. That texts were "written" gave them an awesome higher authority. The elite used this to advantage in what we might call "monumental" and "constitutional" writing. Augustus had his *res gestae* inscribed on monuments erected around the empire not to inform but to impress the urban crowds. Texts of Mosaic torah[35] were written on scrolls and laid up in the temple. In the memoirs of Nehemiah (8:4–6) the scribe Ezra, whom the Persian imperial regime sent to Judea, standing on a raised wooden platform, "opened the writing [scroll] in the sight of all the people." The people then acclaimed "'Amen, Amen,' lifting up their hands," and "bowed their heads and worshipped Yahweh with their faces to the ground." This "writing of the torah of Moses" was clearly a sacred object of great power. The people were bowing before a numinous monumental writing that provided divine authority to the temple-state in Jerusalem.

While the fact that some texts were "written" on a scroll gave them authority, ordinary people had no need of writing in the cultivation of their own customs, stories, prayers, songs, ceremonies, and rituals, all of which were oral and deeply ingrained in memory. Written scrolls, which were cumbersome as well as expensive and unintelligible to the nonliterate people, would have been confined to the scribal and priestly circles based in the temple. The picture in Luke 4 of Jesus opening a scroll in a synagogue and reading was a projection perhaps based on what might have happened at a gathering of a well-off Jewish congregation in a Hellenistic city that might have included someone who could read and who possessed a revered written text. In Roman Palestine people were often suspicious of writing, which could be used against them by the wealthy and powerful. In fact, they could be downright hostile to certain kinds of writing. One of the first actions in the popular insurrection in Jerusalem in 66 CE was "to destroy the money-lenders' bonds and prevent the recovery of debts" (Josephus, *War* 2.426–427).

The Oral-Written Scribal Cultivation and Composition of Texts

Recognition that literacy was limited to scribal circles in Judea has led some scholars to draw a distinction between oral and scribal culture. Another recent line of research, however, explains that scribal culture and practice were also oral, or "oral-written." Like their counterparts in ancient Egyptian and Mesopotamian courts, the scribes who served in the Judean temple-state were trained to read and write. They were the literate professionals who made written copies of authoritative texts. But they learned those authoritative texts by repeated recitation, so the texts became "written on the tablet of the heart" as well as inscribed on scrolls.[36] As Martin Jaffee explains, "the oral performative tradition" was not only fundamental in later rabbinic circles but also central in scribal circles such as the Qumran community, which also produced and valued written scrolls.[37] In contrast to the standard translation that projects modern scholars' own practice of "reading," "studying," and "interpreting" written texts, a more appropriate translation of a now-famous passage in the Community Rule would be: "Where the ten are, ... the many shall watch in community for a third of every night of the year, to recite the writing [*lqrw' bspr*] and to search the justice-ruling [*ldwrs mspt*] and to offer communal blessings [*lbrk byhd*]" (1QS 6:6–8). All three of the activities mentioned—reciting, "searching," and uttering blessings—were clearly oral. The "writing" is usually assumed to have been a "book" of "the Torah." But even if a scroll of torah were open before the reciter(s), recitation would have been from memory. Somewhat like scribes in

Judea and in the ancient Near East, the literate Greco-Roman elite also committed to memory all manner of texts that were (also) written.

Recent studies of composition in Greek and Latin in antiquity are confirming the implications of the ubiquitous memorization and recitation of texts,
particularly for how texts were composed. Contrary to previous assumptions
in classical studies as well as biblical studies, the literate elite in the Roman
Empire did not compose their letters or histories or other texts in writing (as
we are accustomed to doing in modern print culture). Pliny the Elder offers a
fascinating account of his own practice (*Ep.* 9.34; 2.10; 3.18; 7.17).[38] Awaking
before daylight, he composed in his head while lying in bed. Arising after some
hours, he called in a capable secretary to take dictation as he spoke his text. To
disseminate his composition he then performed his text to a group of friends or
in public. His "publication" of his composition was thus assisted or "backed up"
by a written text, but the composition was not done in writing. Many texts in
antiquity, including lengthy epics, were "traditional" in the sense that they were
further developed as they were repeatedly performed.

In any case, nearly all of what we think of as "literature" in antiquity, certainly poetry, drama, orations, and philosophical discussion, was recited or performed before a group, not read and certainly not read by an individual silently.
A very fluid relationship existed among composition, performance, and the
writing down of a text. Since performers, like Judean scribes, had the texts in
their memory, they were not dependent on a written text. The existence of texts
in writing did not disrupt the continuity of oral performance and certainly did
not displace it.

Appreciating the Gospels as Texts-in-Performance

If we now bring these clearly related but largely separate lines of research together, they have serious implications for the Gospels and how we might use
them as sources for the historical Jesus. It seems clear from the examination
of the Gospel stories discussed earlier not only that the Gospels were stories
about ordinary people but also that they were produced by ordinary people. If
even the literate scribes cultivated texts, along with the broader cultural tradition, orally, then how much more did the nonliterate ordinary people cultivate
their own popular cultural tradition orally?[39] If even the literate Greco-Roman
elite composed texts in their minds or in performance, how much more would
ordinary people have done so? But it is unnecessary to determine whether or
not the Gospels were composed with the aid of writing, since, even in literate
circles where texts existed in writing, they were recited or performed orally,

as in the scribal-priestly community at Qumran. Correspondingly, even if the Gospels existed in writing, they would have been orally performed in community gatherings.

From the generation in which the Gospels would have been composed we have little evidence other than these stories and speeches themselves. Several studies have explored the many features of oral discourse and performance evident in Mark and the Q speeches, and studies of oral features in John have recently commenced. Evidence from subsequent generations indicate that the communities of Christ and their nascent intellectual leadership did not just prefer orality but were even hesitant about or suspicious of writing.[40] Using comparisons with what is known of performance practices in Greek and Latin sources, Whitney Shiner has explored how performance of Mark's Gospel may have worked.[41] A *lektor* of the Gospels did not need to know how to read from a codex but could simply learn the Gospel from hearing oral performances by others. Justin Martyr reports that at Sunday assemblies "the memoirs of the apostles or the writings of the prophets are read (= recited) for as long as time permits."[42] Hippolytus says that scripture was recited at the beginning of services by a succession of lectors (reciters) until all had gathered. This practice lasted at least to the time of Augustine. He comments that many people had learned to recite (large portions of) the Gospels themselves from hearing them recited in services.[43] Such evidence of how the oral recitation of the Gospels continued for many generations suggests that the Gospel texts would have also been recited in community meetings at the time of their composition (probably in performance).

Most of us who are engaged in the study of the historical Jesus have barely begun to take any of these recent lines of research into account. As we do so, their implications put us in an awkward position. The texts of the Gospels that we have been trained to interpret are the synthetic products of modern Western biblical studies "established" by text critics on the basis of relatively late and complete manuscripts. Established interpretation of Gospel texts, in which we have been trained, focuses on the meaning of words, phrases, individual sayings (verses), and discrete "pericopes" (often "lessons" for a given week in the lectionary). Text critics are now concluding that the wording of phrases, sayings, and episodes in the Gospels was unstable—until a degree of stabilization was established in late antiquity. Given the dominance of oral communication in the ancient world, moreover, in all the aspects just sketched, the Gospel texts, even once they were written, functioned—had life—as texts-in-performance in communities of Christ in particular life circumstances. The texts (the words and phrases) of the sayings and mini-stories that we have been trained to interpret turn out to be unreliable even in the written form that we formerly assumed provided stability. And our training in interpretation of (fragments of) texts-in-print on the basis of the assumptions of print culture has left us ill prepared to understand texts-in-performance.

Help is available, however, from recent studies of "oral-derived texts" and texts-in-performance in other fields. Proliferating studies of one or many aspects of texts-in-performance in fields such as ancient Greek and medieval European epic, sociolinguistics, and the ethnography of performance, along with theoretical reflection based on such studies, are readily available. Some of the recent experiments by biblical scholars to appreciate texts-in-performance have drawn particularly on the work of John Miles Foley, coupled with recent studies of social (cultural) memory.[44] Serious rethinking and retraining will be required for those who study the Gospels and the historical Jesus and who seek to develop an appreciation of texts in oral performance and an appropriate approach for the use of such texts as sources. In the chapters that follow only some preliminary and partial adjustments will be possible. These will concentrate in two areas where the implications of the new research are relatively clear.

The first is a powerful reinforcement of the recognition (discussed earlier) that the Gospel stories and speeches, not separate sayings, are the sources for investigation of the historical Jesus. The results of recent text criticism of the Gospels and recent studies of oral tradition have seriously undermined the previous concentration on individual sayings. The wording in individual sayings was unstable for centuries. Recent studies of oral performances of long epics and other stories, moreover, is showing that the wording of lines and "stanzas" and episodes changes from performance to performance, depending on the audience and the circumstances. Yet these studies find that the overall story tends to remain consistent from performance to performance. Ironically for how Jesus scholars have focused on separate sayings, while treating the Gospels as unreliable and mere containers, the overall Gospel stories turn out to be the most stable and reliable historical sources. It is necessary for investigators of the historical Jesus to "hear" the whole Gospel stories and speeches.

But how to do this? How can we appreciate texts-in-performance in order to use them as historical sources? As discussed, if we are to be investigating a historical figure it is important to move well beyond the narrow confines of separate sayings and individualism to a relational approach to Jesus engaged in communication, interaction, and conflict with people in the social forms and institutions of his society. The Gospels, the primary sources for information about Jesus, portray him as engaged in interaction and conflict. In fact, it would be impossible for an unengaged, nonrelational individual Jesus to stand behind the communications and interactions that were necessary to have led to the composition of the different Gospels. In fact, work with sources that are "texts-in-performance" should dovetail with and reinforce the relational and contextual approach just outlined. In order to keep the presentation and procedure somewhat manageable here, we focus on three key aspects of appreciating texts-in-performance that are derived mainly from the theoretical reflection of Foley and closely related recent reflections on social memory.

Texts-in-performance involve several "extratextual" factors as well as the "text" itself: a *text* is performed before *hearers* (audience) who interact with the performer-and-text in their life circumstances or *context;* the community of hearers is affected by or *resonates* to the performed text as it *references* the cultural *tradition* or social memory in which both performer (and text) and hearers are rooted. The referencing of tradition is usually "metonymic" (i.e., a part signals the whole). To appreciate the Gospels as texts-in-performance, therefore, we focus on the *text* as performed in *context* as it references the cultural *tradition* (memory).

Attempting to hear the *text* of each Gospel leads to taking the whole story into account, leading in turn to an appreciation of its complexity—virtually the opposite of focusing on text fragments taken out of context one at a time and often selected according to theological questions brought to the text. Earlier episodes (including shorter or longer speeches) set up later episodes, which in turn shed new light on the earlier ones. In the course of hearing the text performed, the audience members are engaged with Jesus's interaction with people in life circumstances like their own, both people who become his followers and those he opposes and who oppose him. Jesus's interaction with the people has implications for his conflict with the rulers and their representatives and vice versa. The story is filled with conflict, often multiple conflicts. Jesus's actions and speeches involve multiple interests and issues simultaneously.

Attempting to hear the text of each Gospel *in context* requires Gospel interpreters to become as knowledgeable as possible about ancient history, particularly that of Palestine under Roman rule and the other areas of the Roman Empire into which Jesus movements spread in the first few generations, all in a multidisciplinary way (history, archaeology, political-economy, anthropology). That the performed texts portray such sharp conflict between Jesus and the people on the one hand and the Roman rulers and their clients on the other requires investigation into the political-economic-religious structures and

dynamics of life in Galilee and Judea under Roman rule and those of other
areas in which a Gospel story resonated with people.

Attempting to sense how each Gospel text performed in context may have
resonated with people as it referenced (predominantly Israelite) cultural *tradition* (social memory) requires Gospel interpreters to become as knowledgeable
as possible about Israelite culture. This includes the differences between popular and official tradition, including how Galileans, Judeans, and Samaritans
were impacted by outside forces, both material and cultural. In this connection, as indicated by the cursory survey of recent research in various areas just
presented, the ground is shifting under our feet as we recognize, for example,
that the books of the Hebrew Bible do not provide *direct* sources for Israelite
popular tradition and that Hellenistic philosophical texts do not provide *direct* sources for popular culture in Hellenistic cities, much less the surrounding
villages.

Second, as we shift from focusing on text fragments as objects of interpretation to critical reading of the whole Gospel stories (and speeches) as
sources for Jesus and then to appreciation of texts-in-performance in historical
and cultural context, our goal also changes. Instead of trying to establish the
meaning of the text-fragment-in-itself, we are attempting to recognize and appreciate the *work* that a performed text does in and on the community of hearers in their particular historical situation. What we are after is the effect of the
performed text on the community addressed, as detected from the text in what
is known of the context, including from other sources.

Recognition that our principal sources for Jesus were the Gospel texts-
in-performance might appear to make historical investigation and historical
knowledge virtually impossible. But that would be true only on the old assumptions of biblical studies and the distinctively modern Western individualistic
belief that an individual, and the revealer Jesus in particular, can be known
apart from how he was embedded in societal forms and social interaction in
a political-economic religious context. The idea that an individual person and
what he "actually" or most likely said and did could be isolated was a chimera of
the modern Western, post-Enlightenment, individualistic imagination. It could
be argued that what has led to the revival of interest in the historical Jesus has
been the greater awareness and more precise knowledge of the historical situation in which he lived and worked. What we have hardly begun to do is to
view and explore Jesus as relationally as well as contextually engaged in societal
forms and interaction. Recognition that our principal sources for Jesus were
texts-in-performance only forces us to move toward a relational and contextual
approach.

Since the Gospels were produced by and performed in communities of Jesus movements that responded to Jesus's mission, however, not only can we not extract Jesus as an individual from his interaction with others in historical context; we cannot extract Jesus-in-interaction from the movements that produced and performed the Gospels. This, of course, is the way history works anyhow, as a historically significant figure emerges from interrelationships and interactions with people in complex circumstances in the movements or events thus catalyzed. In attempting to appreciate how particular Gospel stories of Jesus's mission resonated with the movements in which they were performed we can discern how he was understood as interacting with his followers and his opponents in historical context in some of the principal movements that resulted from his mission. We can then make judicious, informed comparisons of those portrayals to ascertain what may have been the main agenda of Jesus's mission in historical context. Because of the very character of the Gospels as the sources (whole stories in performance), however, it is necessary for our investigation of Jesus in historical context to begin with the broad portrayal of Jesus's mission in particular Gospels before we proceed to those comparisons and the conclusions based on them. This is the procedure followed in preparation of the chapters that follow.

2. Jesus and the Politics of Roman Palestine

The obvious starting point is again what seems most certain about the historical Jesus: he was crucified by order of the Roman governor at the time, Pontius Pilate. Since crucifixion was the gruesome form of execution that the Romans used on political agitators in the provinces, it appears that Jesus was at least thought to be an insurgent leader against the Roman imperial order, in Pilate's terms a rebel "king of the Judeans." The theological field of New Testament studies of which study of the historical Jesus is a subfield, however, works on the deeply rooted assumption that Jesus was a religious figure. Understandably, therefore, many interpreters of Jesus give little attention to how Jesus may have operated in the politics of the historical situation.[1]

In this connection, the continuing projection onto antiquity of the modern separation of religion and politics discussed in chapter 1 has special importance. It may be difficult to appreciate the distortion and misunderstanding of ancient history and historical leaders that result from this reductionist projection. But perhaps we can appreciate the resulting distortion of Jesus as a historical figure in antiquity by recalling the ominous results of similar projections of the separation of politics and religion onto people subject to Western (neo) colonial rule by British and American scholars, governments, and their intellectual advisers in two recent cases.

In a now-famous case in the social sciences, specialists on Iran and the Middle East were taken by surprise by the Iranian revolution of 1978–79. This happened because they had not considered Shi'ite Islam in Iran relevant to politics. They therefore paid little attention to the ever-larger funeral processions honoring Shi'ite martyrs killed by the Shah's secret police and to what the Ayatollah Ruhollah Khomeini and other Muslim mullahs were saying and writing publicly, whether in Qum or in Paris.[2]

Particularly relevant to the historical Jesus is a point made by the current generation of Indian historians of modern India who focus on "subaltern studies."[3] They criticize both colonial historians and Marxist historians for failing to discern that the form taken by the often anticolonial political activity of the ordinary people was what Westerners dismissively classified as religious movements, which were therefore supposedly not involved in politics. In this case, Western scholars focused narrowly on what they defined as the political dimension of the anticolonial struggle while ignoring the cultural-religious dimension of life in which subject peoples' identity and dignity were embedded and expressed. The result in both of these cases proved to be distorted views and skewed understandings in which U.S. and British governments' repressive policies and practices of (attempted) military domination were rooted—with continuing reverberations in still-unfolding history.

Similarly, interpreters distort the historical figure of Jesus of Nazareth and the movement(s) of his followers by classifying him as "religious" and ignoring or dismissing the political dimension of his mission and movement(s). As noted in chapter 1, it will be necessary to abandon some of the basic synthetic Christian constructs, such as "(early) Judaism" and "(early) Christianity," that have been obscuring the complex concrete realities of ancient history in order to discern the political dynamics of Roman Palestine where Jesus worked and the ways in which he may have been engaged in those dynamics. Particularly problematic in blocking discernment of Jesus's political engagement has been the standard theological scheme of Christian origins in which Jesus was the revealer but did not himself generate a movement. The Gospel sources, however, present Jesus as actively engaged in catalyzing a movement. He works in village communities, sends his disciples into villages to expand his program of preaching and healing, and appoints the Twelve as representative heads of the people (of Israel in its twelve tribes) undergoing renewal.

Even some attempts to deal with the social context of the historical Jesus have, in effect, avoided dealing with the politics of Roman Palestine. Several decades ago some of the more socially sensitive interpreters emphasized that Jesus focused his ministry particularly on marginalized people such as tax collectors and sinners and prostitutes. The application of sociology focused on social stratification gave this analysis the aura of social science: Jesus was seen to be addressing primarily the lowest class of "expendables" who had dropped down the social ladder to the level of destitution. The use of structural-functional sociology, oriented to how social phenomena are "functional" for the overall social system, paid little attention to political-economic-religious power relations and underplayed social-political conflict.[4]

In order to consider critically the politics of Roman Palestine and how Jesus operated in that context, it is necessary to avoid the synthetic construct of "Judaism" and the Christian theological scheme of Christian origins and to move beyond the limitations of structural-functional sociology. It may then be possible to take a fresh look at how the Gospel sources portray Jesus, in connection with the results of recent research on key aspects of the historical context of Jesus and/or of Jesus's mission, in three steps. First, working directly from a critical reading of sources (other than the Gospels) for people and events in Galilee and Judea in late second-temple times, I sketch what appear to be key facets of the politics of Palestine under Roman rule. Second, I consider how recent cross-cultural studies may offer insight into modes of peasant politics that fall in between the usual dichotomy of acquiescence and revolt. Third, working directly from the Gospels and component Jesus traditions, I probe how Jesus's prophecies and actions fit into the politics of Roman Palestine.

The Politics of Roman Palestine

Textual sources for society and history in Palestine under early Roman imperial rule[5] portray a fundamental division and frequent overt conflict between the Romans and their client Herodian and high priestly rulers on the one hand and the ordinary people on the other. These sources devote considerable attention to the institutions set up by the Romans to hold the people in subjection and to extract revenues from them and to the measures taken by the heads of those institutions to reestablish political order. They also give a surprising amount of attention to the people's protests against Roman provocations and to distinctively Israelite forms of popular movements of resistance and renewal. The portrayal of the temple and the high priesthood in Josephus's histories and in earlier Judean texts raises serious questions about their authority, that is, about the legitimacy of their religious-political power. It should be evident throughout the discussion that the politics of Roman Palestine are inseparable from religious-cultural conflict.

The Expanded Temple-State Taken Over by Rome

The conflict between rulers and ruled in the Israelite areas of ancient Palestine was inherent in the fundamental political-economic-religious structure of this traditional agrarian society. The fundamental social forms were the multigenerational family and the village community consisting of many families.[6] The vast majority of the people lived and worked in hundreds of semi-self-governing village communities scattered around the countryside. Above the village communities was the temple-state in Jerusalem, headed by the high priestly aristocracy (and, later, regional client rulers), which was in turn subject to the Hellenistic imperial regime. The temple-state and, indirectly, the imperial regime exercised political control and were supported economically by tithes and offerings, taxes, and tribute taken from the villagers. Villagers' inability to support themselves on what remained of their crops after the tithes, taxes, and tribute were taken forced them to borrow at high rates of interest from officers of the state. Exploitation of peasants' indebtedness thus became another source of revenues for the elite and a drain on the villagers. Although the rulers did not interfere in village affairs so long as their revenues were forthcoming, the inherent conflict could intensify as villagers were unable to support themselves after yielding up hefty portions of their crops but remained under the coercive control of the rulers.

While there was no "middle class" in ancient Judean society, the rule of the priestly aristocracy was mediated in certain respects by learned scribes. In a lengthy passage in his book of wisdom (Sirach), the learned scribe Jesus ben Sira, active in the early second century BCE, lauds the scribe's role in service of the aristocracy that headed the temple-state. In contrast to the artisans and farmers, on whose labor the city depends, only the learned scribe has the leisure to learn the torah of the Most High, cultivate prophecies, and acquire various kinds of wisdom in his training to advise the "great ones" in their councils (Sir 38:24—39:11).[7] In his accounts of the Hasmonean high priests, who consolidated power following the Maccabean Revolt, Josephus portrays the Pharisees as playing a similar role in the operations of the temple-state, particularly under John Hyrcanus, who conquered Samaria, and Alexandra Salome, who succeeded her husband, Alexander Jannai (*Ant.* 13:171–173, 288–298, 401–409).[8] The Pharisees, in Josephus's accounts, were evidently a faction or party of the scribes who served as advisers to the Judean rulers, at least when they enjoyed political favor. We will return to a discussion of the scribes and Pharisees in relation both to the temple-state and to Jesus in chapter 6; in this chapter we focus on the conflict between rulers and ruled.

The primary conflict inherent in the political-economic-religious structure of the Judean temple-state is illustrated both by the temple as the political-economic as well as the religious center and especially by the celebration of the Passover festival in the temple. The sacrifices and offerings offered to God presided over by the high priestly aristocracy consisted of a portion of the crops yielded up by the villagers. Passover celebrated the deliverance of the people from bondage under a foreign ruler in Egypt, the foundational origins of Israel as a people called to live in independence under the direct rule of God, and was at first celebrated by families in their ancestral households. As a means of centralizing religious-political power in Jerusalem, however, Passover had long since been celebrated in Jerusalem, requiring pilgrims to bring some of their resources to the temple for the festival. Passover was thus a key source of revenue for the temple-state. Yet it was still the people's celebration of their deliverance from foreign domination, which became all the more poignant with their subjection to direct Roman rule. Thus, as Josephus explains, because the celebration of Passover could be a volatile time, it had become standard procedure for the Roman governors to position a cohort of armed soldiers on the porticoes of the temple (*War* 2.223–227; *Ant.* 20.105–122; cf. Matt 26:5). Ostensibly posted to prevent or quell any "uprising," the soldiers would have only reminded the celebrants of their current subjection to the Romans, thus exacerbating the potential for conflict.[9]

When the Romans conquered Palestine, they took over the Judean temple-state that had expanded its own rule over most of Palestine in the previous decades. The temple-state had been set up by the Persian imperial regime centuries before to control and take revenues from the area immediately surrounding Jerusalem.[10] Following the popular revolt against the weakened Seleucid emperor Antiochus IV Epiphanes led by Judas the Maccabee ("hammer"), his brothers in the Hasmonean family maneuvered to get themselves appointed high priests by the further weakened Seleucid imperial regime. Their successors as Hasmonean high priests then proceeded, with their mercenary troops, to conquer the Idumeans to the south and the Samaritans to the north and destroyed the Samaritans' temple (to eliminate any rival political-religious center). In 104 BCE the Hasmonean regime wrested control of Galilee from the Itureans to the north and allowed the inhabitants of the area to remain on their land if they agreed to observe "the laws of the Judeans."

From the viewpoint that dissolves these historical events into religion, this appears to have been a "forced conversion" to "Judaism." In less anachronistic terms, the Hasmonean regime's insistence that the inhabitants of Galilee, like the Idumeans, live according to "the laws of the Judeans" (*Ant.* 13.318–319) was rather the subjection of the people of these areas to the Judean temple-state.[11] The "laws of the Judeans" would presumably have been the regulations requiring tithes, offerings, and other revenues to be yielded to the temple-state in Jerusalem. Josephus's passing mention that prominent Idumean figures who served as high-ranking officers in the Hasmonean regime continued to observe their own Idumean cultural-religious traditions tends to confirm this conclusion. Josephus's references to the Hasmoneans' and, later, Herod the Great's having established fortresses manned by military garrisons at several sites in Galilee to control the area is further confirmation that the Hasmoneans had taken control of the area and people of Galilee.[12] Prior to the Roman conquest, therefore, Hasmonean high priests in the temple-state had exerted control over all of the areas and people of Israelite heritage, the Galileans and Samaritans and people in the trans-Jordan as well as the Judeans.

Partly, perhaps largely, because of the Jerusalem rulers' conquest and destruction of their temple, hostility between Samaritans and Judeans often erupted in the ensuing generations. It has been claimed that Galileans became loyal to both the temple and "the Torah." While brought under the same rulers in Jerusalem as their fellow Israelites in Judea (for the first time in eight centuries), however, Galileans would likely have been ambivalent about their subjection to Jerusalem rule.

Roman Conquest, Roman Tribute, and Client Rulers

Roman imperial rule was by far the most determinative force in the historical conditions of and for Jesus's mission. Roman imperial rule impacted the people of Palestine in three ways that were particularly significant: military (re)conquests, demand for tribute, and imposition of client rulers.

Roman Conquest

Palestine was the last area around the eastern shores of the Mediterranean Sea that the Romans conquered, in 63 BCE. When the Judeans and the Galileans turned out to be resistant, the Roman armies reconquered the land again and again with far more devastation than the original conquest. In recent decades classical historians have brought a more critical perspective and approach to Roman imperial expansion and military practices than previous generations of scholars.[13] Roman armies devastated the countryside, destroyed villages, slaughtered or enslaved the people, and crucified those who resisted, all as ways of terrorizing the conquered peoples into submission. Josephus's accounts of Roman military actions in Galilee and Judea turn out to be quite credible. Galileans usually bore the brunt of Roman retaliation as the legions moved south through Galilee from Syria. Because Roman imperial violence had such a serious impact on the lives of the people in the historical context in which Jesus worked, the next chapter is devoted to its effects and to Jesus's response.

Roman Tribute

After his initial conquest, Pompey laid the subjected people under *trib-ute* (*War* 1.154; *Ant.* 14.74). The tribute was a means of humiliation and subjugation as well as a source of revenue. The Romans viewed failure or even slowness to render the tribute as tantamount to rebellion and re-taliated with a vengeance. According to Josephus, the people subject to the high priest Hyrcanus were required to render one-fourth of the harvest ev-ery second year (except for the sabbatical year), in addition to the tithes to be paid to the high priesthood (*Ant.* 14.202–203). During the great empire-wide Roman civil war, Cassius imposed an extraordinary levy of tribute "beyond the [people's] ability to pay" (*War* 1.219–222; *Ant.* 14.271–275).

The Roman demand for tribute from Judeans and Galileans provides a vivid illustration of the inseparability of politics, economics, and religion. It placed Israelite people in an impossible "catch-22" situation. Under the first two commandments of the Mosaic covenant, God was literally their exclusive ruler, not merely religiously but inseparably also politically and economically. Israelites were to have no other God and were forbidden to "bow down and serve" another god as lord and master with their produce and labor (Exod 20:3, 4–5; Deut 5:7, 8–9). Yet if they did not pay, the Romans would retaliate bru-tally. Precisely this conflict came to a head when Rome deposed Herod's son Archelaus as ruler of Judea and sent out a Roman governor to oversee the high priestly aristocracy that was now charged with maintaining order. Quirinius, the Legate of Syria, conducted an assessment for the tribute (*Ant.* 18.1–2; Luke 2:1). What Josephus calls the "fourth philosophy" of the Judeans, evident-ly a scribal group led by the learned teacher Judas and the Pharisee Saddok, mobilized a collective refusal to pay the tribute, insisting that Judeans' exclusive loyalty to God precluded service to another lord and master (*War* 2.118; *Ant.* 18.4–5, 23). The tribute was clearly a focal point of a fundamental political-economic-religious conflict between people of Israelite heritage and Roman imperial rule.

Client Rulers: Herodian Kings and High Priests

The face of Roman rule in Galilee and Judea was Herodian kingship and/or the Jerusalem high priesthood. Like the Romans themselves, their client rul-ers—Herod the Great, (Herod) Antipas in Galilee and Perea, and the high priests who headed the temple—pursued programs and practices that irritated and exploited their Galilean and Judean subjects.

Herod was attractive to the Romans as a military strongman who could bring Palestine under control. Having risen to prominence by his violent treatment of the Galileans (*War* 1.203–215; *Ant.* 14.158–184), he then conquered his own subjects with the help of Roman troops. Herod became a model Roman client king. In honor of Caesar Augustus he built not only imperial temples but new cities named for the emperor, the seaport city of Caesarea and the military colony in Samaria, named Sebaste (*War* 1.402–421; *Ant.* 15.331–341, 364). He imposed alien Roman institutions such as a theater, an amphitheater (hippodrome), and games in honor of Caesar in Jerusalem (*War* 1.402; 2.44; *Ant.* 15.267–291, 318). He massively rebuilt the temple in Jerusalem in grand Hellenistic-Roman style, with a golden Roman eagle mounted over one of the gates (*War* 1.401; *Ant.* 15.380–425; 17.151). All of these grandiose building projects, in addition to his lavish court and his extreme munificence to the imperial court and to key cities of the empire (*War* 1.422–428; *Ant.* 15.326–330; 16.146–149), required rigorous taxation of his subjects (*Ant.* 15.365). Throughout his reign he maintained tight control through the use of repressive measures that would today be called evidence of a military dictatorship or police state, requiring loyalty oaths to Roman and his own rule, deploying informers, and mercilessly executing dissenters (*Ant.* 15.280–291, 292–298, 323–325, 365–372; 16.235–240; 17.42).[14]

The Romans and, perhaps, diaspora Jewish communities in the cities of the empire on which Herod lavished gifts may have been pleased with Herod, but scribal circles as well as ordinary people in Judea and Galilee were deeply discontented. The Pharisees refused his loyalty oath—and got away with it (*Ant.* 15.370; 17.41–45). Other scribes articulated a yearning for a legitimate king who was indeed the anointed of God (Psalms of Solomon 17). As Herod lay dying, two revered teachers and their students cut down the Roman eagle from atop the temple gate—whereupon Herod had them burned alive (*War* 1.648–650; *Ant.* 17.149–167). Finally, at Herod's death, the popular resentment that had been building burst forth in widespread revolt in every major district of the realm (*War* 2.55–65; *Ant.* 17.271–285).

After Herod died, the Romans placed his son Antipas, who had been raised at the imperial court in Rome, over Galilee and Perea.[15] The Galileans were thus no longer under Jerusalem rule during the life and mission of Jesus. And after having been ruled historically from distant capitals, Galileans were now for the first time ruled by an administration located directly in Galilee. Within twenty-five years Antipas had imposed not just one but two newly built capital cities on the landscape of lower Galilee: Sepphoris, only a few miles from Nazareth, and Tiberias, prominently in view across the lake from villages such as Capernaum and Chorazin. In an unusual touch, Josephus mentions explicitly the disruption and dislocation caused by the construction of Tiberias, overlooking the Sea of Galilee (*Ant.* 18.36–38). Having most Galilean villages within sight of one or another of his capital cities, Antipas could be rigorously "efficient" in collecting the revenues needed to pay for such construction as well as to support his court and administration. As we know from Josephus as well as from the synoptic Gospels, John the Baptist prophesied against his policies and practices so effectively among the people that Antipas arrested and executed him (*Ant.* 18.116–119; Mark 6:17–29). It seems likely that the intense hostility of Galileans toward both Sepphoris and the Herodian administration in Tiberias that Josephus encountered in 66–67 was developing already under Antipas.[16]

Ten years after Herod's death the Romans placed Judea in the custody of an aristocracy composed of the four high priestly families that Herod had elevated to prominence under the oversight of a Roman governor resident in Caesarea Maritima. The Roman governor ordinarily held power to appoint and depose high priests and often had custody of the high priestly vestments. The frequent change of high priests as each successive governor designated his own creature indicates how vulnerable the high priesthood was to its Roman overlords. That Caiaphas lasted so long under Pontius Pilate suggests that he collaborated closely with his superiors, as often observed. A mark of the priestly aristocracy's close cooperation with the Romans was their responsibility to collect the tribute. Like Herod's kingship and Antipas's tetrarchy, the high priesthood was the face of Roman rule. The illegitimacy of the high priests and the high priesthood in the eyes of the people, however, ran far deeper than their dependency on Roman rule. Since the high priests play such a major role in the Gospel sources for the historical Jesus, the issue of their (lack of) authority merits fuller consideration.[17]

High Priesthood and Temple: Declining Authority and Scribal Protests

Once we are no longer reading our sources through the synthetic concept of "Judaism," with the temple as one of the principal components of a religion, the sources lead to a complex picture of the temple headed by the high priesthood as the central, governing institution of Judean society under Roman rule. After the Roman destruction of the temple, rabbinic traditions usually present the temple in very positive, sometimes idealized terms. Second-temple Judean texts, however, indicate that the temple and particularly the high priesthood and priestly aristocracy were controversial and often the center of conflict.

There was a certain ambiguity inherent in the very establishment of the temple-state under Persian imperial sponsorship. The "second temple" was the arrangement whereby Judeans subject to Persian rule were focused on bringing tithes and offerings to their own God ("the God who is in Jerusalem"; Ezra 1:2–4). The elite circles that produced the extant texts articulated a certain ideology of the temple's political-religious autonomy, as headed by the high priest Joshua and the royal pretender Zerubbabel (e.g., Zech 3; 4; 6). But of course the temple was sponsored—and funded—by the Persian imperial court (Ezra 1; 6), to become, in effect, a local instrument of the imperial administration. The officials of the temple were responsible for maintaining order and collecting revenues for the Persians as well as to support themselves (Ezra 4:13, 20; 6:8; 7:24; Neh 5:4; 10:26–29, 40).[18]

Insofar as the temple-state was also a local representative of the imperial regime, the priestly aristocracy in Jerusalem depended on imperial support for their own political power. They were also susceptible to influence from the dominant political culture. The most dramatic case, the Hellenizing reform under the emperor Antiochus IV Epiphanes that transformed Jerusalem into a *polis*, is well rehearsed in scholarly discussion.[19] Less discussed is the fact that Judeans' resistance to and revolt against the enforcement of the reform constituted also a revolt against the high priests in control of the temple.

Judean texts produced just before and during this political-religious crisis reveal serious opposition to the reforming high priesthood and even to the second temple itself.[20] The Epistle of Enoch (1 Enoch 94–105) called down God's judgment on the aristocracy for their blatant oppression of the poor. When the dominant high priestly faction abandoned the traditional covenant with God, several circles of scribes moved into active resistance. Well before the scribal *hasidim* joined the Maccabean Revolt, the *maskilim* had begun their resistance to those who had abandoned the covenant as well as to Antiochus Epiphanes (Dan 11:20–35). The last paragraphs of the "Animal Vision" (1 Enoch 85–90) indicate that a circle of "Enoch" scribes was engaged in parallel resistance. The "Enoch" group, however, had evidently challenged the legitimacy of the second temple for some time (the new "tower" had "polluted bread" on its altar, 1 Enoch 89:73). The Animal Vision pointedly omits a new temple ("tower") from its expectation of the renewal of the people ("house"; 90:29; cf. 89:50, 72–73).[21] It may also be noteworthy that the visions-and-interpretations in Daniel 7, 8, and 10–12 make no mention of the temple in their scenarios of the restoration of the people.

The Hasmonean leaders of the successful Maccabean Revolt attempted to bolster their authority with propaganda, such as 1 Maccabees. But it is unclear that they ever enjoyed much legitimacy after they set themselves up in the high priesthood through negotiations with rival Seleucids. This was evidently what prompted a sizable group of priests and scribes to withdraw to Qumran in protest against the "Wicked Priest" (1QpHab 8.8–11; 4Q448).[22] Large numbers of people, evidently including the Pharisees, opposed the later Hasmonean high priests' expansionist wars in which they conquered Samaria, Idumea, and Galilee with mercenary troops (*War* 1.88–98; *Ant.* 13.372–383). The virtual civil war that his people, again evidently including the Pharisees, mounted against Alexander Jannai indicates how widespread the resistance was (*Ant.* 13:376–378). And his brutal execution of hundreds of the rebels surely undermined any authority he may have had left (*Ant.* 13.380–381). The Psalms of Solomon (esp. psalms 2 and 17) show just how deep the opposition was to the Hasmoneans toward the end.[23]

Appointed "king of the Judeans" by the Romans, Herod retained the temple and the high priesthood, only now as instruments of his own rule. However impressive his massive rebuilding of the temple (one of the "wonders" of the Roman imperial world) may have been, it cannot have enhanced the temple's authority among the people or scribal circles. Herod's erection of the Roman eagle over the main gate and sacrifices on behalf of Rome and Caesar made it all the clearer that the temple was an instrument of imperial rule as well as the sacred shrine in which the priests offered sacrifices to God. As Herod lay dying, some leading scribal teachers staged a daring and dramatic protest (*War* 1.648–655; *Ant.* 17.149–167). Judas ben Saripha and Matthias ben Margala, "the most learned of the Judeans and unrivalled interpreters of the ancestral laws," inspired some of their students to cut down the Roman eagle "to avenge the honor of God." Clearly the Mosaic covenantal law, which required exclusive loyalty to God as Israel's only ruler and forbade visible representation of any other gods or lords, underlay this suicidal action against Rome's client king and the temple he had so grandly rebuilt. With his typical brutality Herod had the scholars and those who had cut down the eagle burned alive—which only inspired far wider protest among the Jerusalem populace.

The men from prominent priestly families in the Egyptian and Babylonian diaspora communities that Herod appointed to the high priesthood would have evoked not submission to authority but rather resentment among Judeans, including the ordinary priests.[24] After the end of Herod's repressive reign, the people clamored for the appointment of a high priest more in keeping with the law (*War* 2.4–13; *Ant.* 17.204–218). But ten years later the Romans gave control of Judea, under the oversight of a Roman governor based in Caesarea Maritima, precisely to the four high priestly families that Herod had brought to prominence. The priestly aristocracy was charged, among other things, with the collection of the tribute to Rome. Setting the tone for the opposition, scribal as well as popular, that they faced for the next several decades, what Josephus calls "the fourth philosophy," led by the "teacher" Judas of Gamla and the Pharisee Saddok, organized a refusal to pay the tribute (*War* 2.118).[25] Josephus thus represents these men as having somewhat the same religious-political importance as the other scribal factions, such as the Pharisees, with whom he says they agreed, except that they were ready to take action on the basis of their conviction that Judeans should be independent of imperial rule. They insisted that since they owed exclusive loyalty to God as their lord and master, they could not render the tribute, which meant acknowledging Caesar as Lord. Clearly they were insisting on living under the direct rule or kingdom of God, whereas the payment of tribute to Caesar would violate the first two commandments (*Ant.* 18.4–5, 23).

Whatever modicum of authority the high priestly aristocracy may have had left eroded in the next few decades.[26] Josephus's accounts indicate that they did not protest Roman provocations of the people but engaged in increasingly predatory behavior against the people (*Ant.* 20.180–181, 206–207; cf. the rabbinic tradition of popular resentment against the high priestly families in b. Pes. 57a). The many popular movements were rejections of the high priesthood as well as of Roman rule (see next section). Increasingly frustrated over their collaboration with the Romans, a scribal group called the *Sicarii* ("Dagger-men") began assassinating key high priestly figures shortly after the middle of the first century (*War* 2.254–256; cf. *Ant.* 20.208–209).[27] Whatever control the high priestly aristocracy may have had over Judean society at the beginning of the first century CE it had lost by midcentury.

Peasant Politics and Distinctively Israelite Movements of Resistance and Renewal

The realities of peasant politics have been neglected by political scientists and historians as well as by historical Jesus studies. For the latter, defining Jesus as a religious figure who dealt with individuals, popular politics was no more relevant than Jerusalem or Roman politics. Historians and political scientists tended to focus on national and international politics, which by definition concerned those who wielded power. The historian John Kautsky, for example, whose study *The Politics of Aristocratic Empires* sheds considerable light on the Roman Empire, says that subordinated peasantries do not participate in politics, at least the politics of those aristocratic empires.[28] That may be true of some or even most aristocratic empires, although one suspects that Kautsky's and other historians' impression that peasants do not make politics is a result of the lack of sources. Peasants, who are ordinarily nonliterate, usually do not produce texts and appear in written sources, which are produced by and/or for the elite, only when they seriously disrupt the established order.

Popular movements, including widespread peasant revolts, however, have certainly made history, as illustrated, for example, by the German peasant revolt in 1524–25 and the Christian-influenced Taiping rebellion in China. As several important studies have documented at length, what were primarily peasant revolts in Mexico, Russia, China, Vietnam, and Central America had decisive and wide-ranging effects on history in the twentieth century.[29] Popular movements, moreover, such as the Waldensians, the Lollards, the Hussites, and the more recent *communidades de base* have figured prominently in the wider history of Europe and Latin America as well as in the history of Christianity.

Politics of Village Communities

What is also often undetected or ignored by historians and historical sociologists as well as by New Testament scholars is local or locally based politics. The field of history as well as that of political science has given extensive consideration to the importance of the state and state formation. But before and well after the formation of the state in traditional agrarian societies, village communities (comprised of many households) continued to be the fundamental form of political-economic-religious life for the ordinary people, the peasantry. Villages are seldom discussed in written sources because the literate elite, like the rulers, had little interaction with them. Yet they are the matrix of popular movements. It is thus an important antidote to the individualistic assumptions of historical Jesus studies to recognize that the vast majority of people in Galilean and Judean society were embedded in village communities as well as patriarchal families. Recent archaeological surveys have confirmed Josephus's passing comment about Galilee's roughly two hundred villages (*Life* 235).[30]

As noted earlier, village communities were semi-independent. The form of self-governance as well as of religious-cultural cohesion was the village assembly, referred to in rabbinic texts by the term *knesset* (assembly) and in the Gospels by the corresponding Greek term *synagoge* (e.g., Mark 1:22–29; 3:1–5).[31] Activities of village assemblies included common prayers, constitution of courts of elders to deal with local conflicts, and appointment of villagers to repair the town water supply. Local community life would have involved interfamily friction and feuding. But a certain degree of communication and cooperation were built in to the social form of community, a basis for potential collective action in times of distress and discontent.

Social historians suggest that the incidence of banditry is a good barometer of social-economic distress among the peasantry. Josephus's histories offer accounts of social banditry, including occasional flare-ups in Galilee in the wake of Roman attacks in the 40s BCE, endemic banditry that escalated to epidemic proportions in Judea under Roman governors and Jerusalem high priests in the mid-first century CE, and an upsurge in the number of incidents in Galilee at the outbreak of the great revolt in 66 CE.[32] In addition, two accounts by Josephus of events he experienced indicate how serious the social disintegration had become by 66. In Jerusalem the people attacked and burned the archives that held records of debts, pointing both to the level of indebtedness and to the level of popular distress and anger (War 2.427). In Galilee the country people were sharply hostile to their rulers in both Sepphoris and Tiberias and would have attacked them were it not for the constraints posed by Herodian forces and Josephus's own armed "body guard" (Life 30, 66–67, 107, 374–378, 381–384, 392).[33] Such levels of indebtedness and resentment would not have emerged suddenly in only a few years but would have developed gradually over a period of decades marked by economic and social pressures on families and their village communities. Such conditions of social distress and disintegration are the circumstances from which popular movements and, much more rarely, wider revolts may emerge.

Popular Movements—Making History

In the histories of Josephus, our principal sources for events in early Roman Palestine, peasants appear not just to have participated in but to have driven historical events. In reaction to the circumstances imposed by their rulers, they took the initiative in making history. Judean and Galilean and Samaritan villagers mounted protests, sizable movements, and even temporarily successful revolts that regularly had their rulers reacting to their initiatives. In these popular protests and movements, moreover, religion and politics are inseparable. They were deeply rooted in Israelite tradition as well as driven by divine inspiration. And they were movements of renewal of Israel as well as of resistance to the rulers of Israel. Of the many popular protests and movements, we take brief note only of those most significant historically, which also happen to be those whose forms were most significant for comparison with Jesus and his movement(s).

Among the many popular protests, the most remarkable was surely the widespread agricultural "strike" organized by Galilean peasants about a decade after Jesus's mission there (*Ant.* 18.261–288; *War* 2.184–203). The new emperor, Gaius (Caligula), had ordered a military expedition to set up his statue in the Jerusalem temple, by force if necessary—a blatant, powerful, and provocative image of the divinized imperial ruler's domination and demand for tribute. As the Roman army came to the west of Galilee, large numbers of peasants refused to plant their fields and sustained their strike for weeks. As the nervous high-ranking advisers to Agrippa I (the newly appointed Herodian ruler of Galilee) pointed out, unless the peasant strike ended, the ominous result would be "a harvest of banditry" (*Ant.* 18.261–274). That is, there would be no crops later that year, hence no payment of tribute to Rome (and, of course, none for Agrippa's administration as well), and the starving peasants would have to resort to banditry. This sustained strike illustrates the peasants' ability to organize across village communities in defense of the Mosaic covenantal commandments of exclusive loyalty to God and refusal to "bow down and serve" any other divine force. Because of the difficulty of such organizing across villages, some of which were physically separated by ridges, the Galilean villagers' organization of this widespread agricultural "strike" is more impressive than the scribal "fourth philosophy's" organization of resistance to the tribute.

Many of the movements and revolts against Roman imperial rule took one or another of two social forms that were distinctive to Israelite tradition and society. That several movements took these same social forms suggests that the Israelite traditions that informed them were very much alive among Israelite villagers at the time of Jesus.

The revolts that erupted in Galilee, Perea, and Judea at the death of Herod all took a readily discernible social form that could be called "messianic movements" (*War* 2.56–65; *Ant.* 17.271–285).[34] Again in the great revolt of 66–70 CE, the largest fighting force took the same form of a messianic movement, as did the Bar Kokhba Revolt seventy years later, in 132–135 CE. In each case, according to Josephus's accounts, large numbers of peasants acclaimed one of their number as "king." This is clearly reminiscent of the Israelite tradition that underlies the accounts in 2 Samuel of how first "the men of Judah . . . anointed ["messiah-ed"] David king" over Judah and then "all the elders of Israel anointed David king" over Israel (2 Sam 2:4; 5:3) to lead their struggle against Philistine domination. The men acclaimed "king" in these movements, such as the shepherd Athronges in Judea (like David in Israelite legend) and the son of the well-known brigand-chieftain Judas son of Hezekias in Galilee, were all of humble origin. That several of these movements were able to establish the people's independence from Roman rule in their areas for periods of up to two or three years indicates that the peasantry was capable of taking collective political action under its own leaders. It is significant that the messianic movement in Galilee was centered in villages around Nazareth in 4 BCE and would have been fresh in the memory of Jesus's contemporaries.

In the mid-first century CE, several movements of deliverance from Roman imperial rule in Judea and one in Samaria took another distinctively Israelite social form, the popular prophetic movement.[35] Like several other prophetic figures who led their followers out into the wilderness in anticipation of new divine acts of deliverance, Theudas "led the masses to follow him to the Jordan River," stating that "at his command the river would be parted and would provide them an easy passage" (*Ant.* 20.97). In similar fashion, "a man from Egypt," claiming that he was a prophet, led his followers up to the Mount of Olives, asserting that at his command the walls of Jerusalem would fall down, providing them an entrance into the city (*Ant.* 20.169–170; cf. *War* 2.259–262).[36] Somewhat earlier, a prophet in Samaria had led his followers up Mount Gerizim, where they would discover the sacred implements of the tabernacle, the shrine and meeting place of the people (*Ant.* 20:85–87). These mid-first-century prophetic movements were clearly informed by and patterned after the acts of liberation and entry into their land in which Israel had been formed as a people led by the prophets Moses and/or Joshua. Again large numbers of peasants proved capable of collective action, under the inspiration and leadership of prophets like the great heroes of Israel's origins.

A Subtler Approach to Peasant Politics

In modern scholarly interpretation of Jesus, as in many academic fields, it has been standard to think of the political order in terms of polar alternatives. The people either accepted the established order or rebelled. If there is no evidence of violent revolt, then social stability prevailed. A principal reason for this overly simple dichotomy is the failure of Western academic fields to take power relations into consideration, the kind of relations of domination and subordination evident in the sketches already presented of Roman conquest, imposition of client rulers, and demand for tribute. Taking power relations into consideration, however, requires subtle analysis of the dynamics of domination, accommodation, and resistance in the historical process that may not be obvious on the surface in most historical sources. With a subtler analysis of people's combination of necessary accommodation and often hidden resistance to domination, following the lead of the political-scientist and anthropologist James C. Scott, it is possible to discern different forms of peasant politics.[37] Odd as it may seem to modern observers who assume the separation of religion and politics, moreover, the key to subtler analysis may be recognition of the inseparability of religion-culture and politics-economics.

Scott has studied the difference between action and attitude among those who are subordinated to social-political superiors and the difference between what they say and do under compulsion, particularly when interacting with superiors, and what they say and think about doing when "off-stage" and out of earshot. The discourse and rules for the face-to-face communication and interaction of the subordinate and the dominant he calls the "public transcript," in which both sides are performing their designated roles, speaking the appropriate "script." The attitudes, deeper feelings, and desires of both the subordinate and the dominant, however, come out when they are off by themselves and feel freer to speak candidly, what Scott calls the "hidden transcript." An extreme case, familiar in U.S. history, was life under slavery, where slaves wore masks of acquiescence and obedience while in direct interaction with slave masters, while developing a discourse and culture of their own when in the slave house and away from surveillance. While not ordinarily subject to beatings and sexual abuse on a regular basis as were slaves, peasants lived under less extreme forms of compulsion such as threats of violent reprisal for failure to render revenues and demands that they show deference to the dominant.

The "public transcript" was determined (produced) by the dominant group. Historians and social scientists, often focused on politics and economics to the exclusion of religion and culture, have emphasized the material aspects of domination. But domination also works through religious-cultural forms, and often the religious-cultural dimension was inseparable from the political-economic in ways that euphemized or concealed the domination. Instead of relying on coercion alone to control the people and to extract revenues from them, elites used religious-cultural ideas, images, and rituals.[38] In the very acts of bringing sacrifices, offerings, and tithes to the temple and priesthood as forms of service to (not just "worship" of) the God of their ancestors, Judeans provided economic support to the priests, who, in turn, sent tributary revenue to the imperial treasury. With our orientation to theology in New Testament studies, we often miss the importance of buildings, images, ceremonies, and a sacred priesthood. These functioned not so much to persuade the people as to induce awe and ritualized customs, which would supposedly help motivate compliance in tithes and offerings.[39] This would presumably have been true for Herod's grandly rebuilt temple, one of the "wonders" of the Roman world, even though its very scale and Hellenistic style, as well as its Roman eagle, may have had a certain "alienation effect" for some of the people.

What may not be evident, however, until we probe under the surface a bit is the difference between the people's action and their attitude. Pomp and ceremony may well have helped motivate them to yield up the required tithes and offerings. But they were also acting under compulsion. So there is the very real possibility that the compliance of many was a mask of acquiescence, a command performance that concealed a resentful acceptance of or even opposition to the established order. Insofar as almost all of our sources, produced by the elite, are expressions of the "public transcript," we have no direct sources for the people's attitudes. Yet several accounts in Josephus's histories provide telling examples of a clear discrepancy between the people's actions and their attitudes. That the teachers and students who cut the Roman eagle down from above the temple gate as Herod lay dying quickly became heroes (*War* 2.5; *Ant.* 17.206, 214) and that after he died the people immediately clamored for a high priest who would act more in keeping with the law (*War* 2.7; *Ant.* 17.207) suggest that considerable discontent with Herod's temple and the high priests had been building up precisely as the people acquiesced in temple ceremonies and requirements under Herodian rule. It seems clear, moreover, that the teachers and their students had been discussing matters such as the Roman eagle over the gate of the temple and Herod's repressive rule well before they formulated the bold plan to cut it down as Herod was about to die. Circles of scribal teachers and students had been cultivating a "hidden transcript" while out of earshot of Herod's informers. In a later illustration, that the priests refused to continue the sacrifices for Rome and Caesar in the summer of 66 as the Romans were losing control in Jerusalem and the people attacked the house of the high priest Ananias (2.409–10, 426) suggests that during the previous years both priests and people, while still acquiescent, had been resentful of the high priests' collaboration with Roman rule.

Galilean and Judean villagers, like peasants in other societies, would also have been talking among themselves in their village communities. Scott focuses most of his discussion on the development and implications of the "hidden transcript" in communities of peasants. In contrast to the heavy concentration on ideas in some disciplines, Scott includes the emotional-cultural dimension of people's lives in his analysis. His own fieldwork among Southeast

Asian villagers confirms studies of peasant communities in other areas of the world that conclude that peasants, like other people, have a desire for dignity. Given their subordination to superiors, however, they are regularly subject to indignities, which generate indignation, frustration, and anger. In dealing with that frustration and resentment they develop a discourse of dignity and justice. The articulation of anger requires language, which imposes a disciplined form and adds a social extension to it. The articulation of anger and frustration in language brings the "hidden transcript" to life in local communities. Scott emphasizes two key requirements for this development. One is a "social space insulated from control, surveillance, and repression from above."[40] While this is often denied to slaves, peasants already have "sequestered sites" in their semi-autonomous village communities. The second requirement is the involvement of particularly articulate people who transform the "raw" anger and resentment into "cooked" indignation, compelling statements of the people's desire for dignity and justice.

The formation and articulation of such a "hidden transcript," says Scott, is also a form of peasant politics, albeit still in the confines of the local community. More important, it is also the basis for other forms of peasant politics, modes of resistance to domination that happen underneath and in between (what appears to be) passive acquiescence and active rebellion. These often are regular features in political processes that are much more diverse and dynamic than previously recognized.[41] Among these "in-between" forms of peasant politics Scott sees particular importance in two forms. One he calls "a politics of disguise and anonymity" in which people protest on the public stage but protect themselves with double meanings and/or shield themselves under the umbrella of a customary cultural form. Much more ominous in its potential for engendering serious political conflict is the second form, the rare act of someone "speaking truth to power" that ruptures the *cordon sanitaire* between the hidden and the public transcripts.

In adjusting Scott's concept of the "hidden transcript" for investigation of Galilean and Judean villagers' attitudes and actions, however, we must take another major step. For peasants of Israelite cultural heritage the development of a discourse of dignity and justice was nothing new. Ongoing cultivation of a hidden transcript in village assemblies (*synagogai*) had for generations presumably drawn on Mosaic covenantal principles of justice and prophetic oracles that condemned oppressive kings and their officers for violating them. Both covenantal principles and prophetic oracles had been included in the books that later became part of the Hebrew Bible and had contributed to the cultivation of those and other traditional legends, law codes, and histories in scribal circles—what anthropologists and others would call the Israelite "great tradition." As noted in chapter 1, it is increasingly evident from recent research that, given that literacy was limited basically to scribal and administrative circles, those books were not directly accessible and known to villagers, who were nonliterate.[42] But, as in other agrarian societies, peasants cultivated the same or parallel cultural tradition orally in their village communities, emphasizing what was important for their own interests—what anthropologists would call the Israelite "little tradition."[43] The content of the hidden transcript of Galilean and Judean villagers would have been this Israelite popular tradition, with further development of a discourse of dignity and justice working from Israelite popular tradition.

While the Galilean-Judean hidden transcript itself remains "hidden from history" (since it was cultivated in sequestered sites), its operation and influence can be discerned in the popular prophetic and messianic movements that arose from the memory of Moses-Joshua and the young David cultivated in the Israelite popular tradition. Israelite tradition cultivated as hidden transcript in village communities also included several examples of "speaking truth to power" that provided a paradigm for a latter-day prophet. Elijah's pronouncement of God's judgment against King Ahab and Jeremiah's pronouncement of God's condemnation of the temple, for example, both clearly arose out of and applied Mosaic covenantal principles.

The Mission and Movement of Jesus in the Politics of Roman Palestine

As discussed in chapter 1, the Gospels can thus be used as historical sources *through a combination of critical analysis of the viewpoint and agenda of each, critical comparison of the different versions of events presented in each Gospel, critical comparison with the Gospel "materials" that they incorporate, and critical consideration in historical context(s)*—an extremely complex procedure still being worked out, including in these chapters. This way of proceeding from the Gospel sources happens to fit well the more fully relational and contextual approach to Jesus-in-movement also outlined in chapter 1. The most important aspects of that approach here are the particular historical conditions that had produced a crisis for the Galilean and Judean people (outlined in the preceding section), the Israelite cultural tradition in which Jesus and his followers were rooted, and Jesus's interaction with followers and opponents that resulted in the formation of a movement and his own crucifixion. Much of the following discussion of Jesus-in-movement-in-context is based mainly on "projections" or "triangulations" from the remarkably parallel portrayals in Mark and the speeches in Q, usually considered the earliest Gospel sources.

Jesus's Mission in the Villages of Galilee and Beyond

Contrary to the assumption of much scholarship, Gospel sources represent Jesus not primarily as a teacher and healer of individuals but rather as a teacher and healer in the context of village communities. These communities, with their constituent households, were the fundamental social forms in which people lived and worked. This is evident at several levels in the Gospels and Gospel materials. Summary statements in Mark (and Matthew and Luke) repeatedly have Jesus proclaiming the gospel of the kingdom and healing and/or exorcising in villages or "places," village assemblies (*synagogai*), and houses (e.g., Mark 1:38–39; 6:6b). Many speeches of Jesus, "pronouncement stories," and even healing episodes also, explicitly or implicitly, represent Jesus as working in synagogues, houses, or fields or addressing people in their village communities (e.g., Mark 2:1–12; 2:23–28; 3:1–5; Q/Luke 6:27–42; 11:2–4). In the mission speeches, moreover, Jesus sends his disciples into villages or places and instructs them to stay in local houses (Mark 6:7–13; Q/Luke 10:2–16).[44] On the basis of the parallel presentations of Jesus's mission in Mark and Q, we can project that Jesus focused his mission on village communities.

As is explored more fully in chapter 5, the Gospel stories and their component episodes and speeches confirm our sense from other sources that village communities in Galilee and Judea were disintegrating under the political and economic pressures of Roman rule.[45] Given the devastation of houses, the slaughter and enslavement of villagers in the Roman reconquests, and the multiple demands for revenue, the constituent families of the village communities were struggling. The central petitions in the Lord's Prayer and the blessings at the beginning of the covenant renewal speech in Q (Q/Luke 6:20–22; 11:2–4) indicate that many people were poor, in debt, and hungry. Hunger and debt, however, were not simply an individual family problem but factors in the disintegration of community life. With families under economic pressure, local resources were quickly exhausted. In order to support themselves after meeting their rulers' demands for produce, families were forced to borrow from creditors outside their village who had access to stores of grain and oil.

Whereas the contemporary popular prophets mentioned by Josephus led their followers out of their village communities to experience wondrous new acts of divine deliverance, Jesus focused on the renewal of village communities themselves in both his healings and his teachings as presented in the Gospels. In the healing stories, Jesus performs healings in public (villages, assemblies, or houses where people are gathered) and restores people to their families and communities (Mark 2:1–12; 3:1–5; 5:21–42; 7:24–30; 9:20–27). In the speeches, as well, Jesus addresses people in the context of their village communities, exhorting them to cancel their neighbors' debts as they petition God for cancellation of debts and to trust that subsistence food and shelter would somehow materialize if they gave priority to seeking the direct rule of God (Q/Luke 11:2–4; 12:22–31). Countering the village disintegration, people who would do the will of God would form mutually supportive familial community (Mark 3:31–35).

The emphasis on doing the will of God in both the Lord's Prayer and the dialogue about familial community points to what appears to be the very center of Jesus's mission as portrayed in the Gospel sources: the renewal of the Mosaic covenant. As is examined more fully in chapter 5, in both the Q speeches and in Mark's story Jesus's most sustained teaching is in fact a covenant renewal speech. Given their usual focus on individual sayings, interpreters of Jesus usually miss the broader patterns evident in Gospel materials. It has sometimes been noted that the Sermon on the Mount (Matthew 5–7) is a renewal of the Mosaic covenant. Most obvious is the intensification of the commandments in the antitheses (Matt 5:20–48). It goes unnoted, however, that the overall structure of the Sermon includes the components of the Mosaic covenant known from Israelite tradition (Exod 20; Deut; Joshua 24). But the first and longest speech in Q (6:20–49) has the same structure, indeed was what the Gospel of Matthew expanded with other Q speeches. As indicated in the content of the admonitions in Q/Luke 6:27–38, moreover, the context of the covenant renewal speech is the local village community. Villagers are quarreling over previous borrowing and lending, suing one another for repayment of loans, insulting one another in their desperation, and condemning one another. The first and longest speech in the Q series is thus a covenant renewal speech addressed to the disintegration of village communities. Having pronounced the blessings of God's (imminent) new deliverance, Jesus insists that the people renew their commitment to traditional covenantal principles of cooperation and mutual support: "Love your enemies, do good, and lend." ← real

A somewhat parallel renewal of covenant appears at a crucial stage in Mark's Gospel. It has long been discerned that the series of dialogues in Mark 10:2–45 features regular law-like statements (10:9,11–12,15,25,29–30,43–44). If we note further that two of those four dialogues cite covenantal commandments explicitly as the basis of Jesus's exhortations (Mark 10:11–12, 19), it is evident that these dialogues constitute a covenantal speech focused on familial integrity and political-economic interaction in renewed village communities (restoration of fields, houses, families).[46]

Both the covenant renewal speech in Q and the law-like declarations in the covenantal dialogues in Mark, moreover, are not just "teachings" but also "performative speech," that is speech-acts that make something happen, that affect reality (as when a judge pronounces the accused "innocent" or "guilty"). These covenantal speeches, (re)performed repeatedly by Jesus and/or "Jesus speakers," enact the renewal of the covenant. Jesus was not just articulating a "well-cooked" hidden transcript but enacting a program of covenant renewal in the village communities of Galilee and beyond. On the basis of the covenant renewal speech in Q and the explicitly covenantal dialogues in Mark, both of which are performative speech, we can project that Jesus was carrying out a covenant renewal in the village communities of Galilee, as is discussed more fully in chapter 5.

In the covenant renewal speeches/dialogues, Jesus also pointedly juxtaposes God's new deliverance and demand of mutual sharing and God's condemnation of the wealthy who have been defrauding and exploiting the people: "Woe to the rich!" It will be impossible for the wealthy "to enter the kingdom of God." In this further development of a "discourse of dignity" on the basis of Israelite covenantal tradition, Jesus is creatively transforming the anger of the people about their exploitation into motivation for recommitment to cooperation and mutual support.

Some of Jesus's condemnations of the scribes and Pharisees also contribute to this further "cooking" of the popular discourse of covenant-based justice.[47] Countering the Pharisees' insistence that even the ordinary people of Galilee observe their "traditions of the elders," Jesus condemns them for voiding the commandment of God to "honor father and mother" by encouraging people to "devote to God" (i.e., to support of the temple) the produce of the land that they need to support families in local communities (Mark 7:1–13). He further condemns the scribes for "devouring widows' houses," evidently by precisely such devices (Mark 12:38–42). The Q speeches have a parallel condemnation of the Pharisees. In a series of woes pronounced on "the scribes and Pharisees" that resembles some of the indictments of the (earlier) Israelite prophets, Jesus indicts them for their exploitation of the people in carrying out their political-economic-religious role in the temple-state (Q/Luke 11:39–52). Again on the basis of the parallels in Mark and Q (all the more striking because stated in somewhat different forms), we can project that Jesus himself articulated prophetic condemnation of the Pharisees (explored more fully in chapter 6).

While Jesus's articulation of "well-cooked" discourse of covenantal justice and covenant renewal was focused on village communities, his mission of renewal cut across and included many villages communities. This was clearly partly by design, as he commissioned envoys to extend his mission of proclaiming the kingdom and healing to more and more villages. But it evidently also had something to do with what happens as charismatic prophetic figures cause a stir and generate a following. Studies of popular movements in other agrarian societies have shown how "rumor" spreads from village to village, for example in *la grande peur* toward the beginning of the French Revolution. Something similar may well have happened to generate the hundreds or thousands of people that Josephus says joined in the popular prophetic movements in rural Judea and Samaria. Mark's portrayal of the excitement that Jesus's mission generated across village communities thus resonates with a certain historical verisimilitude.[48] The extent to which we might (critically) allow that symbolic "legendary" episodes such as the mass feedings might reflect such a trans-village movement is unclear. Yet it is clear from the overall story of the Gospels as well as from the designation of the Twelve and the covenant renewal that Jesus's mission constituted a renewal of Israel as a people in and across its many village communities.

Jesus's Direct Opposition to the Institutions of the Roman Imperial Order

Jesus's renewal of Israel under the direct rule of God, however, had implications for the rulers of people of Israelite heritage. That Jesus was engaged in a program of restoration or renewal of Israel has been one of the most prominent lines of interpretation in study of the historical Jesus in the past three decades.[49] The restoration of Israel under the direct rule (kingdom) of God requires deliverance from (judgment of) the rulers of Israel. This has been easier for modern Western interpreters to grasp with regard to client Herodian rulers and the Romans, on whom there is less material in the Gospel sources, than with regard to the client high priestly rulers and the temple in Jerusalem, on which there are many pertinent passages in the Gospels. Insofar as the restored Israel is conceived in terms of the synthetic modern construct of "Judaism," it is imagined to include a rebuilt temple. However, it seems highly unlikely that Jesus would have looked for a rebuilt temple in a political situation where both popular movements and even some scribal circles excluded a future for the temple and the high priesthood just as they opposed the current high priesthood's operation of the temple, as discussed earlier in this chapter.[50]

Jesus versus Herod Antipas

If Jesus's agenda were merely opposition to exploitative rulers, then it is surprising that the Gospel tradition does not include some condemnation of the Rome-educated Tetrarch who ruled Galilee throughout his lifetime. The few passing references in the Gospel tradition to Antipas indicate sharp (mutual) hostility. In discussion of the significance of John the Baptist, Jesus mocks and disdains Antipas as "dressed in soft robes" and living "in luxury in a royal palace" (Q/Luke 7:25). Luke's introduction to Jesus's prophetic lament over Jerusalem (Luke 13:31–33) states that Antipas was out to kill Jesus and that Jesus defiantly continued his program of healing and exorcism. The latter would have been a threat to Antipas as well as to the scribes and high priests insofar as Jesus was acting with divine authority that transcended the Roman authorization of the Herodian and high priestly rulers (as in Mark 1:20–28; 11:27–33). This brief passage in Luke reinforces the implications of the story of Antipas's arrest and execution of John the Baptist (Mark 6:14–29 & par.), that is, that Jesus, like John, was a threat to Antipas, who presumably wanted to eliminate Jesus as well. As signaled by the same Lucan passage, however, the scope of Jesus's project extended beyond Galilee and opposition to and by Antipas.

Jesus versus the High Priests and the Temple

The Gospels and the materials they incorporate portray Jesus as adamantly opposed to the high priests and the temple and portray the high priests and scribal-Pharisaic representatives of the temple-state as eager to destroy Jesus. This is particularly vivid in Mark. No sooner has Jesus begun his healing and exorcism in Galilee than the Pharisees and Herodians plot to destroy him (3:1–5). The Pharisees, who have come down from Jerusalem, continue to accuse him during his mission in Galilee. After he stages an entry into Jerusalem (a "messianic demonstration"?),[51] he disrupts the standard conduct of business in the temple in a forcible prophetic demonstration and then engages in a confrontation with the high priests and their representatives in the temple, at the end of which he prophesies the temple's destruction (Mark 11–12). Desperate to destroy him, the high priests and scribes lay a plot to arrest him surreptitiously, charge him with threatening to destroy the temple, and turn him over to the Roman governor for crucifixion, at which time he is again said to have threatened to destroy the temple (Mark 14–15). The other Gospels portray Jesus's opposition to the high priests and their opposition to him in similar terms. And there is an abundance of material in the Gospels (including John) about Jesus's prophetic pronouncement of God's judgment of the Jerusalem rulers and/or the temple (which scholars generally do not judge to have originated after the Roman destruction of the temple, in 70 CE). Although it is difficult to imagine that the high priests and the temple could have been separated historically, interpreters still working with the broad synthetic construct of "Judaism" often argue that while Jesus may have opposed the high priests, he did not oppose the temple. So it may be best to consider the passages focused on the high priests and the (closely related) passages focused on the temple in successive steps.

The parable of the tenants, in all three synoptic Gospels, is addressed to and directed against the high priests (and scribes and elders), with the rhetorical question calling them to draw the obvious application to themselves (Mark 12:1–12; 12:9). The parable itself and its framing in the Gospels do not suggest that "Christianity" succeeded "Judaism." The fundamental conflict is rather rulers (represented by the tenants) versus ruled (the others, other tenants, a people that produces fruits). In the previous episode in the Gospels' narrative sequence, Jesus has just demonstrated that the high priests lack authority with the people, in contrast to John and, by implication, himself. This parable resonates deeply with Israelite prophetic tradition, focusing on a familiar prophetic image and a famous prophecy (Ps 80:8–13; Jer 2:21; 12:10; Ezek 15:1–6; 19:10; Hos 10:1) and particularly on Isaiah's famous "love song" that turns into a prophetic condemnation of the rulers for oppressing indebted peasants (Isa 5).[52] Obviously the master of the vineyard would not stand idly by. God is coming to destroy the tenants and give the vineyard to others, which in context would have strongly suggested restoring to their land the Israelites who been forced into tenancy by their high priestly (and other) rulers.[53] This parable announcing God's condemnation of the high priests for exploiting the people is closely linked with Jesus's condemnation of the scribes and Pharisees who, as representatives of the temple and high priesthood, manipulated peasants into "devoting" (qorban) produce to the temple that was needed locally and "devoured" widows' houses (livings). If we thus also consider how the temple-state worked, it is clear that the temple is implicated in the charge of exploitation.

The prophetic oracle from the Q speeches (Q/Luke 13:34–35) pronounces a similar judgment on the Jerusalem ruling house. In the form of a prophetic lament (cf. Amos 5:2–3), the oracle both assumes and announces that Jerusalem is already desolate (destroyed) in anticipation of God's imminent judgment. It resonates with developing Israelite popular tradition that not only Elijah and Uriah son of Shemiah and Jeremiah (1 Kgs 18:17; 19; Jer 26:7–23) but also many other prophets were persecuted and killed (Lives of the Prophets).[54] And of course the recent beheading of John the Baptist would have been a vivid memory in the minds of the audience. Adapting the image of God acting in the exodus as a warrior-like eagle spreading its wings (in the Song of Moses, Deut 32:11), Jesus envisions God as a more caring, maternal figure, like a mother hen attempting to protect her young ("children" was a standing metaphor for villages subject to a city) from the predatory Jerusalem rulers. Again the primary addressees are the high priestly rulers in Jerusalem, but the temple they head is clearly implicated, particularly in the reference to "your (ruling) house."

The Gospel sources offer plentiful attestation that Jesus prophesied the destruction of the temple (or "house") and the "rebuilding" of the "temple" or "house" (Mark 13:1–2; 14:58; 15:39; John 2:19; Gospel of Thomas 71). All except the saying in the Gospel of Thomas 71 are shaped in particular narrative contexts. Yet a certain parallel poetic structure of a prophetic oracle is discernible that has four components in two lines:

> destruction of a temple/house that is material ("made with hands")
> (in three days) rebuilding of a temple/house that is metaphorical ("not made with hands")

As suggested by the passive formulation in Mark 13:1–2 (and perhaps the indefinite in John 2:19), Jesus is presumably speaking prophetically as spokesperson for God ("I will . . ."), which his opponents in Mark 14:28 and 15:29 construe as Jesus himself having threatened to destroy the temple. In approaching these versions of Jesus's prophecy about the temple it is important to recognize that the words for "house," "temple," "body," and "assembly" overlapped and often functioned as synonyms, with the people often referred to as a "house" or "body." Enoch texts used "house" for the people and "tower" for the temple, as noted earlier. The Qumranites, having rejected and withdrawn from the Jerusalem temple, understood their own community in terms of temple-ritual imagery (1QS 5:5–7; 8:4–20; 9:3–6; 4QFlor 1:1–13). All of the versions agree that the house/temple that is to be destroyed is the material one. In the Markan passages this is clearly the temple in Jerusalem; in the Gospel of Thomas 71 it is ambiguous whether the "house" is the temple or Jesus's body; and in John the dialogue depends on the double meaning of "temple" as the Jerusalem temple and Jesus's "body." While the Gospel of Thomas version simply reverses the statement of rebuilding with a negative, the Markan and John passages agree that the rebuilt temple is metaphorical or figurative, evidently the people and Jesus's resurrected "body," respectively. The memory of Jesus having prophesied the destruction of the temple (house) and the re-building (in three days) of the people is thus strong in the Gospel tradition.

For Jesus's demonstration in the temple there is no need to debate whether the narrative details in John or in Mark and the other synoptic Gospels are trustworthy reports. The gist of the different narratives can be distilled into four key features of the demonstration. First, Jesus acts in the role of a prophet, as in the Gospel narratives generally and as in many of his speeches in particular. He carries out a symbolic prophetic action, in a long tradition of prophetic actions such as Isaiah's (Isa 20) and Jeremiah's (Jer 27–28) that symbolize God's action of judgment. Second, his demonstration is a forcible disruption, even a blockage, of the standard activities conducted in the temple instrumental to the sacrifices. Third, the demonstration resonates with Israelite tradition. As indicated by the direct citation of Jeremiah's charge that the heads of the temple were hiding like bandits in the sacred fortress after stealing from the people, Jesus's demonstration is strikingly reminiscent of Jeremiah's pronouncement of God's condemnation of the temple for having violated the Mosaic covenantal commandments (Jer 7; 26). Fourth, as suggested by the reference to Jeremiah's prophecy against the temple but dramatically reinforced by the framing of the action in the temple with Jesus's cursing of the fig tree, the demonstration is a symbolic prophetic announcement of God's condemnation of the temple.

Jesus's Opposition to the Roman Tribute

The episode in which the Pharisees and the Herodians ask a question designed to entrap Jesus and he offers a crafty reply is an integral component of Mark's (and Matthew's and Luke's) narrative of Jesus's "speaking truth to power" that leads to his arrest, trial, and crucifixion. The Gospel narrative makes no particular distinction between Jesus's condemnation of the temple and high priests and his statement about the legality of paying the tribute to Caesar (as if the temple and high priests were part of "Judaism" or religion, while the tribute to Caesar pertained instead to Roman rule or politics). Even taken out of the context of the Gospel narrative and considered by itself, however, Jesus's statement on the legality of the tribute fits into the politics of Roman Palestine, as represented in non-Gospel sources. As with the episode of Jesus's demonstration in the temple, the gist of the entrapment and Jesus's statement is evident; there is no need to imagine that the confrontation happened exactly as narrated (for example, that Jesus actually manipulated his challengers into "showing their hand" by having a Roman coin on their person).[55]

How the question sets a trap for Jesus is clear from the brief discussion of the tribute presented earlier. The tribute was absolutely against Mosaic covenantal law, the first two commandments of which forbid Israelites, in their exclusive loyalty to God, to have any other god or to bow down and serve (with tribute) an "idol," which represents another god. The Pharisees, of course, knew this very well. Some of their colleagues, led by the Pharisee Saddok and the scribal teacher Judas of Gamla, had organized the refusal to pay the tribute when the Romans instituted their direct rule through a governor in 6 CE. The Romans, however, viewed failure to pay the tribute as tantamount to rebellion and retaliated accordingly. If Jesus had responded to the question as posed, he would presumably have been seized immediately for fomenting revolt. But he shrewdly gives an indirect response: "Give to Caesar the things that are Caesar's, and the God the things that are God's." What he was saying, in effect, depends on how it was heard by the audience. And there would have been no doubt among people of Israelite heritage, whether the Pharisees or the ordinary people, as to what his statement meant. "The things that are God's" in Israelite tradition were all-inclusive, leaving nothing for "the things that are Caesar's." While he did not tell the people not to yield up the tribute, for which he would have been subject to immediate seizure, Jesus stated simply and bluntly that the people did not owe tribute to Caesar.

Between Acquiescence and Revolt: Jesus's Politics of Resistance and Renewal

If we trust the memory of Jesus's speech and action as represented in the Gospels, then he prophetically announced God's condemnation of the high priests and the temple, enacted that condemnation of the temple in a symbolic prophetic demonstration, and declared that the people did not owe tribute to Caesar. The priestly aristocracy and the Roman governor had reasons aplenty to seize and execute him for active opposition to the Roman imperial order. Yet his statements and even his demonstration do not amount to fomenting a revolt against the Romans and their client rulers. As sketched earlier, however, peasants and other subordinate people have long practiced modes of politics that fall between passive acquiescence in the dominant order and revolt against it. Jesus's mission, as remembered in the Gospel tradition, is a parade example of these other modes. As portrayed in the Gospels, Jesus shows how a leader and a movement can move and develop and grow, from a well-cooked discourse of justice in sequestered local sites to renewal of cooperative community among subordinated people and then to a politics of disguise and finally to speaking truth to power that, in turn, reinvigorates the movement of renewal and resistance.

Like the popular prophets and messiahs who led contemporary movements of renewal of Israel, Jesus was deeply rooted in the Israelite popular tradition that featured ancestral movements in which Moses and Joshua or the young David led movements of resistance to oppressive rulers as the people established an independent life under the direct rule of God. Unlike Theudas and the "Egyptian" prophet, however, Jesus developed the discourse of justice rooted in the Mosaic covenant into a program of renewal of local village communities. Like those other popular movements of renewal and resistance, Jesus's program of renewal for Israel not only engaged people across the many village communities of Israel but also encouraged and enabled resistance to the rulers and ruling institutions, as implied by the proclamation of a life of justice directly under the kingdom of God. Unlike the popularly acclaimed "kings" who led the messianic movements, however, Jesus did not lead a revolt. He rather followed in the Israelite prophetic tradition of "speaking truth to power" in the traditional prophetic forms of pronouncing and symbolically acting out God's condemnation of exploitative rulers and ruling institutions.

If we follow the social memory of Jesus in the Gospels (including John), Jesus appears to have shrewdly used the religious-political festival of Passover celebrated in Jerusalem as the occasion and context for speaking truth to power. The weeklong celebration of deliverance from bondage under foreign rulers, during which thousands of pilgrims streamed into Jerusalem and gathered in the large outer courtyard of the temple (the city's "public square"), provided an audience highly receptive to a message of new deliverance and the protection of (what Scott calls) the disguise and anonymity of the crowd. While the Roman governors and high priests took extraordinary measures of security and crowd control, they (like rulers of other preindustrial capital cities) knew that precipitous repressive action against enthusiastic cries in the crowds might only provoke a more serious riot.[56] Again, we need not imagine that the events happened just as portrayed in the Gospels (they are quite different in Mark and in John). But the narratives have considerable historical verisimilitude, given what we know of similar situations in other societies.

While it is highly unlikely that Jesus spoke directly to the high priests, elders, Pharisees, and so on, as portrayed in the Gospels, he would have been speaking and acting "in the face of power," with the high priests presiding in the temple and the Roman soldiers standing atop the porticoes of the temple during the weeklong Passover celebration. We do not have to imagine that events unfolded more or less as portrayed in the Gospels to recognize that his own followers and/or others in the crowd gathered to celebrate the historical deliverance from bondage under the Pharaoh would have responded to new pronouncements against the present rulers. As Scott explains, on those rare occasions when a spokesperson for a group of subordinated people speaks out publicly against the dominant power, it can become a breakthrough moment that crystallizes the people's resentment and mobilizes their energies for a wider and longer-lasting movement of resistance. The Gospel narratives have the disciples themselves abandoning and denying Jesus in the episodes immediately following his arrest, with only the women remaining nearby. But the fact that the Gospel tradition contains such a rich array of Jesus's pronouncements and actions against the rulers suggests that their significance reaches beyond a mere indication of why he was arrested and executed. Jesus's prophetic condemnation of the high priests and the temple may well have served as a breakthrough moment that crystallized the movement he had begun in Galilee, which was then followed by the ensuing breakthrough moment of visions of the exalted, vindicated Jesus who had become a martyr for the renewal of Israel that he spearheaded.

3. Jesus and Imperial Violence

The politics of Roman Palestine was set up and maintained by imperial violence. In Galilee during the century before the mission of Jesus, the people suffered repeated conquest, with the slaughter of people and the destruction of villages leaving collective trauma in their wake. When the Galilean and Judean people persistently resisted Roman rule and periodically revolted, Roman armies reconquered them with ever-greater vengeance. The mission of Jesus and the emergence of Jesus movements were framed by popular revolts and Roman reconquests in 4 BCE and again in 66–70 CE. Beyond that, they were framed by the initial Roman conquest in 63 BCE and by the Bar Kokhba Revolt and the final Roman reconquest in 132–135 CE. That period of more than two centuries of Roman rule, moreover, featured protests and resistance movements and regular acts of military repression by the Roman authorities.

The Jesus books that proliferated during the 1990s, however, give little attention to this military violence and its effects or to the way(s) in which Jesus may have been responding.[1] Given the proclivity of interpreters of Jesus to avoid political issues, one often finds reassurances that things were quiet at the time of Jesus's ministry, that there were no occupying Roman troops in Galilee or Judea at the time. This lack of interest in imperial violence among interpreters of "the historical Jesus" is puzzling; it leaves out of consideration the harshest realities of life in the context in which Jesus lived and worked. From the more candid recent discussions of the Romans' brutal treatment of conquered peoples by historians of ancient Rome it is increasingly clear that Roman military violence created the very conditions of and for Jesus's mission and the emergence of Jesus movements.[2] The most obvious illustration is the ending of Jesus's mission through his execution by crucifixion, carried out by the Roman governor and his military.[3]

Prior to the recent proliferation of Jesus books the issue of Jesus and violence received a good deal more attention. Pacifists, whether individuals or members of traditionally pacifist churches such as the Mennonites, had looked to Jesus as a teacher of nonviolence ("turn the other cheek"), even nonresistance ("do not resist [the] evil [one]"). Mohandas Gandhi and Martin Luther King and other civil rights leaders understood Jesus as the prophet of nonviolent direct action guided by the principle "love your enemies."

After the social-political turmoil of the 1960s, leading New Testament scholars argued strongly for an apolitical as well as a nonviolent Jesus.[4] At the level of academic debate, they were responding to the argument by that outsider from the history of religions S. G. F. Brandon, who suggested that Jesus might have been sympathetic to "the Zealots."[5] But more was at stake in that time of "national liberation movements" against European imperial rule in the "Third World" and also of widespread protests against the US war in Vietnam and other counterinsurgency wars.

In retrospect, it seems like no mere coincidence that European scholars constructed an elaborate synthetic picture of "the Zealots" as a long-standing and widespread movement of violent revolt against Roman rule, as a kind of ancient Jewish "National Liberation Front."[6] As practitioners of anti-Roman violence, "the Zealots" provided a useful foil against which Jesus could be portrayed as a sober teacher of pacifist nonresistance. It seems no mere coincidence, moreover, that New Testament scholars thus focused the issue of violence on resistance to foreign imperial rule rather than on the violence of imperial rule itself. Like many other academic fields, New Testament studies originated in late nineteenth- and early twentieth-century Western European countries during the heyday of imperialism. Western imperial rule of subject peoples was simply assumed as the order of things.[7] Roman imperial rule was viewed as a benign civilizing influence, even idealized, as Western imperial powers understood themselves to be the successors of Rome. It was also assumed that the Gospels belonged to European Christians, whose responsibility it was to take them as the Word of God to subject peoples. Thus, as colonial rule was being effectively challenged, the portrayal of Jesus as a sober advocate of nonresistance in opposition to the revolutionary violence of "the Zealots" was an argument against the use of violence by anticolonial movements in the Third World as well as by student demonstrations in Western metropolises.

It is now recognized that behind the modern scholarly construct of "the Zealots" was a variety of scribal and peasant movements of resistance that took different forms and many of which were nonviolent.[8] The band of scribal teachers who organized resistance to the Roman tribute in 6 CE (Josephus's "fourth philosophy"), the scribal clique of "dagger men" who assassinated high priestly figures fifty years later, and the popular messianic movements in 4 BCE and again in 67–70 CE and popular prophetic movements in the mid-first century are all discussed briefly in chapter 2. The people whom the historian Josephus actually labels hoi Zelotai, who had no direct relation with any of those earlier movements, emerged during the great revolt of 66–70 CE. As the Romans advanced into the hill country of northwestern Judea, destroying villages and slaughtering their inhabitants, some villagers fled into Jerusalem for refuge and formed a coalition to resist further Roman advances.[9] Although few interpreters of Jesus have picked up on it, the demise of "the Zealots" as a foil for an interpretation of Jesus as a teacher of nonresistance should have cleared the way for a closer look at the issue of Jesus and violence.[10] More recently, however, the U.S. invasion and occupation of Iraq evoked a considerable upsurge of interest among biblical scholars and other academics in imperial violence and its effects.[11]

Much of the earlier discussion of Jesus and violence, like the more general discussion of violence in individualistic Western societies, was narrow in its scope, focusing on individual overt acts of violence. The more serious, debilitating, and destructive violence suffered by large numbers of people in both the ancient and the modern worlds is structural, systemic. In the dominant political-economic structuring of life and the ways in which power is wielded, people are denied even the opportunity for an adequate livelihood, exploited, displaced, and/or thrown into illness in ways that are not directly caused by an individual act of overt violence. Such structural violence can lead to protest, which usually leads to repressive violence by those who hold power, which rarely but occasionally leads to violent revolt in a kind of "spiral of violence."[12] In ancient Palestine the Romans used military violence to set up and maintain the political-economic-religious structure and power relations that meant systemic violence for most of the people. Since Roman imperial military violence had such a severe impact on the people, however, it is important to focus attention on some of its effects.

One aspect of violence that has only recently received critical attention is verbal or rhetorical violence and the (ritual and rhetorical) celebration of violence. This was a prominent feature of Roman imperial violence and, while much less lurid, also of Judean and "early Christian" texts that were later included in the Hebrew Bible and in the New Testament—thus at points "inscribing" rhetorical violence in the sacred scripture.

Imperial Violence

Roman conquest of Palestine set up the conditions of and for Jesus's mission of renewal. The hundred or so years prior to his mission were a time of repeated devastation and killing, especially for the Galileans.

The prolonged period of imperial violence, however, began prior to the Roman conquest. After the conquest of Alexander the Great, the rival dynasties of his successors, the Ptolemies and the Seleucids, battled back and forth for control of Jerusalem. Imperial violence in Jerusalem and Judea began with a vengeance with the repeated military invasions led by Antiochus IV Epiphanes to support the Hellenizing "reform" carried out by the dominant faction of the priestly aristocracy. This unprecedented imperial violence was the occasion for the ominous visions of the *maskilim* and other scribal circles that were resisting the departure from the traditional covenantal way of life. "I saw . . . a fourth beast, terrifying and dreadful and exceedingly strong. It had great iron teeth and was devouring, breaking in pieces, and stamping what was left with its feet. It was different from all the beasts that preceded it" (Dan 7:7). Even with substantial forces that included fearsome war elephants, however, Antiochus was unable to suppress the Maccabean Revolt, led by the Hasmonean family, and its guerrilla tactics.

The Hasmoneans then set themselves up as the heads of the Judean temple-state and began to imitate imperial rulers. Expanding their army with mercenaries, they conquered the Idumeans and the Samaritans and destroyed the Samaritans' temple. They then took over Galilee from the Itureans, as well, although Josephus's brief account does not suggest that they made war on the Galileans themselves. The expansionist wars of the Hasmonean rulers, however, led to a series of wars between rival factions of the dynasty that entailed repeated destruction and forcible appropriation of people's resources.

The Roman Culture of Conquest

Long before Rome moved into the eastern Mediterranean it had indicated how it would expand its empire. Still smarting from its defeat by Hannibal, Rome goaded Carthage into attacking one of its allies and proceeded to destroy the city, in 146 BCE.[13] About the same time, aiming to take control of Greece, the Romans provoked war with the Achaean league of cities and ruthlessly destroyed the great classical city of Corinth, enslaved its populace, and despoiled its great works of art and architecture.[14]

Modern Western intellectuals, including classics scholars on whom New Testament interpreters are dependent, have long idealized Rome. Only recently have Roman historians, taking a more critical perspective, made it clear that such brutal military violence against subject peoples was standard practice among the Romans.[15] The Romans believed that their own "national security" depended on the subjection of other peoples by superior military force and the extraction of "loyalty" (*fides/pistis*) from them, as well as tribute, which was a symbol of humiliation as well as a source of revenue. They were afraid that any sign of weakness, such as failure to punish a revolt, would invite further insurrection. Roman warlords became particularly vengeful in retaliating for rebellions, even for tardiness in payment of tribute. In their initial conquests and again in retaliation for any rebellion, the Roman armies purposely devastated the countryside, burned villages, pillaged towns, and slaughtered and enslaved the people (Tacitus, *Ann.* 1.51, 56; 2.21; Cassius Dio 67.4.6; Augustus, *Res Gestae*). As the Roman historian Tacitus has a Caledonian chieftan exclaim, "[The Romans are] the plunderers of the world. . . . If the enemy is rich, they are rapacious, if poor, they lust for dominion. Not East, not West has sated them. . . . They rob, butcher, plunder, and call it 'empire'; and where they make a desolation, they call it 'peace'" (*Agricola* 30). A century earlier, the (pro-Roman) Hellenistic historian Polybius, having witnessed a horrifying scene of human and animal corpses littering a city destroyed by the Romans, seems to have grasped the purpose of it all: "It seems to me that they do this for the sake of terror" (*Hist.* 10:15–17; cf. Julius Caesar, *Bell. Gall.* 4.19; Cassius Dio 68.6.1–2; Pliny, *Ep.* 2.7.2).[16] More familiar to readers of the Gospels is crucifixion, the slow, torturous public execution of rebels in prominent places designed to terrorize the surviving population into acquiescence in Roman domination (Josephus, *War* 5.449–451).

Rome had long since intervened in the interempire politics of the Middle East, weakening both the Ptolemaic regime in Egypt and the Seleucid regime in Syria by defeating them in key battles. Only in the early first century BCE did the Romans move to take direct control of the areas around the southeastern shores of the Mediterranean, undertaking military action on an unprecedented scale.[17] Among the factors driving their military conquest of the peoples in this area, three in particular stand out as particularly prominent.

First, the wealthy and powerful patricians, the senators who controlled the Roman Republic, expanded their understanding of and justification for their conquest and control of other peoples to include their economic self-interest as well as political control of peoples and kings. Regional kings, such as Mithridates in central Asia Minor, had been interfering with Roman magnates' "investments" in the area, and pesky pirates (the dastardly *latrones/lestai* in Roman oratory) were raiding shipments of luxury goods and grain to the metropolis. Political orators such as Cicero used the piracy as a symbolic pretext in their patriotic appeals (Cicero, *Leg. Man.* 33, 53, 56; cf. Plutarch, *Pomp.* 24.4–6; Appian, *Mith.* 94). To secure real peace and prosperity, the Romans had to expand their *imperium* to include control not just of shipping but of the territories from which goods flowed to the metropolis. As Cicero declared (*Leg. Man.* 4–6, 17), it is necessary to protect "your revenues" (*vestra vestigalia*) and "adornments of peace" (a veiled reference to games, public buildings, grain subsidies, and distribution of lands) and also "resources for war."[18]

Second, the Roman elite looked down on other peoples, particularly "oriental" peoples, as decadent, cowardly, and enslaved to despotic kings, in contrast to the way of life enjoyed by the Romans, with their liberty and their supposedly participatory "republic."[19] Like earlier Greek elites, the Romans derided the Persians and the Parthians as shameless and untrustworthy (Horace, *Carm.* 4.14.41–43; 4.15.1; Trogus 40.3.1; 41.2.4; 41.3.2–3; Lucan 8.397–401; Strabo, *Geogr.* 2.9.1). They looked upon Syrians and Judeans in particular as good for nothing but slavery ("born slaves"; e.g., Cicero, *Prov. cons.* 10; Livy 35.49.8; 36.17.5).

The third prominent factor driving the new wave of conquest was the ambition of rival warlords to achieve a great victory over the enemy in order to celebrate and be celebrated in a grand procession in Rome that displayed the military might of the victors and the humiliating defeat of the vanquished. This *triumph*, which was the ultimate honor that a Roman could achieve, moreover, stood at the center of a whole culture of imperial violence. More than three hundred triumphal arches survive or are known from coins and inscriptions. Other "ritual paraphernalia of conquest," such as trophies, public funerals, and triumphal statues with appropriate inscriptions, figured prominently in public life.[20] Julius Caesar achieved his glory in the conquest of Gaul. Pompey sought his in the war against Mithridates, the defeat of the pirates, and the conquest of Syria-Palestine—on the basis of which he became "Pompey the Great."

Roman Conquest and Reconquest of Palestine

The effects of the initial Roman conquest led by Pompey in 63 BCE were nowhere near as severe for the Galilean and Judean countryside as were those of later reconquests. Even without a blow-by-blow description of Roman brutality in the next ninety-some years leading up to the time of Jesus's mission, a selective sketch of successive reconquests and other major acts of violence can help us appreciate their cumulative effect on the people among whom Jesus worked.

After the initial conquest, the Romans kept the temple-state in place, with the Hasmonean Hyrcanus II as client ruler. But this turned into an unsettled situation in which the people were subject to repeated wars between rival Hasmoneans that were later mixed up with the Roman "civil war" between rival warlords, new invasions of Palestine by the Romans to restore their rule, and the predatory practices of Roman warlords. One of the most infamous acts of gratuitous vengeance by a Roman warlord must have left a collective trauma among the people along the western shore of the Sea of Galilee, the very area of Jesus's mission. Eager to reassert Roman power in Palestine after the loss of a whole army by Crassus to the Parthians and an insurgency by one of the rival Hasmoneans, Cassius enslaved thousands of people in and around Tarichaeae, (i.e., Magdala), on the Sea of Galilee, in 53–52 BCE (Josephus says thirty thousand were enslaved, *War* 1.180; *Ant.* 14.120). The memory of this mass enslavement would hardly have faded by the time of Mary of Magdala and people in other villages along the shore, such as Capernaum and Chorazin (including the families of Cephas and Andrew, James and John).

Herod's impressive performance as a military strongman led to his appointment by the Roman Senate in 40 BCE as "the king of the Judeans." Supplied with troops by the Romans, he proceeded to conquer his own subjects (*War* 2.290, 294, 327, 345–346, 351–352; *Ant.* 14.468–469). Because of the widespread resistance, it took him three years, including three invasions into Galilee, where he finally had his troops simply slaughter the people who failed to submit (*War* 1.303–313, 315–316, 326; *Ant.* 14.413–433, 450; vs. *War* 1.291; *Ant.* 14.295).[21] To supply his own and the Roman troops, he raided villages for provisions (*War* 1.299; *Ant.* 14.408). At points, he carried out extensive slaughter in villages and towns, such as Emmaus (*War* 1.219, 334; *Ant.* 14.435–436, 457–461). When he finally managed to take Jerusalem, with a huge army, his frustrated troops butchered people in the alleys (*War* 1.351). As a model client-king of the Romans, he proceeded to establish an intense network of security, with impregnable fortresses around his realm (Masada the most famous), secret informants, and brutal punishments such as burning alive for those who resisted—what today would be called a "police state" (see especially Josephus's summary, *Ant.* 15.366–369).[22] The story of "the massacre of the innocents" in Matthew 2 is a legend, of course, yet it has considerable verisimilitude, judging from Josephus's extensive accounts of Herod's brutally repressive rule. Herod, the face of imperial rule in Palestine, was the very symbol of terrorizing violence against the people.

In response to the uprisings that erupted in every major area at Herod's death, in 4 BCE, the Roman general Varus led a large army in reconquest, burning towns and villages, devastating the countryside, and enslaving the inhabitants. He first sent his army to subdue the Galileans, and his forces burned the fortress town of Sepphoris, which the rebels had seized, and enslaved the inhabitants (*War* 2.68; *Ant.* 17.288–289). Thus, just about the time Jesus was born, the Romans wrought devastation and death in the area that included villages such as Nazareth in retaliation for the revolt led by the popularly acclaimed "king" Judas son of Hezekias. Many villagers in the area would have lost relatives and friends and perhaps seen their villages ravaged.

Moving south to suppress the revolt in Judea (also one of the "messianic" movements), he burned the town of Emmaus, whose inhabitants had fled. He had his army scour the countryside for rebel leaders and, says Josephus, had two thousand crucified (*War* 2.71, 75; *Ant.* 17.291, 295). Even if Josephus has exaggerated the numbers killed in this way, it seems clear that this practice of terrorizing the populace into submission would have been well known in the experience of the Galileans and Judeans in Jesus's lifetime. The Romans deliberately used this excruciatingly painful form of execution by torture (basically suffocation) on upstart slaves and rebellious provincials. It was usually accompanied by other forms of torture, such as severe beatings. Often the victims were never buried but simply left on the crosses as carrion for wild beasts and birds of prey.[23] As with other forms of imperial terrorism, crucifixions were displayed in prominent places for their "demonstration effect" on the rest of the population.[24] Seeing their relatives, friends, and other fellow villagers suffering such agonizing deaths would presumably intimidate the surviving populace into acquiescence in the reestablished Roman imperial order. This "demonstration effect" of crucifixion is dramatically illustrated in Josephus's account of the Roman general Titus's order that his cavalry seize people fleeing the besieged Jerusalem toward the end of the Roman reconquest in 70 CE. Hundreds of the fugitives "were beaten and subjected to torture of every description . . . and then crucified opposite the walls [in the hope] that the spectacle might induce the Judeans to surrender" (*War* 5.449–451).

While there are no reports of such systematic Roman brutality during the decades after the reconquest by Varus, the Roman governors of Judea frequently sent out their military to suppress periodic protests and resistance movements. Some governors perpetrated provocative acts of violence that Josephus blames as one of the factors exacerbating the political turmoil. And after the steady deterioration in both economic and political conditions at midcentury, when widespread revolt erupted again, the Romans systematically devastated villages and countryside, slaughtered and enslaved the people, and destroyed

Jerusalem and the temple (66–70 CE; described extensively in Josephus's *War*). The important recognition in any analysis of the sources and understanding of Jesus's mission, which resonated with villagers in Galilee and beyond, is that the imperial violence of the preceding generations had a serious impact on the people of Palestine. Some of the effects are discernible on the basis of the accounts of Josephus and/or on the basis of comparison with peoples subjected to similar circumstances.

The Effects of Imperial Violence

The killing or enslavement of relatives and neighbors and the destruction of villages would have left collective as well as personal trauma in their wake. We are perhaps more aware of the effect of violence from the aftermath of holocausts and genocide in ethnic conflicts in Armenia, central Europe, East Africa, and the Balkans in the course of the twentieth century. Compounded by the economic pressures of taxation (discussed further in chapter 5), Roman brutality thus contributed to the disintegration of village communities.

Another effect of the imperial violence on the people was the fratricidal violence that erupted periodically. Historians, social scientists, and novelists have long since recognized that subject peoples who somehow know that active resistance to repressive rule would be suicidal direct violence at other subjected peoples. The best-known case in Roman Palestine is the conflict between Judeans and Samaritans. Jesus's parable of "the Good Samaritan" illustrates the underlying hostility between these two groups. That long-standing hostility erupted most dramatically in the mid-first century (*Ant.* 20.118–136; *War* 2.232–246). Some Samaritans attacked and killed a (some) Galilean(s) en route to Jerusalem for the Passover festival. In retaliation, a number of Judeans, led by the well-known brigand leader Eleazar ben Dinai, attacked some Samaritan villages. The Roman answer, to restore order, was military violence, which touched off a wider insurrection. The governor Cumanus sent out his troops, who killed many of the Judeans and captured many others, while brigand raids and local insurrections erupted around the countryside. When Quadratus, the Roman legate in Syria, came to restore order, he crucified the prisoners taken by Cumanus, executed other Judeans supposedly involved in the conflict, and sent both the Jerusalem high priestly officers and the Samaritan nobles, who had failed to maintain order, to Rome in chains.

Another indication of the social disintegration resulting from imperial violence was the rise in banditry in the wake of imperial reconquest. A certain amount of banditry is endemic to agrarian societies in which some families, already economically marginal, simply cannot feed themselves after rendering taxes and tribute. Military destruction of villages and the flight of villagers who did not wait around to be killed or enslaved often created epidemics of banditry. Josephus's accounts offer several illustrations, some explicit, some implicit.[25] The epidemic banditry along the western frontier of Galilee that the newly appointed military governor Herod brutally suppressed would have been one result of the repeated Roman military expeditions into Palestine, usually starting in western Galilee, in the previous decades. In a related effect of the impact on the social memory of the Galileans, in this case, Judas the son of the brigand chief Hezekias whom Herod had killed was the obvious leader for the people to acclaim as "king" to lead their revolt when Herod died, in 4 BCE. The Roman reconquest would have left more banditry in its wake, as would the repeated military strikes that the Roman governors sent against popular protests and movements (illustrated also by what happened after Cumanus's violence, meant to quell the fratricidal violence). While it became epidemic in the next few decades, banditry was already widespread during the mission of Jesus, who was crucified between two bandits (not thieves; Mark 15:27).

An effect that is difficult to "document" but is increasingly apparent on the basis of studies of similar historical circumstances—and of special importance for Jesus's mission—was spirit possession and the upsurge of illnesses such as blindness and paralysis. This is the subject of the next chapter. Perhaps it is sufficient here to recognize that the ("biblically" unprecedented) appearance of destructive heavenly or other spiritual forces ("fallen angels," "demons") in Judean scribal texts coincides with the increase in military invasions by Hellenistic and then Roman imperial armies.[26] Studies of spirit possession and exorcism cults in Africa and elsewhere indicate a parallel relationship between spirit possession and invasion by foreign rulers.[27] People subject to colonial invasion somehow knew, sometimes by bitter experience, that counterviolence against the outsiders' rule would result only in further destruction and death. Possession by alien spirits became, in effect, a self-preservative mechanism, diverting attention from the concrete imperial invaders to invasion by spirit agents.

Something similar seems to have been happening among the Galileans and the Judeans at the time of Jesus. Their fear of and possession by demons diverted their resentment and anger from the Romans, their own expression of violence being directed against themselves and other villagers. That the spirit Jesus expels from a possessed man who is doing violence to himself and his fellow villagers turns out to have the name/identity of "Legion" (Mark 5:1–20) is a very suggestive parallel (as is discussed in chapter 4).

Violence and Nonviolence in Resistance to Roman Rule

Judeans and Galileans sustained their resistance to Roman rule longer than any other conquered people. After the persistent struggle against Herod's conquest in 40–37 BCE came the widespread revolts in 4 BCE, the great revolt of 66–70 CE, and finally the Bar Kokhba Revolt in 132–135.

The revolts of 4 BCE and 66 CE were largely composed of popular movements. In contrast to the earlier Maccabean Revolt, however, these were not insurgencies of sustained guerrilla warfare. The messianic movements in Galilee and the trans-Jordan in 4 BCE seized Herodian fortresses and the goods taken and stored there, then lived free of rulers for a time—until Varus and his army resubjugated them.[28] Except for attacking a Roman baggage train, the villagers in northwest Judea were similarly interested mainly in a life independent of rulers, in some locales for nearly three years, despite Varus's mass crucifixions. In the summer of 66, the ordinary people of Jerusalem also revolted and cooperated with rural fighters in driving back the Romans' initial military attempt at "restoring order" and enjoyed several months free of imperial rule. When the Romans mounted their massive reconquest in 67–68, their systematic campaign of violence produced what became popular movements as people fled to Jerusalem for refuge and fought back against the Romans' prolonged siege in 70. The Zealots proper were a coalition of fugitives from the Roman attacks on villages in northwest Judea, joined by fugitives from Galilee; the Idumeans were a coalition of semitribal groups; and the largest force was the messianic movement headed by Simon bar Giora from the villages of Judea. Theirs was basically a self-defensive fight, punctuated by rivalry among the leaders.

The other popular movements among the Judeans and the Samaritans and most of the protests were nonviolent and were often remarkable illustrations of how people could organize and sustain disciplined resistance in the face of threatening imperial violence. With the exception of the movement led by the Samaritan prophet, Josephus gives no indication that the movements led by prophets appearing as the new Moses and/or the new Joshua at midcentury threatened violence. They were evidently convinced that God was about to carry out a new act of deliverance like the exodus or the collapse of the walls of Jericho (*Ant.* 18.85–87; 20.97–98, 168, 261–263; *War* 2.259–263).[29] Violence came from Pilate and subsequent Roman governors who sent out their cavalry to kill the prophets and their followers.

Remarkable for their nonviolent discipline were two popular protests generated by the people against provocative Roman actions that violated the most basic principles of the traditional Israelite way of life, exclusive loyalty to God. When Pilate sent a company of troops into Jerusalem carrying standards with the images of their gods on them, large numbers of "people from the countryside," along with some Jerusalemites, gathered round his residence in Caesarea on the coast in protest (*Ant.* 18.55–59; *War* 2.169–174).[30] In the face of Pilate's threat to have his soldiers kill them if they refused to admit Caesar's images, the people held their ground, baring their necks, and Pilate finally relented. In a remarkably measured and disciplined mass demonstration, the Judean protesters thus demonstrated the depth of their commitment to the covenantal principles of their traditional way of life.

A decade later Galilean peasants organized a wider and prolonged protest against an even more blantant Roman provocation (*Ant.* 18.261–88; *War* 2.184–203).[31] The new emperor Gaius (Caligula) ordered Petronius, his legate in Syria, to set up his image in the Jerusalem temple. If people resisted, "he was to subdue them by force of arms." As Petronius advanced toward Galilee, large numbers of peasants refused to plant their fields and then sustained the "strike" for weeks (as discussed in chapter 2). This action not only highlights the villagers' ability to organize themselves but also manifests a remarkable collective discipline supporting nonviolent resistance in the face of the Roman military, which was poised to slaughter them, as well as the risk of mass starvation. This event is also remarkable for the highly unusual response of a high-ranking Roman officer. Warned by the ranking officials of Agrippa I that continuation of the strike (or an attack on the villagers) would result in "a harvest of banditry" (no crops, hence no tribute), Petronius was persuaded to defy his emperor. Gaius's sudden (and timely) death saved him from suicide and, far more significant historically, saved Galilee and Judea from actions that would likely have resulted in another revolt and another Roman devastation.

Certain scribal circles also mounted protests and organized resistance.[32] Because scribes served the temple-state, making them dependent on the high priestly rulers who, in turn, were dependent on their imperial sponsors, scribal protests were rare and risky, even though they were nonviolent. The *maskilim* who produced Daniel 7–12 had set the example in their steadfast resistance to Antiochus Epiphanes. In a bold protest against Roman rule, a later generation of scribal teachers inspired their students to cut down the golden Roman eagle from atop the great gate of the temple, an act of direct defiance for which Herod had them burned alive (*War* 1.648–655; *Ant.* 17.149–158).

By far the best-known protest by a group of scribes was the organization of a refusal to pay the tribute to Rome by the group Josephus labels the "fourth" philosophy (*Ant.* 18.4–25). Partly because Josephus blames them for planting the seeds of the great revolt of 66–70, modern scholars have misunderstood their organized protest as a "revolt" and/or taken Judas of Gamla, one of their leaders, as the founder of "the Zealots."[33] A more careful reading of Josephus's accounts indicates an organization of nonviolent resistance. Josephus says that they agreed basically with the views of the Pharisees (one of whom was their other leader), except that they were adamant about adherence to the covenant principles of exclusive loyalty to God as their sole ruler and master—which made it impossible for them to pay the tribute to Caesar. Since the Romans viewed failure to pay the tribute as tantamount to revolt, they were risking violent Roman retaliation. But, says Josephus, in their refusal to acknowledge another lord and master, they were willing to suffer martyrdom and reprisals against their families. Theirs was committed nonviolent resistance.

A half-century later, however, their successors, having become frustrated by the deterioration of the imperial situation and the intransigence of the high priestly aristocracy, moved from organizing nonviolent resistance to a kind of counterterrorism.[34] Because they assassinated prominent high priestly figures at festival times using curved daggers known as *sicae*, they became known as *Sicarii*, "Dagger-men" (*War* 2.254–257; *Ant.* 20.186–187). This was a new, unprecedented, violent phase of scribal resistance, which might justifiably be labeled counterterrorism. At its outset, in the summer of 66, the Sicarii attempted to take over leadership of the revolt. But the Jerusalem populace turned against them, whereupon they simply withdrew to the fortress of Masada and sat out the rest of the revolt.

While active scribal resistance was rather limited, scribal circles did articulate opposition to imperial rule and its violence in texts. They anticipated an ultimate judgment in which violent imperial rule would be ended and the rulers punished. Their images of the judgment are usually fairly simple, with no lurid scenarios. While they may not ascribe agency to God or God's agent, they do assume that there will be counterimperial destruction.

Standard scholarly constructions of "apocalypticism" and its scenario of Last Judgment, such as those articulated a century ago by Albert Schweitzer, followed by Rudolf Bultmann, have misrepresented these texts as anticipating the "end of the world" in fiery judgment, a "cosmic catastrophe." This misunderstanding is rooted in an overly literal reading of traditional prophetic imagery of theophany, the "earthshaking" appearance of God coming to deliver Israel and defeat imperial oppressors. One of Isaiah's oracles against Babylon provides a particularly vivid illustration (Isa 13). When Yahweh of hosts comes "with wrath and fierce anger to make the earth a desolation, [that is,] to destroy sinners, . . . the sun will be dark . . . , the heavens tremble . . ." (Isa 13:9–13). All this, however, is hyperbole pointing to the coming historical deliverance by God in "stirring up the Medes" to defeat the Babylonians, who had invaded and oppressed Judah. The repetition of such images is fairly rare in "apocalyptic" texts (T. Mos. 10; 1 Enoch 57:1–3; cf. Mark 13:22–26), and they were not meant literally, as if the world were about to end in cosmic cataclysm.

More significant is that, while scribes understood themselves as the heirs of the prophets, "apocalyptic" and other scribal texts in late second-temple times do not perpetuate much of the language of God's destruction of imperial invaders. The Testament of Moses, a second-century "apocalyptic" text that was updated around the time of Jesus (chaps. 6–7), condemns the violent oppression by both imperial and client Judean rulers and anticipates God's judgment and deliverance.[35] After one of the rare rehearsals of the earthshaking appearance of God in judgment comes the simple declaration that "he will come to work vengeance on the nations" and destroy their idols (10:3–7). The earlier dream vision in Daniel 7 that represents Antiochus Epiphanes as a horribly destructive beast anticipates the beast's destruction "with fire" (Dan 7:11, 26). Following the rehearsal of the imperial invasion of Jerusalem and the killing of the *maskilim* in the vision-and-interpretation in Daniel 10–12, on the other hand, comes the simple statement that Antiochus Epiphanes "shall come to his end, with no one to help him" (11:45).

The Parables of Enoch (1 Enoch 31–37), probably from the first century CE, speak of punitive divine judgment, but with a few exceptions the imagery is not fiery.[36] The visionary parables anticipate that God will transform the earth and make it a blessing, not destroy it in a fearsome fiery judgment (45:5). When the Head of Days ascends the throne of judgment, the kings and the mighty will be toppled from their thrones and will "burn before the faces of the holy ones" (46:5; 47:3; 48:9; cf. 53:1–6). On the other hand, his "Chosen One" will slay the sinners with "the word of his mouth," not with a sword, and the kings and the mighty will acknowledge the divine sovereignty before the Lord of the Spirits delivers them to the angels for (unspecified) punishment (62:1–2, 3–9, 10–12).

The (nonapocalyptic) Psalms of Solomon, probably from early in the Herodian period,[37] after condemning the Romans for their violent "trampling" of Jerusalem, represent the defeat and death of Pompey the Great, conqueror of Jerusalem, as the result of his own arrogance, under the ultimate sovereignty of God as king over the heavens (2:15–30). Psalms of Solomon 17 is another text that has been misrepresented in the previous Christian theological construction of "Judaism" as having expected the Messiah, Son of David, to be a military victor. The psalm does look for the anointed one "to destroy unjust rulers, purging Jerusalem from nations who trample her to destruction" (17:22). But his "rod of iron" (alluding to the imperial image of the Davidic king in Psalm 2) will be "the word of his mouth" (17:24), upon which he will rely instead of war chariots (17:33–36). While the military images are taken from earlier imperial psalms, this is a scribal, not a military, messiah.

The Judean scribal texts that engage in considerable rhetorical violence are from the Qumran community, mainly the War Scroll (1QM). These scribes and priests who had formed a renewed covenantal community in the wilderness in protest against the regime of "the Wicked Priest" in Jerusalem were also adamantly opposed to the Romans ("the Kittim"). Rather than actively resist either the Romans or their client rulers in Jerusalem, however, they withdrew from participation in politics altogether and were evidently not suppressed by either the Jerusalem rulers or the Romans. Their nonresistant "pacifism," however, was rooted in the conviction that the solution to imperial violence was divine counterviolence. They understood their conflict with the Romans as the earthly manifestation of the larger transhistorical conflict between the Prince of Light and the Prince of Darkness, or Belial. The War Scroll reveals that they expected that God would imminently mount a full-scale war, at both the heavenly-spiritual level and the historical level, against the Prince of Darkness and the Romans. "On the day when the Kittim fall, there shall be battle and terrible carnage before the God of Israel, for that shall be the day appointed from ancient times for the battle of destruction of the sons of darkness" (1QM 1:9–11).[38] In anticipation of their own participation in the conflict, they evidently rehearsed ritual warfare in their community.[39]

This survey of protests, resistance movements, and scribal texts indicates that most resistance to imperial violence was nonviolent, although popular revolt erupted at times of extreme crisis. Dissident scribal literature anticipated God's judgment against the imperial rulers that involved destruction of some sort, either stated or assumed. Yet, with the exception of Qumran literature such as the War Scroll, the anticipated violence does not appear in elaborate, much less lurid images, and agency is generally not attributed to God or God's agent.

Jesus's Response to Imperial Violence
"Love your enemies . . ."

Arguments that Jesus advocated and practiced nonviolence and even nonresistance have been based mainly on individual sayings, especially "love your enemies," "turn the other cheek," "do not resist evil/the evildoer," and "go the second mile."[40] These and other sayings were printed as separate statements in the KJV (Matt 5:39, 41, 44). Devout Christians and professional interpreters became deeply habituated to appropriating Jesus's teachings as separate statements or commands. Some who took Jesus's teachings seriously and undertook to be faithful disciples felt an obligation to practice nonviolence. And whether it was declaring one's stance as a "conscientious objector" to war, observance of the principle of nonviolence in civil rights demonstrations, or drawing conclusions about Jesus's stance toward the use of violence, these sayings provided the basis.

While this has been an important way of appropriating scripture for Christians, however, it is problematic as a starting point and basis for investigation of the historical Jesus (interacting) in historical context. It would not have been possible for Jesus, any more than for anyone else, to have communicated mainly by means of separate sayings (as noted in chapter 1).

The set of sayings grouped with "love your enemies," moreover, provides good illustrations of how focusing on separate sayings is problematic for historical investigation. The meaning of a saying depends on context, and interpreters of Jesus and the Gospels who take sayings separately, out of literary context, then determine the context themselves or perhaps bring their own context to the sayings (for example, "what does Jesus say about violence or war or retaliation?"). One of the bases on which interpreters have taken "love your enemies" (Matt 5:44/Luke 6:27) as pertaining to the Romans (and meaning "do not fight back/revolt") is the saying about going the second mile (Matt 5:41). They claim a historical basis in the Roman practice of pressing subject persons (or their animals) into service to carry burdens such as a soldier's gear, with a limit placed on such service (only "one mile"). Historically, however, after the Romans had conquered or reconquered the people, Galilee and Judea were not occupied by Roman troops during Herod's reign before Jesus's lifetime, nor was Galilee during Jesus's lifetime (Herod Antipas had his own officers). Roman military occupation somewhere at some point may account for the origin of this saying (which may then have become a popular proverb). But if spoken by Jesus, it does not fit the context in Galilee during his lifetime.

While many sayings taken separately give no hint of their historical-social context, however, many others do; if we use our semi-educated historical sensitivities to fundamental forms of an agrarian society, we can discern likely social contexts. This is true of the "love your enemies" set of sayings.[41] The commands to "lend" and "not refuse a loan" and "not take back" (Matt 5:42; Luke 6:30, 35) pertain to lending and borrowing in a local community.

If we then also attend to the cultural context in which Jesus and his audiences would have been living, "love your enemies" and the sayings grouped
with it make multiple allusions to traditional Israelite covenantal teaching that
we are familiar with in the "law codes" of Exodus, Leviticus, and Deuteronomy.
For example, in Matt 5:43–44 "love your enemies" is explicitly connected with
"love your neighbor," which was a standard summary of covenantal instruction (torah; Lev 19:18)—in the same collection of covenantal teachings that
begins with "You shall be holy, for I . . . God am holy" (Lev 19:2), of which
"Be perfect/merciful as your Father is perfect/merciful" in Matt 4:48/Luke
6:36 is a more popular (less "Levitical") variation. Clearest of all the references to traditional Israelite covenantal law in these sayings is the admonition about yielding the tunic when someone seizes the cloak, which pertains
to the custom of taking someone's garment in pledge (as symbolic collateral—but giving it back immediately) when making a loan (see Exod 22:25–26;
Deut 24:10–13; cf. Amos 2:8). From these multiple references to or adaptations of covenantal tradition, it is again clear that the context of the teaching
in these sayings is social-economic interaction in the local village community.

In the sayings where context can be determined, therefore, even when
taken separately they do not pertain to the issue of violence or relations with
the Romans. Only "the golden rule" in Luke 6:31 and "go the second mile" in
Matt 5:41 do not necessarily refer to local interaction. Their being grouped
with the other sayings in both Matthew and Luke, however, suggests that they
too refer to local interaction.

As they appear in the Gospels of Matthew and Luke, however, these
sayings are not only grouped together but constitute a section or sections of
Mosaic covenantal instruction in larger speeches of covenant renewal.[42] This
is clearest in Matthew's "Sermon on the Mount," which begins with the "be-
atitudes" as new declarations of deliverance (5:3–16) and then presents Jesus's
"intensification" of the covenantal commandments in what have been called the
"antitheses" (Matt 5:17–19, 20–48). Each begins with a citation of a commandment (e.g., "you shall not murder"), followed by a command concerning even
the motivation of what is prohibited (e.g., "do not even be angry"). The set of
sayings that appears in Luke's parallel "sermon on the plain" (in Luke 6:27–36)
are divided between the final two "antitheses" in Matthew (5:38–42, 43–48).
This same set of sayings (with certain additions) appears again as the first step
in a larger discourse of covenantal teaching in Didache 1–6. It seems clear that,
in their cultivation of Jesus's teaching, several different early Jesus communities
understood this whole set of sayings as renewed covenantal teachings about
interaction in local communities.

It may be that the tensions addressed in the final antithesis in Matthew's "Sermon" (5:43–48) include those between members of the Matthean community(ies) and "outsiders" in the same town. "Those who "accuse" or "persecute" you might include people outside the community. The implied admonitions to love not just those who love you and to greet not only your brothers also suggest that outsiders are in view. But nothing in this antithesis (or in the preceding one) suggests that the renewed covenantal teaching directly addresses the issue of violence or relations with Romans.

Getting Reoriented to the Gospel Sources

As illustrated in this examination of the renewed covenantal teaching parallel in Matthew 5 and Luke 6—and as discussed in chapter 1—investigation into the historical Jesus (interacting) in historical context must begin from the Gospel sources as whole stories and/or series of speeches.

In the Q series of speeches Jesus teaches and enacts the renewal of Israel in its village communities in opposition to the Jerusalem rulers and their representatives.[43] Most of the speeches deal with issues internal to the movement, such as covenant renewal (Q 6:20–49), commissioning of envoys to extend Jesus's mission to other village communities (9:57–10:16), prayer for subsistence bread and cancellation of debts (11:2–4, 9–13), and anxiety about subsistence living (12:22–31). The opening prophecy by John the Baptist announcing that "the coming one" will bring the fire of judgment (as well as the Spirit of renewal) does seem to apply to the Jerusalem rulers as well as to Jesus's movement itself. Subseqently Jesus pronounces prophetic woes and sentence on the scribes and Pharisees as representatives of the temple-state as well as a prophetic lament over the ruling house of Jerusalem, in both cases because they have persecuted and killed the prophets (11:39–52; 13:34–35a). Both of these prophetic pronouncements seem to assume God's impending destruction of the rulers and their representatives.

Mark's story also presents Jesus as leading a renewal of Israel under the rule of God and against Jerusalem and Roman imperial rule.[44] The exorcism episodes imply that Jesus's casting out of "unclean spirits" is a manifestation of God's "binding" (destruction?) of Satan, the prince of invasive alien spirits (1:21–28; 3:22–28). Early in the story, the Pharisees and the Herodian representatives of the rulers plot to destroy Jesus. Unclean spirits have possessed some of the people, touching off fratricidal social violence, and the unclean spirit(s) named "Legion" self-destructs by "charging" into the Sea (Mark 5:1–20). Antipas beheads John, anticipating Jesus's suffering at the hands of the

Jerusalem rulers (e.g., 6:17–29; 8:32). Because of the rulers' repressive violence, following Jesus will require "taking up the cross" (8:34–38). After he marches up to Jerusalem, Jesus enacts the impending destruction of the temple, implies God's judgment of the high priests, and prophesies and is accused of threatening to destroy the temple (11:12–24; 12:1–12;13:1–2; cf. 14:58; 15:29–30). In his speech to the disciples about the immediate future, Jesus refers to war, military brutality against women and infants, and violence so pervasive that one dare not take time to get a cloak or provisions (13:3–23). Finally, in the climax of the story, the Jerusalem rulers arrest Jesus by force of arms and the Roman governor orders him beaten and executed by torturous crucifixion (14:43–15:32).

The Ways in Which Jesus Responds to Imperial Violence

If we consider all the facets of Jesus's mission of the renewal of Israel, the two most important ways in which he responded to imperial violence were probably his healing and exorcisms and his renewal of covenantal community.

Jesus's healing and exorcism addressed the illnesses and spirit possession that had resulted partly or primarily from the killing and from the destruction of people's houses and livelihood in the periodic Roman reconquests. As noted earlier, belief in and possession by superhuman spirits was an adaptive way of coping with the imperial violence. Jesus's exorcisms that "cast out" the invasive, possessing spirits ("Legion") could thus be understood as a healing of the effects of imperial violence, as is discussed more fully in the next chapter.

Jesus's second major response to the effects of imperial violence was his renewal of covenantal community evident in the covenant renewal speeches such as Matthew's Sermon on the Mount and the parallel in Luke (behind which was a Q speech). Destruction of houses and killing of family members in the Roman reconquests, exacerbated by demands for taxes, tribute, and tithes, led to the disintegration of village communities, with conflicts between desperate families over borrowing and lending to feed themselves. Addressing these tensions, Jesus attempted to generate a recommitment to sharing and cooperation. This recommitment would have strengthened communities that had been disintegrating, mitigating the crisis to a certain extent and leaving local village communities better able to withstand the outside pressures through the sharing and cooperation. This is more fully explored in chapter 5.

Important to examine here are the other ways Jesus (and his followers) dealt with the violence or threatened violence of the Roman rulers and their clients and the potential violence implicit in God's judgment that Jesus pronounced on the temple and high priests.

While the "love your enemies" set of sayings does not provide evidence for whether Jesus was an advocate of nonviolence or his stance vis-à-vis the Romans, other episodes or references in the Gospel stories suggest that while Jesus opposed the Jerusalem rulers, he did so nonviolently, in the main. Judging from the several leaders and movements among the Galilean, Samaritan, and Judean people at the time, there were two distinctive types or models of leadership derived from Israelite popular tradition: a popular king in the tradition of the young David and a popular prophet in tradition of Moses and Joshua. The popular kings and their followers mounted revolts against Roman and Jerusalem rule; the popular prophets and their followers, in nonviolent collective action, were caught up in their conviction of God's new deliverance. The earliest Gospel sources indicate that Jesus and his followers evidently interacted in adaptation of one or both of these familiar models in their relation with the rulers.[45]

The Gospel sources give a few indications that some of his followers, perhaps some of his inner circle of disciples, understood him as a popular messiah, evidently somewhat like the leaders of the messianic movements in the revolts in 4 BCE and 66–70 CE. The Q speeches give no suggestion whatever of Jesus in the role of an anointed king. But a passing reference in the Gospel of John refers to some followers as wanting "to take him and make him king" (John 6:15). And Mark's story juxtaposes Jesus's announcements that he must suffer and die in Jerusalem with the evident assumption among some of the disciples that he was "the messiah," a popular king who would become the new ruler. Peter pronounces him "the messiah" and objects to the suffering role (8:27–33), and James and John want to share Jesus's exercise of power (10:32–45). John's reference to "making him king" and Mark's "correction" of the disciples' (mis)understanding indicate that an understanding of Jesus as a popular king was current among at least some of Jesus's followers. The episode of Jesus's entry into Jerusalem riding on a donkey in allusion to the prophecy (in Zech 9:9–13) seems to present Jesus as a popular king coming to deliver the people (11:1–10)—although this can be explained as a provocative demonstration during the festive procession up to Jerusalem for Passover.

On the other hand, both Mark's story and the Q speeches represent Jesus as a prophet like Moses and Elijah, catalyzing a movement. Unlike the other popular prophets at the time, however, Jesus did not call followers out of the village communities to participate in an act of deliverance but worked on renewal of the common life in those communities. In two episodes in Mark the people and/or Herod Antipas say that Jesus is (like) one of the prophets, and Mark pointedly has Jesus rebuke Peter for acclaiming him the messiah (6:14–16; 8:27–30, 31–33). Thus, judging from the dominant early tradition of Jesus's interaction with his followers, he was evidently (in interaction) adapting the role of a prophet like Moses or Elijah, catalyzing a movement based in the villages of Galilee and pronouncing God's judgment on the rulers and their representatives.

While no evidence of political violence by Jesus is evident in the Gospel sources, however, he is clearly portrayed as bold, even confrontational, in his resistance. Most of his confrontation takes the form of prophetic pronouncements. Both Mark's and John's stories, however, present his prophetic demonstration in the temple as forcible. In Mark's account he "began to drive out those who were selling ... and buying ... and overturned the tables of the money changers" (11:15–16). Similarly, in John's account, "making a whip of cords, he drove ... out of the temple" all of the sellers and moneychangers, poured out the coins, and overturned the tables (2:13–15). While this cannot be described as political violence, it is forcible disruption of temple business. And while it should not be imagined that the disruption happened more or less as portrayed, it seems highly unlikely that Jesus's followers would have invented such a forcible disruption.

On the other hand, it should not be imagined that Jesus somehow took over the whole large area of the outer court of Herod's massively reconstructed temple. It was standard practice at the Passover festival, when the crowds celebrating their historical liberation could be volatile, for the Roman governors of Judea to bring a military cohort up to Jerusalem and to post them atop the colonnade around the temple courtyard. One year, in reaction to a large-scale protest over a provocation by a soldier, the governor Cumanus set his soldiers upon the crowd in the courtyard (Josephus, *War* 2.223–227; *Ant.* 20.105–109).[46] We may speculate that Jesus's disruption would have been on a much smaller scale that did not evoke an immediate response. We may also speculate, however, that it may have been a factor in drawing attention to him, leading to his (surreptitious) arrest.

While Jesus's mission in Galilean villages may not have attracted the attention of the "Herodian" officers of Antipas in his capital cities, Sepphoris and Tiberias, certainly after Jesus's crucifixion and perhaps before as well, Jesus's followers experienced repressive action by the "authorities." And given what is known of rulers' repressive responses to protests and movements, Jesus and his followers probably knew what might happen to those involved in a movement of renewal and resistance. Both Mark's story and the speeches in Q include a

Jesus speech exhorting followers to be steadfast in resistance to such repressive action (Mark 8:34–38; Q/Luke 12:2–9). Jesus warns in both speeches that they might well be killed, perhaps even by crucifixion (that is, the form of execution for rebellion; Mark 8:34; Q/Luke 14:27). The clear implication is that they were engaged in activity that the authorities might consider so disruptive as to warrant execution. Nothing indicates that Jesus's or his followers' activity was violent in some way, but it was sufficiently oppositional or disruptive to evoke repressive action.

Prophetic Pronouncement of God's Judgment

Jesus's prophetic pronouncements of God's imminent judgment of the Jeruslaem rulers, as presented in both the Gospel of Mark and the Q speeches, was a significant aspect of his engagement in the politics of Roman Palestine, as discussed in the previous chapter. It is now important to take a closer look at those pronouncements for how they were responding to the violence of the Roman imperial order, with special attention to the question of destruction of the rulers, attribution of agency to God, and rhetorical violence. In both Jesus's confrontation with the Jerusalem rulers in Mark's story and prophetic oracles in Q, judgment is coming upon the rulers or their representatives explicitly because of the violence they had done to the people and/or to the previous prophets who protested their oppression. Jesus's pronouncements clearly assume that the temple and the high priests are about to be terminated or destroyed. Yet they often do not ascribe agency to God, and they involve little rhetorical violence.

Besides speaking in the traditional prophetic role as the spokesperson for God, Jesus speaks in traditional Israelite prophetic forms such as a series of woes and a prophetic lament. In the oracles of prophets such as the "historical" Elijah, Amos, Micah, and Isaiah, God pronounces indictments of kings and/or their officers for their oppression of the people in violation of covenantal commandments and then pronounces sentence. Very often "the punishment fits the crime"; the rulers will no longer have their own lavish houses because they have coveted and stolen the houses and fields of their subjects. Punishment is often anticipated to come in the form of defeat by other rulers, and there is little rhetorical elaboration about violent destruction. Isaiah's prophecy pronouncing God's imminent punishment of the Babylonian imperial conquerors by bringing the Medes against them (Isa 13) is unusual in the rhetorical violence with which it embellishes both the appearance of God and what will happen to the Babylonian rulers. Jesus's prophetic pronouncements against the high priestly rulers of Jerusalem, unlike that oracle included in the book of Isaiah, resembles more those of the eighth-century prophets Amos, Micah, and Isaiah of Jerusalem, with virtually no rhetorical elaboration about violent destruction.

In the Q speeches, most references to God's judgment are brief, functioning as sanctions on Jesus's admonitions to the communities of the movement itself (not to outsiders), as in the references to Gehenna and the heavenly court in the exhortation to solidarity when on trial (Q/Luke 12:5, 6–9). The Q speech behind Luke 17:22–37 is directed not at "all Israel" but at participants in the Q movement itself, as a speech sanctioning all of the preceding speeches in Q. However, Q/Luke 11:39–52 is a series of woes and sentence against the scribes and Pharisees as servants of the temple-state, and Q/Luke 13:34–35a is an oracle against the Jerusalem ruling house, perhaps linked with another oracle and the "great supper" parable.[47]

One of the woes against the scribes and Pharisees indicts them and, by implication, their patrons in the priestly aristocracy with being complicit in their ancestors' killing of the prophets (11:47–48, 49–51). This indictment appears to be closely related to the representation of John the Baptist and Jesus as the greatest in the line of Israelite prophets, now also martyred at the hands of the Jerusalem authorities (cf. Q/Luke 7:18–35). Although it is not explicitly articulated but remains implicit in the pronouncement of the sentence, the declaration that "the blood of all the prophets will be required of/charged against this generation" (11:49–51) is a death sentence, according to the traditional prophetic principle that the sentence corresponds to the violent crime of the rulers. As often in prophetic oracles, the passive verb ("will be required of") implies God's agency in the judgment. In contrast with some of the series of woes in the Epistle of Enoch (1 Enoch 94–106), however, the pronouncement of the sentence includes no description of the punishment and does not involve the persecuted people or prophets as agents or witnesses of the punishment.

The oracle in Q/Luke 13:34–35a was perhaps central in a larger speech that included the oracle in 13:28–29 and the parable in 14:16–24, both of which deliver somewhat the same judgment.

> O Jerusalem! Jerusalem!
> City that kills the prophets and stones those sent to it.
> How often have I desired to gather your children together
> as a hen gathers her brood under her wings—
> But you were not willing.
> Behold! Your House is desolate!
>   (Luke 13:34–35/Matt 23:37–39; author's trans.)

This is a prophetic lament, like a funeral dirge, the kind that Amos and Jeremiah pronounced against the rulers of Israel. The prophet is the spokesperson for God. God is deeply saddened that it is necessary for the ruling house to be destroyed in punishment for its oppression of the people. The imagery is maternal and caring. Like a protective mother hen, God had attempted to protect her "children," that is, the peasant villages under the power of the ruling house. But the rulers refused God's attempts, even killed the prophets she sent, and continued to oppress the villagers. As a result, it is implied, the rulers are to be destroyed in punishment. God, through the prophet, anticipating the destruction, is now lamenting that it had to happen. Such laments anticipate God's destruction. But they do not trade in rhetorical violence.

The Gospel of Mark also presents Jesus as pronouncing and even symbolically acting out God's judgment of the temple and the high priests as well. In Mark the destruction involved is explicit, although it involves God's agency in only some of the prophecies. Mark's story also insinuates, at least, the self-destruction of the Romans.

Jesus's forcible obstruction of temple business was also a prophetic demonstration, a symbolic prophetic action (instead of an oracle) that signified God's impending destruction of the temple. This has been avoided in the anachronistic Christian interpretation of Jesus's action as a "cleansing," as if the temple were only a religious institution. The citation in this Markan episode from Jeremiah's oracle of God's impending destruction of the temple indicts the priestly rulers for violently oppressing the people. Like brigands, they have been robbing the people of their produce (on the pretense that it is owed to God and the priests as offerings and tithes) and then fleeing into their "brigands' stronghold" (the temple) for protection (they assume, hypocritically, by God). Just in case the hearers of the story might not recognize that the action symbolized destruction, Mark frames the episode with Jesus's cursing of the fig tree and explicitly states its lesson about "this mountain" being thrown into the Sea (11:12–14, 20–24).

Three different episodes in Mark, some paralleled in other sources, all cite or refer to Jesus's prophetic oracle pronouncing the destruction (and rebuilding) of the temple. Almost as a summary statement of his series of confrontations in the temple, Jesus says, in reference to the massively reconstructed edifice, that "not one stone will be left here upon another, all will be thrown down" (13:1–2). Some of the witnesses at his trial in Mark say they heard him say, "I will destroy this temple that is made with hands and in three days I will build another, not made with hands" (Mark 14:58). Passersby at his crucifixion deride him, saying,

"Aha! You who would destroy the temple and build it in three days" (15:29). The simplest version of the oracle is in the Gospel of Thomas 71: "Jesus said: 'I shall de[stroy this] house, and no one will be able to build it [again],'" which is close to the reports in Acts 6:13–14 that Stephen had said "that this Jesus of Nazareth will destroy this place." That Jesus had prophesied the destruction (and rebuilding) of the temple was so deeply embedded in the tradition that the Gospel of John carefully explained that Jesus was referring to his body rather than suppress the prophecy (cf. John 2:19–21).

Several attempts have been made to explain and to explain away this prophecy. Some have dismissed it as prophecy after the fact. This is based on the dating of the Gospel of Mark to after the Roman destruction of the temple in 70 CE by reading the "war and rumors of war" and "desolating sacrilege" as references to events of the great revolt of 66–70. However, judging from Josephus's histories, Jesus and his contemporaries would have been experiencing "wars and rumors of wars" and "desolating sacrileges" aplenty in the mid-first century at the hands of the Roman governors and military. This leaves no compelling reason to date the Gospel of Mark after 70 CE and the prophetic pronouncement against the temple as "after the fact."

Jesus's prophecy of the destruction of the temple has also been dismissed on the grounds that at Jesus's trial in Mark the paraphrase of his prophecy is presented as false testimony. Mark's narrative ("But even on this point their testimony did not agree"; 15:59) does not really say that. The assumption at the crucifixion scene is that Jesus had indeed spoken about destroying the temple. And Mark's story had earlier presented Jesus as declaring that the stones would all "be thrown down" (13:2). It is possible that the "falseness" of the testimony pertains (subtly) to its form. The Markan narrative may be portraying the high priests and elders as unacquainted with the form of prophetic pronouncements and as uncomprehending of their ominous import, assuming that Jesus meant that he himself would do so. If he had been uttering prophecy as the mouthpiece of God, in the same way that earlier Israelite prophets had done and in the same way as in Q/Luke 13:34, then it was God who was about to destroy the temple.[48]

The form of the prophecy in two of the Markan episodes and in John is a double saying, about the destruction and the rebuilding of the temple. Another attempt to mitigate the severity of the prophecy of destruction has been to claim that there was a long-standing expectation of a new temple and that the destruction in Jesus's prophecy was to prepare for the rebuilt temple.[49] This is a misreading of several second-temple Judean texts.[50] In some of those adduced, terms such as "Zion" and "the house" are symbols for the restored people, not the rebuilt temple. In others the temple is conspicuously missing in images of the fulfillment of history (e.g., 1 Enoch 90:28–29).

The temple "not made with hands" was taken as a "spiritual" or "heavenly" temple in earlier Christian interpretation. The appearance of "house" in the Gospel of Thomas 71 version, however, suggests another possibility for understanding the prophecy in its double-saying form. As noted in chapter 2, "house (of God)" was used in second-temple Judean texts not only for the temple and for the ruling house but also for the people and often for the restored people of Israel. The discovery of the Dead Sea Scrolls has provided evidence of a Judean community contemporary to the Jesus movement that understood itself as the "temple" (1QS 5:5–7; 8:4–10; 9:3–6; 4QFlor 1:1–13). Terms such as "house," "temple," body," and "assembly" could all function as synonyms, usually with reference to a social body (the people).

Jesus's prophecy of destroying and rebuilding the temple can thus be understood as playing on the double meaning of the term "temple" or (more likely, as in the Gospel of Thomas version) "house." His prophecy declared that God was destroying the "house/temple made with hands" in Jerusalem but rebuilding the/God's "house/temple not made with hands," the people of Israel. This would fit well with the agenda of Jesus's mission, as attested in Q as well as in Mark, of spearheading a renewal of Israel in opposition to its rulers. If the renewed people were understood as the rebuilt "temple" or "house" of God, then of course there would be no need for a temple-state, which, as an instrument of imperial control, was widely resented among the people (see the discussion in chapter 2 of how even scribes viewed the current high priests and even the temple as illegitimate). The oracle was apparently a simple statement, with no elaboration on the destruction. But it is well attested in the Gospel sources that Jesus prophesied the destruction of the temple.

The way Jesus confronts the high priests is somewhat subtler than his explicit prophecy of the destruction of the temple, but the message is parallel. In telling a parable, Jesus sets the hearers up to draw the implication or application. Internal to the parable of the tenants (Mark 12:1–9) is the conclusion that after the tenants have expropriated for themselves the produce of the vineyard and then killed the messengers, the owner will destroy the tenants in retaliation for their theft and violence. The high priestly addressees recognize immediately that they are implicated. It is unnecessary to name God as the agent, and the impact of the parable in particular draws on the well-known prophecy of Isaiah that began in the form of "the song of the vineyard" (Isa 5:1–7). As the love song shifts into a lawsuit against the hearers, the rulers of Jerusalem ("inhabitants" is NRSV's depoliticizing translation), the speaker (God) declares that he will "make it a waste." There would have been no question who "the owner" of the vineyard was and who were the predatory tenants.[51]

The Gospel of Mark also includes at least the insinuation of destruction for the invasive Romans, although it is nothing like direct divine condemnation of the temple and high priests. In the exorcism where the identity of the unclean spirit turns out to be "Legion," that is, Roman troops (note the following military imagery), the latter ask Jesus to "dismiss" them to enter the great "troop" of swine there on the hillside, which then suddenly "charge" down the steep bank "into the Sea" and "were drowned in the Sea" (5:1–20). Exposed and confronted by the divine power working through Jesus, the Roman military becomes self-destructive in its desperation.

Jesus and Imperial Violence in Historical Context

Dealing with the issue of Jesus and (non)violence is far more complicated than was discerned forty or fifty years ago. The imperial military violence of Roman conquest and reconquest, about which historians of ancient Rome have been much more candid in recent decades, set the conditions of and for Jesus's mission and nascent movement(s). Compounding the destruction and social trauma left in the wake of military conquest, the structural violence of the Roman imperial order further exacerbated the disintegration of the fundamental social forms of family and village community.

Organized collective responses to imperial violence, obscured by the old synthetic construct of "the Zealots," was diverse in it forms. In the widespread revolts that historically framed Jesus's mission, Galilean and Judean villagers drove the Roman military and/or Herodian garrisons out of their fortresses. After enjoying a few months or years of life without rulers, they then fought or fled the destruction and slaughter of Roman reconquest, many of them ending up hung on crosses. In some areas those revolts took the form of popular messianic movements, which were also forms of regional self-governance patterned on memories of the young David. The popular prophetic movements in the mid-first century, patterned on memories of Moses and/or Joshua, were not violent movements. The Roman governors made no distinctions, however, and wiped them out in military action. Especially impressive as examples of the ability of Judean and Galilean villagers to organize themselves and maintain collective discipline in the face of threatened Roman violence were the protest against Pilate in Caesarea and the agricultural "strike" against the military expedition sent to install Gaius's statue in the temple.

Despite their dependency on their high priestly patrons who headed the temple-state, small circles of scribal teachers, evidently including a few Pharisees, also organized resistance. In contrast to continuing claims that the "fourth philosophy" mounted a "revolt," their refusal to pay the tribute was disciplined nonviolent "civil disobedience," like the nonviolent peasant protests, that consciously risked official repression and death. Forty-some years later, in utter frustration with Roman intransigence and high priestly collaboration, a small circle of scribal teachers began assassinating key high priestly figures in a sort of counterterrorism.

Jesus's mission was similar in many ways to the nonviolent prophetic movements, but, instead of drawing people out of their villages, Jesus focused on renewal of village communities. This would presumably have appeared less threatening to the Herodian, high priestly, and Roman rulers. Although the sayings previously taken as principles of nonresistance turn out to be components of covenant renewal speeches, there is no indication in the Gospel sources that Jesus engaged in political violence in his opposition to the Roman imperial order. Consistently pursuing his role and recognition as a prophet, however, he pronounced God's judgment against the Jerusalem rulers for their oppression of the people and their violence against the prophets. Given the seriousness with which pronouncements by prophets were taken (as in the arrest and beheading of John the Baptist by Herod Antipas), this constituted what today would be called nonviolent direct action. From the accounts in Mark and John, it is evident that Jesus went even further in this confrontation in carrying out a prophetic action that forcibly blocked temple business, symbolizing God's judgment on the temple.

While Jesus's forcible demonstration in the temple may not have been that much of a disruption in the festive atmosphere of the Passover festival, it would have been sufficient provocation to evoke reaction by the high priests and Roman governor—especially if he had also declared that the people did not owe tribute to Caesar (see chapter 2 again). Not surprisingly, from what we know of Roman practice, the governor ordered him crucified. This highly charged act of imperial violence, however, became a source of motivation and commitment among Jesus's followers. Jesus's "speaking truth to power" would already have been a "breakthrough" event for them. The martyrdom of their prophet further evoked their solidarity and commitment to his program of renewal and resistance. This is clearly expressed in both Mark's story (the open ending calling the followers to continue the movement in Galilee) and in the Q speeches (where the hearers understand themselves as continuing Jesus's prophetic program).

Considering the broader conditions in Roman Palestine that had been set up by Roman imperial violence, however, the most important ways in which Jesus responded were his attempts to deal with its effects in the healing of sickness and the exorcism of spirits and in his renewal of covenantal community—which are the subjects of chapters 4 and 5.

4. Illness and Possession, Healing and Exorcism

The way interpreters of Jesus and the Gospels deal with Jesus's healings and exorcisms has not changed much since Rudolf Bultmann's influential presentation in the 1920s. Treating the Gospels as mere containers or collections of discrete sayings and stories, they sort the materials by categories such as individual sayings and various kinds of stories. While they classify Jesus traditions ostensibly by (literary) form (sayings, parables, controversy/pronouncement stories), modern Western rationalist criteria are also determinative. Thus, stories that deal with healings, exorcisms, "nature miracles," and "raising the dead" are all lumped together in the controlling category of "miracle stories," before being separated into subcategories (e.g., healing stories, exorcism stories). Then, partly because "the sayings tradition" also attests healings and exorcisms, contemporary scholars such as John Meier and Robert Funk (and the Jesus Seminar)[1] repeat Bultmann's conclusion of 1926: that while most of the miracle stories are legendary, "there can be no doubt that Jesus did the kind of deeds which were miracles . . . , that is, deeds which were attributed to a supernatural, divine cause; undoubtedly he healed the sick and cast out demons."[2]

But these same scholars then ignore Bultmann's other conclusion from 1926: that there is "no great value in investigating more closely how much in the gospel miracle tales is historical."[3] They devote great energy and hundreds of pages to ferreting out fragmentary "historical facts" or elements that "have a chance of going back to some event in the life of . . . Jesus."[4] Meier devoted twice as much space (530 pages) to the "miracle stories" as to Jesus's message, and Funk and the Jesus Seminar devoted 500 pages and five years of research, discussion, and voting (1991–96) to the task. As the result of this painstaking analysis of the "miracle stories," however, they find few elements that they deem "authentic." Meanwhile, they give little or no attention to the historical social context or to spirit possession and exorcism or to the significance of the healings and exorcisms in Jesus's mission.

Interpretation of Jesus's healing and exorcism has thus been severely limited by a combination of a fragmenting approach to the Gospel sources for Jesus and the rationalist assumptions of modern Western culture. Recent developments in other fields suggest that it may be possible to take some provisional steps toward a broader and more historically appropriate approach to Jesus's healing and exorcism.

A first crucial step is to move beyond the modern rationalist "scientific" reduction of reality toward a more comprehensive perspective on and approach to illness and spirit possession and healing and exorcism. This involves learning from medical anthropology how to recognize that illness and healing are culturally defined and that political-economic factors significantly affect illness and healing, including spirit possession and exorcism.

Second, studies of spirit possession and exorcism in African societies have found that they are related, as recent medical anthropological studies suggest, to the impact of colonial rule, as indigenous societies make cultural adjustments to cope with this impact.

This suggests, third, that it would be particularly pertinent to attend to the effects of Roman imperial conquest and rule on Judean and Galilean society, discussed in chapters 2 and 3, and to investigate late second-temple Judean culture for how it may have been adjusting to those effects.

Finally, with an appropriately broadened perspective on and approach to the historical context and determinative factors in illness and spirit possession, we can better appreciate how key healings and exorcisms of Jesus are represented in Mark, often considered the earliest (narrative) Gospel source.

Broadening Our Approach to Healing and Exorcism
Problematic Projections

It is nowhere more evident that the standard interpretation of Jesus is rooted in Western Enlightenment culture than in the treatment of his healings and exorcisms. The Enlightenment reduced reality to rationally apprehensible terms. Only the natural was allowed as knowable, that is, as empirically or scientifically knowable. Only what was humanly possible was deemed natural; phenomena and causation beyond human capability were classed as "supernatural" or "miracles." Christian believers and theologically trained scholars alike were understandably placed on the defensive. As Enlightenment Reason became dominant in Western culture, many Christians took comfort in the stories of Jesus's "miracles" as evidence of his divine empowerment and as proofs that he was indeed the Messiah and the Son of God. By the end of the nineteenth century, however, liberal theologians preferred either to ignore the "miracle stories" or to ascribe them to later stages in the development of the traditions about Jesus and to view them as therefore unreliable as evidence for the historical Jesus. The concept of miracles and miracle stories, however, had taken deep root in New Testament studies. While even more "moderate" scholars now agree with "liberal" interpreters that most "miracle stories" contain few elements that "go back to Jesus," there is a consensus that Jesus must indeed have performed "miracles" of healing and exorcism.[5]

The Gospels, however, have no equivalent for the modern English term or concept of "miracle/miraculous," certainly no equivalent for the modern Western dichotomy between the natural and the miraculous or supernatural. The Gospels speak of "wonders," "signs," and especially of "powers" (often translated as "mighty acts"), not "miracles." It is thus modern interpreters, not the Gospel sources, who think of Jesus as having performed miracles. And since the very concept of miracle is loaded with connotations of the supernatural or divine, as opposed to the natural and human, it imposes a peculiar modern Western viewpoint and valuation on the world, culture, and activities of Jesus.

It has recently been claimed, even by serious scholars, that Jesus was working magic, that he was a magician.[6] Some ancient Greek and Latin sources do have a seemingly equivalent concept in the cognate term *magos/ mageia* and *magus/magia*, although these terms do not appear as often as has been assumed. As in the modern Western world, the term was highly ambivalent, positive in some circles but used primarily in polemics. The *Magoi*, ancestors of those who play a cameo role in Matthew's story of the threatened Herod's massacre of the children in Bethlehem, were renowned priestly advisers at the court of the Persian emperor.[7] In the Roman Empire, however, the imperial elite and intellectuals denigrated popular religion or foreign practices as "magic."[8] By the mid-second century, opponents of the nascent "Christians" were charging that Jesus had indeed been working magic.[9]

Once Christianity had become the established religion, theologians appropriated the term for their own attempts to suppress popular religious beliefs and practices. In the great European witch hunts of the sixteenth and seventeenth centuries, Christian and secular officials alike tried to ferret out and kill those who practiced "magic."[10] Then, as Western European explorers, missionaries, and the agents of nascent European imperial projects came into contact with other peoples in Africa and Asia and the Americas, the beliefs and practices of those peoples were categorized as magic (Sir James Frazer had a huge influence on theological fields such as biblical studies, as well as on other fields). The concept continued to play a major role in the grand schematic thinking of social scientists, including those who recently influenced New Testament scholars.[11]

The concept of "magic/magician" is thus highly problematic in general and especially in its application to Jesus's healings and exorcisms. In antiquity, except for its use by some intellectuals who admired the Magi, the terms related to "magic" were mainly polemical. Herbalists who developed medicines were accused of peddling "potions" (same term, *pharmakeia*). Poets who chanted hymns were accused of using "charms" and "incantations" (same terms). But medicines and hymns to divine forces are hardly magic. The discovery of the so-called Magical Papyri in Egypt that date to late antiquity was taken, right through the end of the twentieth century, as evidence for the practice of magic. When interpreting the "miracle stories" or "miracles" of Jesus, New Testament scholars cited brief passages from the these papyri as evidence that Jesus is represented as performing magic in his healings and exorcisms.[12] Perhaps what is most striking about the contents of the texts inscribed on those papyri, however, is that very few of the "spells" pertain to healing and virtually none pertain to exorcism.[13] If the term *mageia* is even applicable to what the users of the texts found in these papyri were practicing, their practice did not include exorcism and included the healing only of simple problems such as headache. Many of the "spells" are designed to manipulate women into sexual submission or to cause harm to others. These texts thus appear singularly incomparable and inapplicable to Jesus's healing and exorcism.

Finally, the Gospel sources for Jesus's healings and exorcisms offer no suggestion that the term "magic" would have been applicable. Jesus is castigated for healing on the Sabbath and is accused of casting out demons by Beelzebul, the Prince of Demons, and he is executed after his conviction on the charge of posing as the (rebel) "king of the Judeans." But he is not accused of practicing magic. That was a charge leveled at Jesus by elite intellectuals of the second century in attacks against his followers.

Seemingly at odds with the claim that Jesus was performing miracles and/or practicing magic, but equally reductionist and misleading, is the interpretation of Jesus in the standard (scholarly) translations that impose the concepts of Western biomedicine on the context and activities of Jesus. The people he healed are represented as having had "diseases," and Jesus is represented as having "cured" those diseases. These terms/concepts now appear even in the most widely used "authorized" translations (such as NRSV and the NJB). Modern interpreters simply assumed that the "leper" (of Mark 1:40–45) was suffering from what is known as "leprosy" in modern medicine. Such "domestication" of ancient experiences continues into the pathologizing of demon possession as "hysteria." In modern medicine, however, "disease" suggests primarily the dis/malfunction of organs and processes of the individual human body, which must be "cured" if possible by medical intervention such as drugs or surgery, procedures that are "natural" and "scientific." Ironically, such a translation reinforces the sense that Jesus must have been performing "miracles." If Jesus, who could not have known scientific medicine, was curing diseases, he must have been doing so by supernatural means—unless of course in some cases it was "faith healing." Again we impose modern assumptions and concepts alien to the Gospel sources and to Jesus's culture.[14]

Learning from Medical Anthropology

Investigation of Jesus's healing and exorcism may be able to move beyond such projections of modern Western concepts and toward a much broader perspective on ancient society and culture by learning from recent developments in medical anthropology. In their encounter with other cultures, including traditional indigenous forms of healing, medical anthropologists have become increasingly critical of the ethnocentrism and reductionism of "scientific" Western medicine.

The very starting point of "cultural" or "meaning-centered" medical anthropology is to distinguish "disease" and "illness" and to recognize that they are not natural, that is, in nature, but are culturally constructed. "*Disease* refers to a malfunctioning of biological and/or psychological processes," which Western medical practitioners attempt to diagnose and *cure*. *Illness* involves "personal and social responses to such primary malfunctioning," including emotions and valuations and interpersonal interaction, "particularly within the context of the family and social network."[15] Perhaps partly because they work within "health-care systems" that include biomedicine as well as other "sectors," cultural medical anthropologists are not always clear whether they conceive of *illness* as separate from or inclusive of *disease*.[16] Since biomedicine is a very recent development and there was no such cultural construction in ancient Galilee and Judea, however, investigation of Jesus's mission requires a concept or term that holds together bodily malfunctioning and the broader personal-social dimensions and does not slip back into the modern Western body-mind dualism and the attendant separation of the "individual" from the social matrix. Thus I will use the terms "illness"/"sickness" as a concept that includes the bodily malfunctioning that biomedicine constructs as "disease" as well as the personal and social dimensions.

The response that corresponds to *illness* is *healing*. Western medical science has developed sophisticated means of diagnosing and attempting to cure the malfunctions of bodies and their organs and dysfunctional psychological processes but tends to ignore or slight the wider psychosocial experiences involved in *illness*. While lacking the scientific analysis and intervention techniques of Western biomedicine, many societies have traditional ways of diagnosing and *healing* the more broadly conceived *illness*. As is quickly evident from reading healing and exorcism episodes in the context of the larger Gospel stories, *healing* is the appropriate concept, not the narrower biomedical *cure* that has become standard in recent Bible translations.

In adapting "meaning-centered" medical anthropology for an approach to Jesus's mission, it is important to keep in mind that *disease* and *illness* are not entities and not labels of things *in themselves* but are culturally constructed explanatory concepts. It would be singularly inappropriate for us modern interpreters to assume, for example, that the man in Mark 1:40–45 had the disease leprosy (simply because the ancient Greek cognate term *lepros* is used in the episode). We may suspect that something like what we moderns call the "disease" psoriasis was involved. To understand the episode more broadly in terms of *illness* and *healing*, however, we must pick up the various allusions to ancient Judean cultural traditions and social relations. Such pointers suggest further investigation into the ancient Judean/Galilean cultural construction of illness and healing.[17]

With more complex societies in mind, cultural medical anthropologists such as Kleinman also think in terms of an overall "health-care system," analogous to religion or language as a cultural system, that has various sectors. Most illness is first defined and care initiated in the family or local network. This is also the context to which people return for further healing if they do go to professional or specialist practitioners. Most prestigious—and costly—in more complex societies is the *professional sector*, the highly educated and trained "physicians" of high civilizations. In addition, there are various forms of *folk healing*, ranging from the sacred, such as ritual healing practices, to the secular, such as herbal medicine, which are often not separate.

The distinction among the popular, professional, and folk modes of healing may be helpful in historical investigation of Jesus's mission. In the Gospel healing episodes it is clear that family members and wider village networks of kin and/or neighbors had been caring for the (e.g., paralyzed, deaf and dumb) people who were brought to Jesus for healing. Professional healers (*hiatroi*) are mentioned as being very costly and not very effective in the episode of the woman who had been hemorrhaging for years. And other "folk healers" besides Jesus crop up here and there in these episodes. It makes no sense, however, to speak of "the health-care system" of ancient Galilee-Judea as if it were a cultural system distinguishable from others. Except perhaps for the costly professional healers who catered mainly to the wealthy elite, health care was embedded in the basic social forms of family, village community, and the central religious-political-economic institution of the temple. Sickness and healing were not separate from religion, which was not separate from the domestic and political economy.

While cultural medical anthropologists such as Kleinman have suggested that factors "external" to the health-care system, including historical, social structural, political, and economic influences, could have important effects on illness and healing, it remained for "critical" medical anthropologists to explore these more fully.[18] Their efforts were part of a general interest among anthropologists in integrating analysis of historical forces, such as colonialism, political-economic structures, and "subaltern" studies of indigenous resistance movements, into their ethnography. Realizing that these factors have generally gone unattended or simply denied in Western medicine, critical medical anthropologists are attempting to understand "health issues in light of the larger political and economic forces that pattern interpersonal relationships, shape social behavior, generate social meanings, and condition collective experience."[19] Such forces contribute to the "social production" of illness or the "manufacture" of madness.[20] A burgeoning number of complex studies focus on how wider social and political-economic influences, including colonial and now global economic forces, contribute to the production of illness in given societies and can be traced to the local experiences of living and dying.[21]

Critical medical anthropologists also point out that cultures are not simply systems of meaning that orient humans to one another and to their world. They are also often "webs of mystification" that disguise political and economic realities, particularly the power relations that determine sickness and the possibility of healing.[22] Certain representations of illness may well be "misrepresentations" that serve the interests of the elites who control cultural production.[23] The dominant cultural constructions may serve the interests of those in power, whether colonial powers, social-economic elites, or those who benefit from existing dominant economic arrangements. Cultural representations need to be probed for such influences. I would add that cultural representations of peoples subject to seemingly unchallengeable power may be defensive, even self-protective, precisely as they "mystify" or distract attention from the concrete power-relations.[24]

Many of these "critical" anthropologists also point out that various forms of illness, such as nervous disorders or "hysteria" or "possession," are (also) forms of resistance. This interpretation has been reinforced by Foucault's insistence that "where there is power, there is [also] resistance."[25] Also influential have been James C. Scott's analysis of "everyday forms of resistance" that are hidden from the dominant and his analysis of how subordinated people have traditionally honed certain "arts of resistance" that may operate in culturally disguised forms.[26] Trances and/or spirit possession can be the only safe way of expressing fear, anxiety, and anger about circumstances imposed by outside forces.[27] In outbreaks of spirit possession in factories of multinational corporations in Malaysia, for example, the young women workers brought production to a halt as they resisted their working conditions and forced change of identity.[28] A growing body of research explains nervous disorders in various circumstances as culturally constituted expressions of malaise with political and economic origins and, sometimes, even a way of negotiating working and living conditions.[29]

What medical anthropologists do not seem to pick up from Scott—and might have picked up from the prophetic books of the Hebrew Bible—is that where there is power, there can also be *creative* resistance. As Scott points out, people under domination suffering various forms of indignity can develop a discourse of dignity, including images of a new social order of justice. Similarly, people suffering various forms of illness are capable of imagining and dreaming of healing and wholeness. And leaders of people in crisis situations, who are in tune with the people in distress, often include healing in their repertoire of leadership.

In order for interpreters of Jesus to understand his healing and exorcism it may help if we attempt "to step outside of the cultural rules governing [our] beliefs and behaviors," as medical ethnologists try to do.[30] The illnesses and demon possession that Jesus dealt with, as represented in the Gospels, were culturally constructed in their own historical situation. Thus, investigators must attempt, insofar as possible, to learn about and to understand the cultural situation in ancient Galilee and nearby areas where Jesus operated and Gospel accounts of Jesus's healing activities were formulated. That situation, moreover, had been seriously impacted by Roman conquest and the pressures of Roman rule. And, as critical medical anthropologists point out, illnesses and demon possession in their cultural situation cannot be adequately understood without factoring in historical changes and the impact of political-economic power relations. That impact, moreover, may have evoked a "web of mystification" that served partly to disguise while it culturally constructed those power relations. An understanding of the ancient Judean and Galilean cultural construction of those power relations is essential for our investigation insofar as it also determined the possibility and, to a degree, the form of healing.

Possession and Exorcism among African Peoples

Western biblical interpreters, perhaps largely because they tend to project the separation of religion from political-economic life in their own societies back into antiquity, have difficulty entertaining how possessing spirits could be related to political powers. Davies, for example, who seeks modern Western psychological explanations of Jesus's exorcism, bluntly rejects the suggestion that the demon possession addressed by Jesus could have been related to Roman rule in Palestine.[31] Studies of spirit possession and other illnesses among African peoples, however, find that influences of and invasions by outside peoples and colonial powers were of central importance. These studies of how African peoples adjusted to outside influences, including Arab-Islamic rule and European incursions, may provide helpful comparative material for discerning how Judeans and Galileans may have responded to Roman imperial rule.

A wide range of African peoples, both prior to and after European incursions, represented strangers as aspects of their own culture, expressed in various rites in which the strangers' spirits played a role.[32] Among the Shona, for example, in what is today Zimbabwe, the spirits of indigenous heroes protected the well-being of the land and the political fortunes of the inhabitants. Yet the hierarchy of those heroes and their spirits reflected the political system of outside conquerors.[33] Other rituals were carried out by conventicles of people who, possessed by the *shave*, or alien spirits, assumed the characteristics of foreigners, such as the Europeans or traders from the coast.[34] It is not difficult to discern the identity of the spirit Varungu, for example, who incited the people to meticulous cleanliness and whose hosts' clothes and food were those of Europeans.[35] The hero cults were constitutive of the social order as it appropriated outside influences, the *shave* cults largely a defensive or self-protective measure by those in whom those outside influences happen to become manifest in possession by the spirits of strangers.[36]

Swahili peoples interpreted sickness and grief as signs that the spirits of strangers (*pepo*) wished to embody themselves in persons and to demand sacrifices and worship.[37] They referred to the *pepo* with the Arabic word *sheit-ani* (satans), which misled Christian missionaries to believe the possession was demonic, rather than that the possessed persons were hosting the spirits of the Arabs or the Europeans (*Kizungu*).[38] In cases where the alien spirits were experienced as threatening, the possession appears to have had a defensive or self-protective character. For example, early in the twentieth century, sections of the Kamba people were possessed by *Kijesu*, the spirit not just of Jesus but of the whole invasive Christian mission, the whole alien culture that posed a serious threat to their own traditional way of life. This powerful invasion of strangers was not easily manageable in a regularized cult.[39] Possession by the spirit of Jesus was an *alternative* to conversion.

How a people, in its constituent local village communities, deals with the cumulative effect of domination by outside forces is exemplified in the *zar* cult in Sudan. In this cult can be seen the enduring results of how an Africa people adjusted to the conversion of its males to Islam and to the influence of Arabic culture, the relatively more recent incursion of the British military, and the recent influence of American medical and development initiatives. After Islam became dominant among the males of Sudanese villages, the women continued to cultivate traditional African culture, while also developing the *zar* cult, which continued to develop under the impact of European colonial invasions. In special sessions involving drumming and ecstatic dancing, women entertained possession by alien spirits in order then to have them exorcised, in a combination of accommodation, negotiation, and mollification. The anthropologist Janice Boddy explains that such possession and exorcism were both self-protective measures and protests against the invasion of their lives by the outside forces.[40]

The more imposing and threatening *zayran* were outsiders. The most frequent outsider *zayran* are the *Habish*, or spirit parallels of Arabic-speaking Muslims, who exemplified political power.[41] The *Bashawat* spirits represented the Pashas, Turks, and other malevolent conquerors. The spirit "Lord Cromer" was more ambiguous, since villagers were sometimes allied with British forces.[42] The *Khawajat* were light-skinned spirits representing Europeans or Westerners, alternatively referred to as *nasarin* (i.e., "Nazarenes," Christians). They demanded "clean" Western foods associated with the power of the outside world: bottled beverages, expensive fruits, tinned goods, biscuits, and white bread. They had considerable wealth, yet another aspect of power. Especially notable among the colorful Western spirits was Dona Bey, an American doctor and big-game hunter who drank prodigious amounts of whisky and beer and carried an elephant gun. He clearly represented Western technological overkill, destroying what he hunted, and the hegemony of masculine science situated within a display of unprincipled lascivious action.[43]

The peoples discussed so far, with their older cults of possession, could deal with the impact of European colonialism by enlarging their inventories of alien spirits and adapting their already existing ceremonies of negotiation and exorcism.[44] For other, largely homogeneous peoples less acquainted with alien spirit possession, however, the invasion of European colonization happened far more suddenly and traumatically. Such peoples were more completely and exclusively possessed by spirits corresponding to Western influences. The Tonga along the Zambezi River were invaded by spirits with names such as *maregimenti* and *mapolis* (clearly representations of military regiments and the police) at the height of the invasion of the colonial state.[45] Interestingly, the healing antidotes were also derived from invasive influences. In women's possession dances in Tonga, spirit hosts washed themselves compulsively with scented soaps, and girls "drank soapy water in order to make the insides of their bodies clean and sweet-smelling."[46]

The sudden impact of European colonization and development was also felt by homogeneous peoples with centralized political authority, such as the Zulu. The rapid impact of mining operations under the control of overwhelming European power exacerbated the disintegration of traditional social forms. A bewildering array of new alien spirits suddenly attacked people, who would become possessed. Spirit hosts would rage uncontrollably, run back and forth in a daze, tear clothes off their bodies, or attempt to kill themselves. "There was no appeasing these raving hordes of spirits, let alone domesticating them as helpful spirits."[47] When the *izangoma*, the traditional healers and possessed mediums of the Zulu ancestors, exorcised the hordes of alien spirits, they also "inoculated" their subjects with "soldier" spirits (*amabutho*) to defend them against further attack.[48] When the "soldiers" spoke through their subjects, they used foreign languages, such as English, or railroad sounds, and the spirit hosts used symbols of alien origins, such as machine oil or white men's hair to express their new, protected identity.[49] The Zulus made alien powers their own in order to resist and ward off the greater alien powers that were destroying them.

While many of the more traditional possession cults that expanded their register of alien spirits to include those representing European colonial forces operated mainly among women and had little direct political influence, men began organizing possession dances, evidently in response to the escalating European colonial invasion. Among the most significant was the hybrid

beni ngoma ("band-dance") that began in the 1890s and spread and contin-
ued through the 1920s. These dances placed great emphasis on colonial attire.
Possessed participants in the *hauka* cult that spread in West Africa in the 1920s
imitated not only Islamic authority figures from the Near East and French and
British colonial officers but also the flag, uniforms, and drill formations of the
British army.[50]

More potentially political in their implications and effects were the charismatic possession cults led by prophets who countered the divisive effects of
the colonial impact early in the past century. These cults formed a wider community of peoples against the effects of colonial invasion and repression, moving from a local focus and diverging interests to the more general interests in
opposition to the colonizing forces. New in these charismatic movements led
by prophets was their claim to exclusive and unlimited authority, which they
appropriated from the corresponding claim by the colonizing power and/or
Christian mission. The African prophetic movements demanded selfless devotion to a broader cause and unity. It is not merely circumstantial that many of
these prophetic movements were the precursors to and prepared the way for
more politically oriented anticolonial movements.

This survey of various African peoples suggests that illness and particularly spirit possession have everything to do with invasion of alien forces,
particularly colonial conquest and domination. Possession by and exorcism of
spirits is important in the ways subordinated peoples deal with the invasive
effects that outside forces far beyond their own comprehension, let alone control, have on their lives. As illustrated in the cases just sketched, one of the
principal ways that African peoples dealt with invasion and influences from
the outside was to incorporate the invasive spirits of the invasive powers
into their own culture, which they dealt with in possession cults and, sometimes, exorcism cults and dances in which the invasive spirits were identified
and driven out so that the hosts were (at least temporarily) relieved. In many
cases it is evident that these were ways that peoples could resist the invasive
influences as they attempted to maintain their threatened traditional way
of life. And in some cases the possession cults developed into wider movements of renewal of the indigenous society and resistance to colonial rule.

The Judean-Galilean Cultural Response
to the Impact of Imperial Rule

The impact of colonial domination on African peoples suggests the importance of taking into account the impact of Hellenistic and Roman imperial

rule on the people among whom Jesus worked. The military invasions of Judea by Hellenistic imperial armies and particularly the repeated conquest and reconquest of Galilee and Judea by the Romans not only devastated the countryside but left collective trauma in their wake (as discussed in chapter 3). Compounding the impact of imperial violence, the drain of economic resources from villagers by the demands for tribute, taxes, and tithes by multiple layers of rulers led to irrecoverable indebtedness, loss of land, and the resulting disintegration of families and village communities. The impact of Roman imperial violence was probably most severe on the villagers whose family members and neighbors were killed or enslaved and whose houses were destroyed or who became impoverished. But imperial rule also affected scribal circles who were dedicated to the cultivation of Israelite-Judean tradition and the high priestly rulers whose position was dependent on continuing Roman approval and appointment. It is difficult to discern an aspect of life that Roman rule did not affect.

As discussed earlier, recent studies by critical medical anthropologists suggests that the effects of imperial rule may well have been a factor in the illnesses experienced by Galileans and Judeans. These illnesses, however, would have been culturally defined, suggesting that to understand them we would need knowledge of Galilean-Judean (Israelite) culture as it responded to the impact of imperial rule. Insofar as interpreters of Jesus have not posed questions about illness and healing (including spirit possession and exorcism) in terms of cultural definition, we have not previously carried out the necessary analysis of Galilean-Judean culture at the time, let alone explored how it might illuminate Jesus's healings and exorcisms. It is impossible to mount an extensive investigation in this chapter. But we can recognize at least a few of the more easily discernible aspects of Israelite culture in Galilee and Judea that seem pertinent, taking into account the inevitable differences between scribal culture (for which we have written sources) and popular culture (for which we have limited sources, mainly the Gospels).

The cultural ideal, as is evident in many Judean texts, including the books that later became biblical, was that the people should be independent of foreign rule, living directly under the rule of God, who had liberated them from bondage under Pharaoh in Egypt and given them the Mosaic covenant as a guide for their independent political-economic-religious life. Israelite peoples, however, had been subject to one empire after another for centuries and longed for the time in the future when the debilitating effects of oppressive rule would be overcome and the people would be made personally and collectively whole (for example, Isa 35:5–20; 40:1–11; 61:1–4; 65:17–25). Not surprisingly they remembered the stories of Moses, the original prophet of liberation, through whom God had wrought acts of power for the people, and stories of Elijah, whose program of renewal of Israel had included healings and multiplication of food for a suffering people (Deut 18:15–18; Sir 48:1–11).

Galilean and Judean culture also had explanations for their personal and collective malaise, the debilitating effects of their situation. Perhaps the most prominent was that illness and misfortune were divine punishment for not having kept the covenantal commandments—the result of "sins" committed by either themselves or their ancestors This was rooted in the motivating sanctions of the Mosaic covenant, in which the people called down curses on themselves and their children if they failed to keep the provisions of the covenant. We can see how this sense of sin, this tendency to blame themselves for the effects of their subjection, may have become intensified under Roman imperial rule in the scribal Psalms of Solomon (see psalms 3, 9, 10). This same sense of self-blame—the belief that their poverty and their debilitating illnesses were related to their own or their parents' sinning—is clearly a major issue in Jesus's covenantal renewal speech in Q/Luke 6:20–49 (discussed in chapter 5) as well as in his healings, as discussed later in this chapter.

Under the impact of foreign imperial rule, Israelite culture creatively developed other ways of explaining and adjusting to the new forces affecting people's lives. It has been standard in the fields of (early) Jewish history and New Testament to contrast the "apocalypticism" of later second-temple times with the "biblical" worldview of the books of torah and prophetic books that were later included in the Hebrew Bible. The standard scholarly construction of "apocalypticism" focuses on its supposed dualism and determinism, its alienation from history and its expectation of "the end of the world" in "cosmic catastrophe." I have argued recently that such characterizations of "apocalypticism" are not readily evident in the texts that are usually classified as "apocalyptic."[51] What is evident in certain "apocalyptic" texts and in key texts from the Qumran community found among the Dead Sea Scrolls is a dramatic shift from prophetic books in the understanding of the divine governance of the world.

In earlier Israelite tradition divine beings do not play prominent roles in the governance of the world. Coinciding with the takeover of the area by the Western empires, the Seleucids and particularly the Romans, however, Judean literature portrays a wide array of both benign and malign heavenly forces or spirits. Like the African peoples, Judeans and Galileans incorporated alien spirits or powers into their cultural representations. The scribal circles that produced "apocalyptic" texts did this in a way that differs dramatically from the way it was done in the temple headed by the high priestly aristocracy. For the Judean and Galilean peasantry among which Jesus worked, largely villagers who were nonliterate, however, we lack sources except for the Gospels, whose representations can be compared with the somewhat parallel representations in Judean scribal texts.

The members of the priestly aristocracy, who owed their position of power and privilege to their imperial overlords, honored imperial power in their temple and in their sacrifices. As has been recognized more clearly in recent decades, the rebuilt temple in Jerusalem and its restored priesthood were established by the Persians as an instrument of imperial rule.[52] As explicitly stated in Ezra 1, the "god who is in Jerusalem" was one of the gods of the empire and was represented with appropriate imperial symbolism while simultaneously being presented as the "God of Israel." The Romans, like the Ptolemies and Seleucids before them, simply perpetuated the arrangement (discussed in chapter 2). The high priesthood collected and transmitted the imperial tribute and conducted sacrifices for the emperor and the imperial regime. When Herod rebuilt the temple in grand Hellenistic-Roman style, he installed a golden Roman eagle over the gate of the temple and constructed other Roman political-religious institutions in Jerusalem.

By contrast, scribal circles, while appropriating imperial schemes into their representation of the ultimate sovereignty of the God of Israel, portrayed Hellenistic and Roman imperial power as hostile and destructive of the traditional common life. Since they served as retainers to the priestly aristocracy, they represented the interests of their patrons to a considerable extent. Yet, as those responsible for cultivation of Israelite cultural tradition, they also developed a sense of their own authority, not derivative from the priesthood but directly under the God of Israel.[53] In the early centuries of the second-temple period they continued to develop the books of the Pentateuch and the historical and other "prophetic" books. These texts included earlier traditions such as the Mosaic covenant in which God (YHWH) is the transcendent and exclusive king of Israel. Not only service to "other gods" but appropriation of alien influences is forbidden. The primary representation of God as their exclusive ruler or king, which supposedly excluded their submission to foreign human kings, was seen in terms of the ancient Near Eastern kingship that their God forbade them to have. They represented God as an ancient Near Eastern king in the heavens, who fights for his people with heavenly armies (YHWH Sebbaoth). He ruled his people and the historical process from a heavenly imperial court, attended by a host of "sons of God" (*bene-elohim*; 1 Kgs 22:19–23; Isa 40:1–6). Yet YHWH himself held exclusive power and authority over Israel. In most texts later included in the Bible, moreover, YHWH wielded kingly power in a fairly direct way in the events of Israel's struggles to maintain its independence from foreign rule.

In "apocalyptic" texts of later second-temple times under the Hellenistic empires, however, representation of God and of foreign powers changed significantly. In "apocalyptic" texts generally, "the Most High" is represented as the great emperor of the world, seated in his remote heavenly court and governing through a host of heavenly forces (spirits) to which he has delegated certain responsibilities or jurisdictions (see especially Dan 7:1–13 and the Book of Watchers, 1 Enoch 1–36). In the Enoch literature and some of the principal Dead Sea Scrolls from the Qumran community in particular we can see the effects of the invasion of imperial forces in the increased prominence of heavenly spiritual forces. The effects of and the attempt to come to grips with the invasive wars between the Ptolemaic and the Seleucid empires that raged through Palestine appear fairly clearly in "The Book of the Watchers," particularly in the rebellion of the Watchers (1 Enoch 6–11).[54] The Watchers, sons of heaven, attracted by the beautiful daughters of men, descended to earth and conceived from them great giants, who imposed imperial warfare and expropriated peoples' goods on the plane of earthly life. The imagery is readily transparent as representing the typical practices of the Hellenistic imperial regimes.

> They were devouring the labor of all the sons of men, and men were not able to supply them. And the giants conspired to kill men and to devour them . . . Asael taught men to make swords of iron and weapons and shields and breastplates and every instrument of war . . . He showed them metals of the earth and how they should work gold to fashion it suitably, and concerning silver, to fashion it for bracelets and ornaments for women. (1 Enoch 7:3; 8:1–2; Nickelsburg trans.)

In a desperate attempt to restore order to the governance of the world, however, the Most High delegated other heavenly forces, the highest ranking, to check and punish the renegade forces. The "sons of God" in the prophetic books were a vague set of spirits in YHWH's heavenly court. In the Book of Watchers the heavenly powers have specific personalities and roles in the divine governance, some directly associated with imperial warfare, exploitation, and courtly culture, and they generate a host of additional shadowy spirits or demons that haunt historical affairs.

The most elaborate Judean scribal-priestly attempt to come to grips with the impact of imperial conquest and domination of Israel/Judea was the grand scheme of opposed spirits in the Qumran Community Rule and the War Scroll found among the Dead Sea Scrolls in 1947. In attempting to explain how the God of Israel could still be ultimately in control of history, while at present foreign empires dominated their lives, the Qumranites articulated a world-historical struggle between two controlling spirits:

> All the children of righteousness are ruled by the Prince of Light and walk in the ways of light, but all the children of injustice are ruled by the Angel of Darkness and walk in the ways of darkness. The Angel of Darkness leads all the children of righteousness astray, . . . for all his allotted spirits seek the overthrow of the sons of light. But the God of Israel and His Angel of Truth will succour all the sons of light" (1QS 3:18–24; 4:18–19; Vermes trans.).

In contrast to the more diffuse spirits of African peoples under the impact of foreigners, the scribes and priests at Qumran articulated a generalized abstract scheme of quasi-divine spirits to symbolize and explain their historical situation. The scheme of the two spirits explains and symbolizes both how historical developments and the experience of these Judeans had become so utterly "out of control" of God and their belief that ultimately God remained in control and would (imminently) assert control over the destructive and seductive forces of Belial/the Angel of Darkness. This grand scheme went together with and framed the experience of the scribal-priestly group that produced it. While they were (potentially) attacked and tempted by the Spirit of Darkness, they lived under the guidance and protection of the Spirit of Truth. Since they were already "possessed," as it were, by the Spirit of Truth, they were not individually possessed, hence had no need to practice exorcism. Moreover, they anticipated that the God of Israel would soon act to resolve the extreme crisis of historical life by terminating the rule and power of the Angel of Darkness.

The War Scroll found at Qumran (1QM) makes a direct connection between the hostile heavenly spirits and the Romans, for whom the code name is "Kittim," who have conquered them. In fact, most of the text consists of an elaborate scenario in which the final battle between the company of Belial, along with the Kittim, and the sons of light aided by the heavenly forces that fight for them will be conducted. In anticipation of the final battle, members of the Qumran community evidently engaged in elaborate rituals drills, ostensibly in imitation of Israelite holy-war tradition but clearly also influenced by the drills of the Roman legions.

These expressions of ancient Judean scribal circles differ in significant ways from the possession cults of African peoples in their attempts to come to grips with the impact of outside imperial forces on the indigenous societal life. The African peoples negotiated a combination of adjustment and resistance to the impact of and domination by outside colonial powers. By contrast, these Judean scribal circles, while representing their God in increasingly imperial imagery, rejected imperial cultural and political domination as unacceptable and as impossible to reconcile with their traditional value of independence under the exclusive rule of their God.

In ways unprecedented in their own cultural tradition, they came to believe that imperial rule and imperial rulers were operating as the historical political instruments of transcendent demonic powers directly opposed to God's will for their people. In their attempt to affirm that their God was truly transcendent and ultimately in control of history, they imagined the demonic power(s) as ultimately created by God and ultimately to be defeated by God. But demonic power(s) were currently on a rampage in the historical process, out of the effective control of a remote imperial God. Their own situation, living under debilitating invasive power(s) and yet faithful to a God they believed ultimately in control, had to be understood as a struggle between two superhuman spiritual forces.

It is interesting to compare the Qumran people in particular with the way two particular groups of African people dealt with the impact of foreign invasion. The Qumranites' collective possession by the Spirit of Truth was a comprehensive means of protection parallel to the individual protective "soldiers" with which the *izangoma* inoculated possessed Zulus. And the Qumranites drills of ritual warfare against the Romans resemble the West Africa Hauka cult's parades in the uniforms and drill formations of the British army.

For Galilean and Judean culture at the popular level we have few sources other than stories and speeches in the Gospels, which derive mainly from popular culture in Galilee. Because there are significant differences between what anthropologists have called "the great tradition" and "the little tradition," we cannot use books produced by scribal circles, whether in Jerusalem or Qumran, as direct sources for villagers, particularly for Galileans, who were brought under Jerusalem rule only about a hundred years before the lifetime of Jesus. Yet sources produced by the literate elite, such as Josephus, do provide some evidence for popular beliefs and particularly actions, such as "prophetic" and "messianic" movements rooted in social memory of Moses and Joshua or of the young David and Galilean protests of violations of covenantal commandments.[55] On the basis of such sources we can confidently posit the operation of Israelite popular tradition in the lives of Galilean and Judean villagers and can justify a critical extrapolation from scribal sources to cultural traditions that may have figured in a popular movements such as the one spearheaded by Jesus of Nazareth. For more direct access to popular culture we depend on the Gospels, which are also our sources for Jesus and his followers, in this case the accounts of Jesus's healings and exorcisms.

Jesus's Exorcism and Healing as Represented in the Gospel of Mark

The Gospel sources that provide access to the historical Jesus are extended narratives and/or series of speeches, not mere containers of sayings and "miracle stories," as discussed in chapter 1. The starting point for understanding Jesus's exorcism and healing, therefore, cannot be particular elements of individual "miracle stories" that might "go back to Jesus" just as we cannot use these sources to establish the "authenticity" of particular separate sayings of Jesus. What our Gospel sources offer are thus overall stories, with many speeches, that portray several related aspects of Jesus's mission. We can access Jesus's healing and exorcism only through the healing and exorcism "stories" as integral components of the larger Gospel narratives and their component speeches. To keep this provisional investigation manageable, we will focus mainly on the representation of Jesus's exorcism and healing in the Gospel of Mark, with some attention to that in a few Q speeches.

In Mark's story the overall plot focuses on Jesus spearheading a renewal of the people in opposition to and by the rulers and ruling institution in Jerusalem, as discussed in chapter 2. Particularly striking in the Gospel of Mark is that the first two narrative steps of the story (1:16–3:35; 4:35–8:26) are composed overwhelmingly of episodes of exorcisms and healings. The third narrative step is framed by two healings and features an exorcism (8:22–26; 9:14–29; 10:46–52). In fact, the renewal of Israel that is happening in Jesus's mission and that is opposed by the rulers and their representatives is, in effect, manifested largely in the healings and exorcisms. The "chains" of stories of sea crossings, exorcisms, healings, and wilderness feedings that some scholars discern behind the Gospel's second narrative step (4:35–8:26) also represent Jesus as a new Moses-and-Elijah leading a renewal of Israel.

The illnesses that appear in the Gospels, particularly those in Mark, were understood as interrelated, insofar as exorcisms and healings appear as episodes (or in summaries) in complete stories with overall plots and agenda (or in a series of speeches). In fact, some of the illnesses/healings and spirit possessions/exorcisms appeared in relation to others in the parallel chains of episodes, that is, in a coherent narrative pattern and meaning-context that predate Mark's Gospel. That exorcisms precede healing stories in those pre-Markan chains suggests that it is significant as a narrative pattern when exorcisms precede healings in the narrative steps of Mark's Gospel both prior to and following the step where Mark reproduces the two chains. That the expulsions of the demons, as it were, happened prior to the healings of illnesses set them up, prepared the way, made them possible.

The Illnesses and Spirit Possession and Their Diagnosis

The illnesses in the narrative chains are astounding when considered in the context of agrarian village life. In Mark's first narrative step (1:16–3:35), following the exorcism of "a man with an unclean spirit" in a village assembly, appear Peter's mother, suffering a fever; a socially ostracized "leper"; a man who is paralyzed; and a man with a withered hand. Mark's second narrative step (4:35–8:26) has the two sequences of acts of power.[56] After the alien spirit that, possessing a man, makes him so violent against himself and others that he cannot be restrained even with chains in the cemetery, come the woman who has been hemorrhaging for twelve years (and who in her desperation for relief has exhausted all of her resources) and a young woman, daughter of the leader of the local village assembly, who has come to "the point of death" just as she reaches puberty (the threshold of becoming a productive and reproductive member of her people). Then, following the Syrophoenician woman's daughter, who is described simply as possessed by a demon, come a man who is both deaf and has a speech impediment and a man who is blind. The one cannot communicate in his social interaction, since both his hearing and his speech have become closed down (rather than being "opened up"). The blind man, of course, would have been completely dysfunctional in a village community with an agrarian economy. Finally, in the third narrative step (8:22–10:52), following the exorcism of an alien spirit that, possessing a man, "makes him unable to speak and, whenever it seizes him, dashes him down, and he foams and grinds his teeth and becomes rigid," comes another blind man, Bar-Timaeus, who has become a beggar.

The illnesses in the two chains of episodes and in the rest of Mark's story clearly cannot be reduced to diseases in the modern Western medical sense that doctors could cure. All of the cases of spirit possession and illness in Mark's story are presented and understood in the context of family and village life. All of them are fundamentally debilitating in the social-economic as well as the personal sense. The sicknesses that appear in the earliest Gospel texts all consist of some kind of serious disabling of the basic personal functions necessary for productive social life in an agrarian society. That the blind Bar-Timaeus had become a beggar beside the road, for example, gives a clear indication of how blindness left people utterly incapable of productive activity and normal participation in family and community. Blindness, deafness, paralyzed legs, withered hands, and demon possession are all long-term disablings of the most fundamental functions of personal and social life, without which a person cannot function in social-economic life and without which a society cannot long survive. Indeed, the illnesses in the two chains that may provide the earliest attestation of the illnesses dealt with by Jesus point to just such social disintegration. A society in which the constituent villagers were unable to communicate with each other, blind, with their life blood draining away, close to death, and (in the case of those possessed by a spirit) so violent that they must be physically restrained and banished from ordinary social interaction, would have simply disintegrated, falling apart, indeed "dying" as a viable society.

The speech of Jesus in Q/Luke 7:18–28, 31–35 offers a list of the illnesses he has been healing that is not only parallel to that in the episodes of Mark's Gospel but suggestive of the circumstances of the social disintegration of which they are symptoms. In response to John's disciples' question whether he is "the one who is to come," Jesus points to what is happening in his mission: "the blind recover their sight, the lame walk, lepers are cleansed, and the deaf hear, the dead are raised up, the poor are given good news" (Q/Luke 7:18–19, 22). His response is usually understood as pointing to a fulfillment of prophecy in the book of Isaiah. It is not, however, a fulfillment of the particular prophecy in Isa 35:5–6 or the one in Isa 42:6–7 or the one in Isa 61:1. The similar but somewhat different lists of illnesses and other forms of malaise (prisoners, captives, poor) to be overcome in those passages from sections of Isaiah that originated in or refer to Judean society after the Babylonian conquest suggest illnesses typical of an imperially conquered society. In his list of illnesses that are being healed, Jesus must be referencing a widespread expression of longing for deliverance that were also referenced centuries before in those passages in the book of Isaiah.[57]

In their concern not to reduce other peoples' experience of sickness and possession to the terms of Western biomedicine and psychology, medical anthropologists and ethnographers emphasize the importance of culture in illness and healing, as noted earlier. They insist on taking seriously whatever indications indigenous peoples give of what they are experiencing in illness. And they discover that the key to healing illness is the diagnosis of illness, such as a discernment of its cause or etiology. While the healing episodes in Gospel texts provide little by way of diagnosis, it does appear in a few cases. The etiology or "diagnosis" of the cause of the man's paralysis—that he had sinned—is deeply rooted in Israelite covenantal tradition, but it becomes clear that it is the scribal representatives of the temple-state who were pressing that diagnosis. Jesus's forgiveness of sins offers a clear alternative, and suggests a more general overcoming of this debilitating cause of illness. The portrayal of Jesus's dealings with the "leper" suggests popular resentment of or conflict with the temple, which claimed jurisdiction (and an offering) for "cleansing" blemished areas of the body.

The exorcism episodes, of course, have a built-in diagnosis, that of possession by an alien "unclean spirit" or "demon." Besides this built-in diagnosis, moreover, these episodes indicate a serious attack by and struggle against alien outside forces. In addition to the violent struggle that usually ensues when Jesus confronts an unclean spirit, Jesus's first exorcism in Mark's story is portrayed as a battle in which Jesus is defeating the enemies of the people somewhat as God has defeated Israel's foreign conquerors. In the context of Mark's whole story this suggests that rule by hostile foreign forces is a factor in the sicknesses of the people. In the Markan Beelzebul discourse (with its parallel in Q), the scribal authorities from Jerusalem accuse Jesus of working in the power of Beelzebul, the Prince of Demons.

This is significant for *our* "diagnosis" of the diagnosis of illness in Mark: possession and exorcism are understood in terms of a struggle between powers, the basic opposition being between the power(s) of the demons and their Prince, Satan, and the power of God effecting "acts of power" through Jesus. It is all the more significant, then, that in the next exorcism episode, the demon identifies itself as "Legion," which was the term for a division of the Roman army. The cause of the man's uncontrollable violence turns out to be "invasion/possession" by the outside force of "Roman troops." The narrative sequence, moreover, in which this episode immediately precedes the healing stories in the first five-episode chain, would have suggested that Legion was also a factor in the woman's bleeding and in the case of the young woman who was virtually dead. In the broader context of Mark's story, when Jesus is condemned and executed by Pontius Pilate, the factor of Roman rule and control of the people and country is simply assumed as the brute reality of political power relations in Judea and Galilee.

This analysis of the kinds of sickness represented in the chains of episodes behind Mark and in Mark's story as a whole, combined with the built-in diagnosis of demon possession, suggests a hypothesis about illness as portrayed in the earliest Gospel texts. Judging from the kinds of illnesses represented, Galilean society was undergoing a disintegration, with people plagued by debilitating dysfunctions of blindness, inability to communicate, paralysis, and loss of lifeblood. The people were also experiencing attack and possession by alien outside spirit forces understood as enemies of the people who had to be overcome (Mark 1:22–28), with the identity of one turning out to be "Legion," that is, Roman troops (5:1–20).

The Effect and Significance of Jesus's Exorcisms and Healings

The preceding considerations have, I hope, prepared the way appropriately for a consideration of Jesus's exorcism and healing in their cultural context. It is possible here to deal only briefly with a few representative episodes. In the context of Mark's overall narrative healings and exorcisms are the principal manifestations of the renewal of Israel under the direct kingship of God. Since exorcisms take priority in the narrative and seem to prepare the way for the healings, I will focus first on a few key exorcisms.[58]

The first action Jesus takes after his general announcement that the kingdom of God is at hand and his calling of four disciples is an exorcism in the midst of the village assembly in Capernaum (Mark 1:22–28). This is not a gathering set up purposely for the explicit purpose of exorcism, as in the *zar* cult in northern Sudan. We have no evidence for whether the ancient Galileans and nearby peoples would have had a standard procedure or special "cult" for exorcising spirits, although there were evidently other exorcists about. The episode is similar to experiences in the *zar* cult where the presence of the exorcist is what brings the spirit to the fore. In this episode the presence of Jesus in the midst of the village gathering seems to have provoked the "unclean spirit" to burst forward and cry out, "What have you to do with us, Jesus of Nazareth? Have you come to destroy us? I know who you are, the holy one of God." The spirit recognizes Jesus as an adversary with divine power to destroy him and his compatriots.

A decisive battle has been engaged. Indeed, the language used in this episode is not the usual language of exorcism ("cast out," *ekballein* in Greek). The key term *epitiman*, distinctive among Mark's exorcism episodes and not used in Hellenistic exorcism stories, is rather the Greek equivalent of the Hebrew term *gaʾar* used in Israelite tradition (in the Psalms, Zechariah, and the Dead Sea

Scrolls).[59] Something far stronger than a verbal "rebuke" (NRSV) is involved, something more like "vanquish" or "destroy." In the Psalms, Israelite peoples appealed to God as a divine warrior coming in judgment to "destroy," "root out," or "vanquish" foreign nations or imperial regimes that conquer and take spoil from Israel (Pss 9:6; 68:31; 78:6; 80:16). The term is even used with reference to Satan in a late prophetic text: "The LORD subject you [*ga'ar/epitiman*] O Satan!" (Zech 3:2). In Dead Sea Scroll literature from Qumran, *ga'ar* is used for Abram's or God's subjection of evil spirits (1QapGen) and more ominously with reference to the struggle between God and Belial (= Prince of Darkness, Satan). Perhaps most telling is a passage in the War Scroll (14:9–11, supplemented from 4Q491): "During all the mysteries of his [Belial's] malevolence he has not made us stray from Thy covenant. Thou has driven [*ga'ar*] his spirits [of destruction] far from [us]. Thou hast preserved the soul of Thy redeemed [when the men] of his dominion [acted wickedly]."[60]

Judging from this use of language, therefore, we must conclude that in this Markan episode Jesus is speaking and acting as the agent of God in bringing the destructive demonic forces into submission as the kingdom of God is established and God's people delivered and renewed. This episode gives no attention to thaumaturgical techniques but has Jesus utter the simple command, "Be silent. Come out of him!" The emphasis then falls on the violence of the struggle engaged for control of the possessed person ("convulsing him and crying out with a loud voice, came out of him"). The gist of the episode is that in the first action taken by Jesus in his mission of renewal of Israel, he confronts and defeats the invasive forces that were possessing the people in destructive ways. In Jesus's mission the power/authority (*exousia*) of God is bringing those spirits under subjection, liberating the people in local communities from their debilitating effects.

In the Beelzebul discourse (Mark 3:22–27, with a parallel but somewhat different version in Q/Luke 11:14–22), Jesus offers a programmatic statement of what is happening in his exorcisms. Accused—by the scribes come down from Jerusalem, in Mark—of casting out demons by the Beelzebul, Prince of Demons/Satan, he replies that in his exorcisms the rule of Satan over people is coming to an end as the kingdom of God is being established.[61] Both the charge by the scribal challengers and Jesus's response assume that life's circumstances involve a struggle between God and demonic forces headed by Satan. In the parables of his logical argument for why the opposite of the charge is true, he uses what were already standard political terms for rulers in Israelite culture. "Kingdom," of course, is the same term as is used in "the kingdom of God," and its synonym "house" was a long-standing metaphor for the ruling family or dynasty (as in God's promise to the Davidic "house"/dynasty in 2 Sam 7). It would be absurd to think that Satan would be divided against himself and his "house/rule" thus fall on its own. Therefore, since there are only the two forces, divine and demonic, struggling in the world, Jesus must be battling the demons with the power of God. Since the demons are clearly being cast out, the house/ rule of God is obviously defeating the rule of Satan.

As in the Community Rule and the War Scroll from Qumran, quoted above, Jesus's (and the scribes') argument assumes that what is happening to people's lives is interrelated with, even determined by, the struggle happening at a transcendent level between the spirits, the divine versus the demonic, God versus Satan. What is happening to people, particularly the bizarre behavior of people possessed, is determined, hence explained by the interference of demonic powers. The Qumranites who produced and used the Community Rule and the War Scroll understood not only personal behavior but also contemporary political affairs to be determined by and hence explained by the struggle between transcendent spiritual forces, divine versus demonic. The Roman imperial forces and the incumbent high priesthood were ultimately under the power of the Prince of Darkness/ Belial. Ultimately—and imminently—God would intervene in the historical conflict and subdue the forces of darkness so that the people could finally be free to live directly under the sole rule of God, without attack and interference by the Roman imperial forces.

It is difficult to tell from the Beelzebul discourse in Mark by itself whether the "binding of the Strong Man" and Jesus's "plundering of his property/goods" had implications for Roman rule of the people or just for demon possession. That Jesus's exorcisms are done "by the finger of God," an allusion to Moses's actions in the exodus story, constituted a new exodus from foreign rule in the Q version suggests that indeed Jesus's exorcisms as manifestations of the kingdom of God imply the end of Roman rule. In Mark's story, however, we must wait until the next exorcism episode to recognize this more clearly.

In the exorcism in one of the villages of Gadara/Gerasa (good illustration of different wording in different early manuscripts; Mark 5:1–20), after the demon is expelled from the possessed fellow, it is possible to establish its identity. Its name is "Legion." This is no mere "Latin loan word" meaning "many." The hearers of the Gospel would have recognized the identity of the demon immediately as "Roman Legion," that is, a "battalion" of Roman troops who wrought extreme violence against subjected peoples such as themselves. Other language in the episode also indicates that a military "battalion" is involved, as the "company" "charges" down the slope into the sea (suggesting the Mediterranean Sea, not the Galilean lake). And in that "charge" down the bank "Legion" also self-destructs. The "Roman army" implodes, as it were. Not only do the demons represent the occupying Roman imperial forces in Mark's story, but the implication is that as the kingdom of God is manifested in actions such as Jesus's exorcisms, the days of Roman rule are numbered.[62]

At the end of the episode, finally, the other people in the village, far from exclaiming over what has happened, cannot get Jesus out of their area quickly enough. Why? Apparently they cannot face what has just been revealed. Yet Jesus's followers and the hearers of the Gospel are not particularly worried. The complexity of this episode forces to us to recognize that belief in demons (possession) can be both revelatory and mystifying—and that Jesus's exorcisms may have moved beyond the standard cultural construction of demon possession and exorcism in popular circles in Galilee and nearby areas. The belief that their misfortunes and malaise were caused by demons and not by the Romans or their own sins enabled the people not to blame themselves and not to blame their God. Yet the focus on demons was mystifying insofar as it diverted attention from Roman conquest and imperial rule as the cause of their malaise. That had a self-preservative effect because it kept them from engaging in what would have been suicidal action against their conquerors in their passion for liberty, which was deeply rooted in Israelite cultural tradition. That, combined with the confidence that their God was ultimately in control and would resolve the struggle with demonic forces at some point in the future, enabled them to continue their traditional way of life, however handicapped by demon possession and the imperial domination that demon beliefs obscured.

In the Legion episode, however, Jesus offered a "diagnosis" of the diagnosis of misfortunes as due to demon possession. The force that was bringing such violence upon the people, once the demon could be identified, was Legion, that is, Roman imperial military forces. That revelation, however, disrupted the accommodation that the subjected people had reached with those forces in the imperial situation. It was threatening to recognize that the forces causing their malaise were the Romans. It created a dilemma for the Gadarenes/Gerasenes that they had long avoided as some people hosted the invasive alien spirits: should they simply acquiesce in Roman rule, against their cultural tradition? Or should they resist, even fight? Jesus's mission and the followers offered a third alternative, or perhaps a form of resistance that would not become suicidal (as explored further in the next chapter as well as chapter 2).

By overcoming the superhuman forces that plague the people's personal and community life, the exorcisms prepare the way for other manifestations of the coming of God's kingdom in the healings. We can focus on two in particular that involve social and political dimensions in fundamental ways.

The healing of the paralytic (Mark 2:1–12) involves far more than the healing of the paralysis. Not only is the political-economic context built into the episode, but so are the assumptions and traditional terms in which paralysis is culturally constructed. The "performative speech" of Jesus both indicates that he understands the standard diagnosis of this illness and cuts through that with a diagnosis of the social-psychological and political-economic effects of that standard diagnosis.

The people who come bearing the paralytic constitute some of the social resources already available for healing, a social network of support. The opening of the episode indicates, moreover, that they are already responding to the excitement generated by reports of Jesus's previous exorcisms and healings. In the extreme measures they take to lower the paralytic into the presence of Jesus, they are acting in the hope, even confidence, that healing power is active in and through him. Instead of simply declaring the paralytic healed, however, while presupposing and agreeing with the standard diagnosis, Jesus cuts through it and offers the possibility for the people to take action themselves in transforming the social-political context: "your sins are forgiven."

According to the standard Israelite cultural understanding, illnesses and other misfortunes were the result of, indeed even divine punishment for, either people's sins or those of their parents. In the Mosaic covenantal structure, the people were told to expect curses as God's punishment if they did not keep the basic commandments and laws of the covenant given by God. In the self-governing local communities of a simple agrarian society the "blessings and curses" may well have been an effective sanction that supported the keeping of the covenant principles. Israelite prophets, moreover, appealed to this component in the structure of the Mosaic covenant in their condemnation of Israelite rulers' oppression and exploitation of the peasantry. As an interpretation of misfortune, suffering, and subjugation by foreign empires, however, sinning became problematic. Jeremiah saw its debilitating effects on the people's motivation to persist in covenantal life in the aftermath of the Babylonian destruction of the monarchy and the temple in Jerusalem: "The parents have eaten sour grapes, and the children's teeth are set on edge." Accordingly, he declared that God would write the covenant on the people's hearts so that they would keep it spontaneously and would "forgive their iniquity and remember their sin no more" (Jer 31:29, 34).

The Deuteronomistic interpretation of suffering and misfortune as due to people's or their parents' sin was perpetuated, however. Its domesticating effect on the populace was useful for social control. Accordingly, scribal circles not only interpreted the people's subjection by the Romans as due to their rulers' sins (Psalms of Solomon 17) but insisted that since suffering and misfortune were due to sin, it was all the more necessary to bring offerings to the temple (whose revenues of course supported not only the priestly aristocracy but their own work as scribal retainers of the aristocracy; Sir 38:9–11).

Accordingly, in this healing episode in Mark 2:1–12, the scribal representatives of the temple system stand by ready to charge Jesus with blasphemy: only God can forgive sins. In the episode's portrayal, of course, they ignore that Jesus's passive formulation "your sins are forgiven" refers to God as the agent of the forgiveness. He is declaring God's forgiveness to people who had been blaming themselves for their suffering, thus freeing them to resume a role in the cooperative, mutually supportive life of their communities. His declaration of forgiveness to the paralytic and the principle he annunciates, that "the human one," that is, people themselves, "ha[ve] authority on earth to forgive sins," moreover, bypass and replace the role of the temple and its sacrificial rites in mediating between the sinful people and their God—which is what the scribes are concerned about.

The case of the hemorrhaging woman (Mark 5:25–34) has been the parade example of the Christian stereotype of "Judaism" as obsessed with purity codes that stigmatized female impurity and enabled recent interpreters to heroize Jesus as having broken with such supposed oppression of women.[63] Recent Jewish interpreters have attempted to "set the record straight" by pointing out that the episode has nothing to do with impurity (supposedly of menstrual flow).[64]

It is striking that the narrative pattern in this episode differs from those in the other healing episodes. Typical in the three-step pattern is that the person looking for healing comes into Jesus's presence or makes a request, Jesus heals the person with a gesture or statement, and the healed is dismissed and/or the onlookers exclaim in astonishment. In this episode, by contrast, the description of the woman's illness is very elaborate: "twelve years, . . . many physicians, . . . spent all she had, . . . no better but worse! (5:25–27). Although others do take initiatives in other episodes, the hemorrhaging woman is the sole actor to take initiative in this episode. She takes and heeds her own counsel: "if I but touch his clothes, I shall be made well." She does not hesitate and does not act secretly but confidently takes bold, deliberate action.

Most striking is that her healing is attributed not to Jesus but to her own action! And it is her own experience that confirms the result: "she felt in her body that she was healed of her illness." In contrast with other episodes, in which Jesus makes some gesture or statement of healing, he is passive and unaware here, until at her touch he becomes aware that power has flowed through him. Then he simply confirms what she is already fully aware of, that it is her own trust that has made her whole. In the story, in her trust that healing power would flow through Jesus to herself she becomes a paradigm for all others so that they can now "take heart, refuse to despair, and act" for themselves and one another.[65] Her case demonstrates that, while mediated through Jesus, God's healing power is relational in its operation, that healing is produced not by Jesus's action alone but through people's trust that power will work through him and on them. The woman who had been hemorrhaging for "twelve" years and is healed through her own trust in God's healing power now available, moreover, is a figure representative of Israel generally, which can follow her example and trust that healing power is happening in Jesus and the Jesus movement.

The exorcisms and healings of Jesus are narrated in Mark's Gospel as the manifestations of the kingdom of God, that is, of the renewal of the people in opposition to their rulers. People are healed not as isolated individuals but as members of families and communities. The exorcisms and healings take place in the midst of public meetings, and the people healed are restored to their communities as integral and productive members. Not only does the first exorcism happen in a village assembly (synagogue), but the people know and exclaim that this action demonstrates how Jesus "teaches" with "authority/power" for the people, in contrast to the scribes, who represent the "authorities"/power holders. The healing of the paralytic, who is already embedded in a supportive network of family and friends, becomes the occasion for Jesus's declaration that the people themselves are authorized to "forgive sins on earth" on behalf of God and are not confined to or dependent on the sacrifices in the temple controlled by the Jerusalem priests represented by the scribes. The woman who had been hemorrhaging for twelve years and the twelve-year-old woman who is almost dead both represent Israel as a whole, healed by the power working through Jesus. The women and the people they represent are restored to life, including symbolically the reproductive potential represented by the young woman just restored to life as she becomes a mature woman capable of bearing children.

ŋ ŋ ŋ

In all of this analysis and discussion of the exorcism and healing episodes in Mark and Jesus's Beelzebul speech in Q, I am in no way suggesting that particular exorcisms or healings happened more or less in the way presented in the Gospel sources. Rather, I am suggesting that the Gospel representation of Jesus's exorcisms and healings gives important indications of features of the illnesses Jesus encountered, of the social and even political relations involved, and of the significance that the exorcisms and healing were understood to have among the people the movement(s) that formed.

The illnesses cannot be reduced to "diseases" that could have been "cured" by modern biomedicine but rather were illnesses typical (and symbolic) of peoples impacted by colonial/imperial invasion or conquest, the most striking of which is possession by alien spirits but which also include paralysis, blindness, hemorrhaging, and extreme weakness (being virtually dead). These were symptoms of a whole society undergoing disintegration—as in the title of Chinua Achebe's novel *Things Fall Apart*.

Contrary to the way that scholars have treated the "miracle stories" as Jesus's one-on-one encounters with a diseased person, Jesus's exorcisms and healings would have happened in a network of social relations and political pressures, as represented in the Gospels. People with illnesses already had support networks in which care had been taking place. Jesus was the effective agent or the channel of healing power, not the sole agent. The suffering persons and/or the friends and/or family of their support network took initiative. Healing and exorcism were able to happen because Jesus was playing the role of a prophet-healer with a reputation for having healing power *and* because people trusted both him and that power (had "faith"). On the other (political) side of the relational aspects of the exorcisms and healings were the effects of the rulers on the people, illustrated most vividly in the exorcism of "Legion" and the scribes charge of "blasphemy" against Jesus's declaration that the people have power to forgive sin. Jesus's declaration transformed self-blame into healing energy, in the context of the supportive network of family, friends, and village community.

Jesus's exorcism and healing cannot be separated from the other aspects and the general agenda of his mission. As portrayed in both Mark and the Q speeches, followed by Matthew and Luke and paralleled by John, this was evidently the renewal of the people in opposition to the rulers. No amount of close analysis of healing episodes will produce reliable historical tidbits of knowledge about particular healings, such as of the hemorrhaging woman or the twelve-year-old woman. But, as indicated in the symbolism of "twelve" (years) and the "hemorrhaging" and of the women just approaching puberty but nearly dead and their restoration to health/life, these episodes were shaped and told as indications of the renewal of the people of Israel that was happening in the healings. What is more, even prior to the composition-and-performance of the Gospel of Mark, the exorcism and healing episodes were included in "chains" of acts of power (*dynameis*) in which they were understood and retold, along with sea crossings and feedings in the wilderness, as indications of the renewal of Israel by Jesus as a Moses- and Elijah-like prophet. The "punchline" of Jesus's response to the charge that he was possessed by Beelzebul, moreover, alluding to Moses and the exodus—"since I am casting our demons 'by the finger of God', the kingdom of God has come upon you"—suggests the same: that the exorcisms were manifestations of the renewal of Israel. In terms of recent medical anthropological analysis, the illnesses, including spirit possession, that Jesus addressed were evidently symptoms of the impact of imperial domination, and his healings and exorcisms both presupposed supportive social networks and helped bring social as well as personal restoration and renewal.

In most episodes of healing and exorcism Jesus restores the sufferers to their supportive families and village communities, important aspects of the healing of illnesses, according to medical anthropologists. It is significant therefore that Jesus, as portrayed in the Gospel sources, also worked at the renewal of those disintegrating village communities themselves—the subject of the next chapter.

5. Renewal of Covenantal Community

In ancient history, the battle of Actium, off the western shore of the Greek peninsula in 31 BCE, became a watershed event. Octavian, representing the rational moderate political-cultural forces of the West, defeated Marc Antony, who represented the dark tyrannical forces of the East, according to the prevailing imperial propaganda. The Roman patricians and the elite of the cities of Greece and Asia Minor acclaimed Octavian, "the August One," as the "Savior" who had brought "Salvation" and "Peace and Security" to the whole world, which had been falling into chaos. It was a new world order in which Rome was now the sole superpower. Political and economic power were increasingly centralized under the control of the imperial and provincial rulers.[1]

This new world *order* for those of power and privilege in the Roman empire, however, was experienced as a devastating and debilitating new world *disorder* by the peoples subject to the empire. The economic base for the "Peace and Security" and "Salvation" (that is, prosperity) of the imperial and provincial rulers was the peasantry of the subject peoples. Whether the tribute that provided the "bread and circuses" for the Roman plebs, the rents that funded the temples and shrines to Caesar in the Greek cities, or the taxes that supported Herod's massive building projects in honor of Caesar, it was the produce of the peasants that supported the imperial order. The more that was siphoned off by the elite, however, the less was left to support the producers. The result was the disintegration of the fundamental social forms of family and village community. To better appreciate the mission of Jesus we focus in this chapter on the increasing disorder among Judeans and Galileans that resulted from the recently imposed Roman imperial order.

The New World Disorder

A review of the shifting Roman arrangements for the control and extraction of revenues from Judea and Galilee may clarify the interrelated ways in which the new world order meant disorder and disintegration for Galilean and Judean villagers.

First, as discussed more fully in chapter 3, Roman conquest and especially reconquests brought devastation to villages, death or enslavement to many of their inhabitants, and continuing collective trauma to the survivors. While other local areas also suffered severely in the several decades leading up to and including the time of the birth of Jesus, the military violence in the areas of Sepphoris-Nazareth in 4 BCE and at Magdala nearly fifty years earlier indicate that the areas of Jesus's life and mission in Galilee had been directly impacted (*War* 2.68–75; *Ant.* 17.291–295).

Second, as discussed in chapter 2, the Romans required the conquered people to pay tribute. After the initial conquest, the Romans set the rate for all of the people subject to the Jerusalem high priesthood at one-fourth of the harvest every second year (except for the sabbatical year; *Ant.* 14.202–203). The rate was presumably similar in later decades. Under the Roman governors the high priestly aristocracy was responsible for the collection of the tribute. Josephus's account of the peasant strike in Galilee (discussed in chapter 2) and his reference to grain silos in northern Galilee (*Life* 71–73) indicate that tribute continued to be taken in Galilee.

Third, the people's economic burden of rendering to Caesar was compounded by two layers of client rulers over the people of Galilee and Judea, both of which also demanded revenues from the people. The high priests in the temple were already in place as the rulers when the Romans conquered. The Romans kept the temple-state in place. Then, when they appointed Herod king, he rebuilt the temple on a massive scale and expanded the priestly aristocracy with the appointment of figures from the diaspora. Thus, in addition to the already existing expectations of tithes and offerings, "first fruits," and the temple tax paid annually by all adult males, considerably expanded revenues were needed, particularly to support the rebuilding of the temple but also to support the high priestly aristocracy of four extended families.

In addition, Herod had need of increased revenues to support his other massive building programs, his extensive security apparatus of mountaintop fortresses, and his lavish court and administration. In addition to adorning his own realm with temples and cities honoring Caesar, Herod gave grandiose gifts to the imperial family and to major cities of the empire. Obviously he had to generate revenues far in excess of what the territory he ruled had previously produced (the Romans estimated his "take" from his territory at nine hundred talents, according to Josephus, *Ant.* 17.318–320). To intensify agricultural production Herod surely ratcheted up demands on the tenants of the "royal estates" in the fertile Great Plain just south of Galilee. He also extended the areas cultivated to include additional lands east of the Sea of Galilee that Caesar placed under his control. And he sponsored the cultivation of specialty crops such as balsam in the Jordan valley, on which the regime had a monopoly.[2]

The peasants in village communities (in Judea, Idumea to the south, Samaria and Galilee to the north, and Perea across the Jordan), however, constituted the principal economic base from which Herod needed to extract greater production. He demanded additional royal taxes on top of the tithes and offerings for the temple and priesthood. He also probably increased the "efficiency" of tax collection. In Galilee, for example, Herod established fortress towns on hilltop sites such as Sepphoris and stored grain and other goods taken in taxes in the "royal fortresses" there. The demands he made on his subjects to meet his extensive expenditures "stimulated" the almost exclusively agricultural economy but also threatened to ruin the basis of the economy in the village communities. The effects of overtaxation were soon felt in the countryside. Josephus mentions that in order not to destroy his economic base, Herod had to grant temporary tax relief and, during a devastating drought and famine, since the heavily taxed villagers had no reserves whatever, had to import food to keep the villagers alive (*Ant.* 15.299–316, 354, 365).

Antipas's estimated "income" from his territories (two hundred talents; *Ant.* 17.318–320) was less than a quarter of what Herod the Great had derived from his realm.[3] Yet, like his father, he launched massive building programs. Within twenty years he built two capital cities, Sepphoris and Tiberias. With pretentions to Hellenistic Roman culture, Antipas built a theater in Sepphoris and an elaborate palace above Tiberias (this is what Jesus mocks in referring to "rulers who wear soft raiment and live in royal palaces," Luke 7:24–25). The "Tetrarch" clearly needed to maximize his income from his subjects. It helped that for the first time in history the ruler of Galilee now resided in the area. Antipas's regime could thus employ far more "efficient" tax collection practices than had previous rulers working from distant capitals. In fact, between them these two capital cities literally had oversight of nearly all of the villages in "lower" Galilee.

After the death of Herod the crowd assembled in the temple courtyard clamored for the appointment of a high priest who would rule more in accordance with the laws of Moses (i.e., justly; *Ant.* 17.206–8). After their ten-year experiment with Herod's son Archelaus as ruler of Judea, however, the Romans installed in power the high priestly aristocracy as expanded by Herod, with the

Roman governor appointing the high priest from among the four dominant families. The high priestly families became not only exploitative but downright predatory in their treatment of the people. According to archaeological findings, they built mansions near the temple. According to accounts of Josephus, particular high priestly figures sent their private gangs of ruffians out to seize the tithes intended for the ordinary priests from the village threshing floors, leaving the ordinary priests to starve (*Ant.* 20:181, 206–7). A telling first-century lament of the people later included in the Talmud indicates the deep popular resentment:

> Woe unto me because of the house of Bathos;
> Woe unto me for their lances!
> Woe unto me because of the house of Hanin (Ananus);
> Woe unto me because of the house of Ishmael ben Phiabi;
> Woe unto me because of their fists!
> For they are high priests, and their sons are treasurers,
> and their sons-in-law are Temple overseers,
> and their servants smite the people with sticks. (b. Pes. 57a)

Fourth, the level of hostility expressed in this lament may also have been rooted in yet another way in which the Roman imperial order meant disorder and disintegration for the people of Judea and Galilee that compounded the ones just discussed: the exploitation of their escalating indebtedness by the Herodian and high priestly families and their officers.

After yielding up portions of their crops as tithes and offerings to priests and temple and paying taxes to Herodian rulers and tribute to Caesar, an increasing number of village families were unable to survive until the next harvest without borrowing. To survive they were forced to take loans from those outside the village community who had control of stores of grain and oil but would lend at interest. Making loans to desperate people at high rates of interest became the principal way that the wealthy and powerful could "grow their wealth" and enhance their luxurious lifestyle. With their debts spiraling out of control, the poor gradually lost control of their (ancestral) land and became tenants or sharecroppers of their creditors.

The process and the result worked similarly but not identically in Judea and Galilee. In first-century CE Judea, collateral branches of the Herodian family and Herodian officers were eager to expand the wealth and control of land they had gained during the long reign of Herod. It has been reasonably surmised that resources coming into the temple from diaspora communities as well as from local revenues created a surplus of funds.[4] Herodian and high priestly families and others with access to storehouses or funds drew upon them to make loans at high interest to villagers who were struggling to feed their families after meeting their obligations for tribute, tithes, and offerings. From the interest charged and/or from "foreclosure" on loans, they increased their own wealth and control of land. This fits two important sets of information from archaeological explorations: the expansion of large estates in the hill country of northwest Judea and an increase in the construction of mansions in the section of Jerusalem just to the west of the temple complex during the first century CE.[5]

Evidence, fragmentary as it is, points to an increase in the impoverishment and indebtedness of the Judean peasantry. Unable to feed themselves after rendering tribute to Caesar in addition to the tithes and offerings to the temple, families were forced to borrow. With the priestly aristocrats and wealthy Herodians eager to lend, the people's poverty led to debts, which in turn led to their losing control of their land to their wealthy creditors. Land in the Judean hill country moved ever more into the control of Herodian and the high priestly families. The prolonged drought and acute famine of the late 40s further exacerbated the people's desperate situation. Some of the impoverished peasants formed bands of brigands. As in the case of Eleazar ben Dinai, some of these were capable of leading local uprisings rooted in the people's discontent (*War* 2.235–238). When revolt erupted in the summer of 66, says Josephus, the rebels set fire to the public archives "in order to destroy the records of debts and to provoke a wider uprising" (*War* 2.427), an indication both of how the impoverished peasantry had been manipulated into debt and loss of land and livelihood and of their resentment about their situation.

The fragmentary evidence suggests that the land in Galilee in the first century CE had not yet been turned into large estates under absentee landlords.[6] But that is exactly what Galilean villagers would have been most anxious about. They would have known about the large royal estates in the Great Plain just to the south, worked by people who would have been dependent laborers, that is, tenants, sharecroppers, or day laborers. Judging from indications in the Gospels and in early rabbinic traditions, many Galileans must still have been living on their ancestral inheritance of land. Under pressure for tithes, taxes, and tribute, however, many had fallen into debt and had long since exhausted the possibility of loans from other villagers who were also having difficulty meeting their own subsistence needs. Their only recourse was to borrow from outsiders, very likely Herodian officials in the cities, who had control of supplies of grain and oil. They might also supplement their income by hiring out as day laborers in addition to continuing work on their own fields. As families and village communities began to disintegrate, villagers found themselves threatened with loss of their land, with the prospect of becoming tenants or completely dependent on employment as day laborers.[7]

Studies of other, similar societies have found that these are precisely the economic circumstances that are conducive to the emergence of popular movements or even, rarely, peasant revolts. In the summer of 66, of course, a widespread revolt did erupt in Galilee as well as in Judea. Thirty-some years earlier indebted and hungry villagers may well have been receptive to a prophet who taught people to pray for the direct kingship of God, which would also mean, economically, that they would have sufficient daily bread and a (mutual) cancellation of their debts.

The Focus of Jesus's Mission on the Economic Distress of the People

This is precisely the situation that Jesus addresses, according to the Gospel stories and speeches: villagers who are poor, hungry, and in debt. Most interpreters hold that the Lord's Prayer was central in Jesus's mission. In this prayer for the coming of the kingdom of God, the focus is on the economic situation of the people. After the main overall petition for the coming of the direct rule of God come the two principal petitions for enough bread to make it from day to day and, in the more concrete Matthean wording, for cancellation of debts (Matt 6:9-13//Luke 11:2-4). In the other speeches of Q as well, Jesus addresses the poor and hungry. In the longest speech (Q/Luke 6:20–49) he declares to the poor that "yours is the kingdom of God." To those worried about both sustenance and shelter, he offers the reassurance that these will be taken care of if they singlemindedly "seek first the kingdom of God" (Q/Luke 12:22–31). In sending envoys to extend his mission to more and more villages, aware of the subsistence level of the component households, he instructs them to be content with whatever the host families can provide (Q/Luke 10:2–16; cf. Mark 6:6–13). In a confrontation with the scribes and Pharisees down from Jerusalem, in Mark's story, he pointedly changes the subject from washing hands to the use of local economic resources needed to support families instead of the temple (Mark 7:1–13). His sustained confrontation with the Jerusalem rulers in Mark 11–12 deals repeatedly with the economic drain on the people created by rulers' excessive demands.

The Gospel of Luke, with perspective and in retrospect, frames the whole story of Jesus in the Roman imperial order that had brought economic distress and dislocation to subject people. The story of Jesus's birth (Luke 2) is legend, hardly an account of an event that happened as portrayed. But legends often give us a sense of the broad pattern of power relations, the gist of things, better than many tidbits of "data." Caesar Augustus, the Lord and Savior, decreed that peoples subjected by the empire must be registered to pay tribute. To do this they were required to go back to their original family land and village, where they were to raise the crops from which the tribute was to be taken from the top of the heap of grain on the threshing floor. Papyri in Egypt indicate that the legend of Jesus's birth has historical verisimilitude on this.[8]

But why had people such as Joseph left their family's land and village? Bethlehem was "shepherd country," so dry that grain might not grow and people had to rely on raising sheep and goats for a living. We may reasonably speculate that, forced off their land by taxes and debt, people like Joseph had left in search of (low-wage) labor, such as in the construction of Antipas's new capital city Sepphoris (a few miles from Nazareth). But Caesar Augustus needed more revenues to support the Roman legions stationed on the frontiers, such as that between Syria and Palestine, and to support the famous "bread and circuses" in Rome, that is, to feed and entertain the people of Rome who had been forced off their land by the wealthy Roman patricians in a similar process in Italy.[9] So Caesar insisted that all subjects of the empire return to their land to raise crops from which the tribute could be taken.

Composed in perspective and in retrospect from popular legends and psalms that had become standard Jesus tradition, Luke's infancy narratives presents how Jesus movements understood the effects of Jesus's mission. The heavenly messenger announces to the destitute shepherds, "*To you* has been born a *Savior*"—an alternative, counterimperial Savior. The "peace" that he brings "to those whom he favors" is pointedly intended to relieve them finally of the disorder brought to them by the imperial Savior who had brought peace and security to the wealthy and powerful. Just prior to the story of Jesus's birth, Luke's story has Mary sing a hymn in praise of God for his previous deliverance and in anticipation of the new deliverance: "He has brought down the powerful from their thrones, and lifted up the lowly. / He has filled the hungry with good things and sent the rich away empty. / He has helped his servant Israel" (Luke 1:52–54). Both the Gospel of Luke and the pre-Lukan song that Mary sings thus indicate that the work of the prophet Jesus as the counterimperial "Savior" was understood in his movement(s) as not only concretely political-*economic* but also collective-societal in its scope.[10] The rest of Luke's story of Jesus's mission, like those of Mark and Matthew, portrays Jesus's mission as concretely and collectively religious, political, and *economic*.

In the Gospels, as in other sources for Judean and Galilean society at the time, the social-economic life of the people had concrete social forms, mainly village communities composed of varying numbers of households. The individualism of standard interpretation of Jesus and its narrow focus on individual sayings means that interpreters simply do not notice the Gospel sources' attention to and Jesus's engagement with the fundamental forms of social-economic life. Rather, they construct a Jesus who is unengaged with or even hostile to these forms. As noted in chapter 1, a highly influential version of this Western individualistic interpretation has been the portrayal of Jesus and his followers as adopting the "lifestyle" of an "itinerant radicalism." Focusing on sayings such as those about "hating father and mother" and "leaving the dead to bury the dead"—taken out of their speech and/or narrative context and out of historical context—such individualistic interpretations conclude that Jesus was calling on individuals to abandon their families and villages to become itinerant beggars.[11] This individualistic interpretation is compounded by the reduction of "the kingdom of God" to an individual spiritual reality.[12]

In ancient Judea and Galilee, however, the life context of the vast majority of people would have been one or another of those hundreds of villages composed of multiple families. The Gospels portray Jesus as pursuing his mission of healing, exorcism, and proclaiming the kingdom precisely in the villages of Galilee and near-by areas. It is only in relation to these concrete social-economic forms of village communities and their component families that the many references in our sources to hunger, loans, debts, day laborers, large estates, absentee landowners, and the hostility of the (indebted) people to debt records and wealthy Herodian and high priestly figures make sense.

Village Communities and Covenantal Principles

So long as the component households of village communities in Galilee and Judea rendered large portions of their crops as tribute, taxes, and tithes, their rulers left the villages more or less alone. Villages were thus semi-independent and self-governing communities. The local form of self-governance as well as social cohesion was the village assembly (*knesset* in Aramaic or Hebrew, *synagoge* in Greek). Community life, including social-economic interactions, were guided by Israelite tradition and customs.

Insofar as the vast majority of people in Galilean and Judean society lived in village communities, there were serious consequences for social order and political-economic-religious conflict if those communities began to disintegrate. Yet the disintegration of village communities and their constituent households, the fundamental forms of social-political-economic-religious life, was precisely the effect of the multiple layers of rulers under Roman rule. Many would have found it difficult to recover, socially and psychologically (religiously) as well as materially (economically), from the loss of members who had been killed or enslaved and of houses and villages destroyed in the Roman campaigns of the 50s and 40s BCE and the reconquests of 40–37 and 4 BCE. Whole villages were displaced by Antipas's construction of his second new capital, Tiberias (*Ant.* 18.34–38). And, as just discussed, demands for revenues from multiple layers of rulers left families in debt and facing loss of their ancestral lands.

As a number of historical and anthropological studies have shown, however, peasants in many agrarian societies had developed customary measures and mechanisms to maintain the minimal economic viability of struggling families. Lending to one another, supposedly at no interest, and the sabbatical fallow and cancellation of debts, for example, appear to have been just such measures in ancient Israelite tradition.[13]

Some of the recent research mentioned in chapter 1, however, has forced us to rethink how this worked. Contrary to previous assumptions of widespread literacy and availability of written texts, recent studies of manuscripts, limited literacy, and the dominant oral communication in antiquity make it seem unlikely that villagers would have had direct contact with scrolls of authoritative texts. Galilean and Judean villagers, rather, cultivated their own version of Israelite tradition orally, as explained in chapter 2. Israelite popular tradition was learned from generation to generation in families and village communities and applied by village elders in local assemblies (*synagogai*) and courts. The exodus stories of Israel's origins, for example, were known from annual celebration of Passover, as well as from other retellings, such as certain psalms. From Josephus's accounts of the popular messianic and prophetic movements, we know that memories of the young David and of Moses and Joshua were very much alive in village communities, so much so that they provided the models for new movements of resistance and renewal.

While villagers probably had no contact with scrolls of authoritative torah texts, they were deeply rooted in the Mosaic covenant and its commandments. Josephus's accounts of incidents in Galilee during the revolt of 66–67 indicate that Galilean villagers' actions against Herodian and other rulers were taken in defense of the covenantal commandments.[14] Jesus's accusation against the Pharisees in Mark 7:9–13 presupposes the people's commitment to, as well as knowledge of, the basic "commandment of God." The petition for cancellation of debts in the Lord's Prayer assumes familiarity with the Mosaic covenantal mechanism of the sabbatical cancellation of debts. That the tribute to Rome made an exception for sabbatical years assumes that the Mosaic covenantal custom of leaving the land fallow every seventh year was widely practiced.

While recent research suggests that the books that were later included in the Hebrew Bible cannot be used as *direct* sources for village life, they can be used critically as *indirect* sources. From these books, for example, we can make judgments about what appear to have been popular Israelite traditions that were taken up into the books produced by the scribes in support of and for the guidance of the temple-state. And these books enable us to see what was evidently current in scribal cultivation of the official Judean tradition. The authoritative written texts of torah and prophets, moreover, enable us to discern certain Israelite cultural patterns far broader than what is evident in particular laws or "verses" of text, cultural patterns that are also evident in the Gospel sources for Jesus—if we can only overcome the habit of focusing only on separate sayings or "verses."

The most striking example is the Mosaic covenant and its component commandments. The basic commandments of the Mosaic covenant and closely related laws, regulations, and practices form the substance of the books of Exodus, Leviticus, Numbers, and Deuteronomy. The exodus story of Israel's origin is the basis of God's demand for keeping the commandments. Many of the laws in the law codes, moreover, are clearly "applications" of one or another covenant commandment to circumstances of village life. And covenant commandments are the criteria on the basis of which prophets condemn the oppressive practices of rulers and their officers. Many of those same connections then appear not only in later texts, such as the Community Rule of the Qumran Community, but also in the actions of popular and scribal protests and of popular movements, as known from the hostile accounts of the elite (Josephus) who left written sources. Both at the level of the written texts, with which we are more familiar, and at the level of village life, for which we have only fragmentary evidence, cultural tradition and its cultivation and application worked in patterns, patterns that we are likely to miss when we focus narrowly on individual verses.

As Hebrew Bible scholars recognized a generation or two ago, the Mosaic covenant has a structure, evident in the key texts in which the Covenant was given (Exod 20; Deut 5:6–21; Josh 24).[15] *First* comes God's declaration of deliverance, originally "I brought you out of bondage in Egypt." This is the basis of the Israelites' obligation to obey God's demands, the *second* part. These commandments consist of ten basic principles; the first require exclusive loyalty to the God of Israel, while the rest govern the people's social-economic interaction. The first commandments insist that God is the sole God and Lord (ruler) of the society, to the exclusion even of human rulers. Gideon's reply when the Israelites want him to become king illustrates the exclusive direct rule of God over the people: No, you already have YHWH as your King (Judg 8:22–23). The second commandment prohibits not only "making images of the powers of heaven and earth, but also bowing down and serving them," that is, giving them taxes and tribute. Then come the commandments that protect the integrity of the family unit (adultery), the rights of elderly family members, and prohibition(s) against scheming to get control of other's goods, that is, coveting and stealing and swearing falsely. What these commandments do is protect people's economic rights, rights to a living on the basis of their land and household and draft animals and such. The *third* step in the covenant structure consists of sanctions to motivate people to keep the commandments, such as the declaration of blessings and curses for complying or not complying.

The same pattern is evident in many other passages and contexts in the books of torah and the prophets. In the context of the instruction of a child, for example, when the child asks about "the decrees and the statutes and the ordinances that YHWH our God has commanded," the parents shall reply with a recitation of the story of YHWH's deliverance of the people from bondage in Egypt and provision of their ancestral land. And this is the basis of the obligation of the people to observe the commandments. The Mosaic covenantal pattern is evident even in a key word used for the components of the covenantal relationship: since God *shaphat* (liberated/established justice for) the people from bondage, the people are obligated to obey the *mishpatim* (the laws/rulings/ordinances, that is, principles of justice). Furthermore, YHWH and human agents inspired to provide leadership to the people are *shophetim* (liberators, those who [re]establish justice for the people).[16]

The Mosaic covenant and the laws and practices linked to it clearly arise from and fit a peasant society of village communities of multiple households.[17] The principle of exclusive loyalty to God as the sole God and ruler/king, which is set directly against bondage under the harsh exploitation by Pharaoh in Egypt, is hardly a constitution for a kingship, as Gideon stated bluntly. The other commandments are clearly principles intended to guide social-economic interaction in village communities composed of families. This is the context in which no-longer-productive elderly family members might need economic support, adultery might threaten the integrity of the component families, and families might need protection against other villagers who might scheme to (covet) gain control of their resources (e.g., animals, produce) by theft, fraud, or false promises. Given its overall pattern and the particular contents of its commandments, the Mosaic covenant provides principles (a "constitution") for social-economic interaction in village communities that have no state ruling over them or that live semi-independently under a state that does not (yet) exert tight control and impose more intensive exploitation.

We see how the Mosaic covenant may have worked in practice much better in the covenantal laws that set up certain mechanisms for others in the community to aid the needy and other mechanisms to protect their economic viability as families when they really get into difficulties, such as indebtedness. Many of these mechanisms are attested in collections of laws edited by scribes, in the Covenant Code, Exod 21–23; the Holiness Code, Lev 17–26; and the Deuteronomic Code, Deut 12–26. A kind of economic "safety net" is set up in the practices of gleaning rights (Lev 19:9–10; 23:22; Deut 24:19–22), leaving the fields fallow every seventh year so that the poor can gather what grows anyhow (Exod 23:10–11; more schematized in Lev 25:2–7), and lending liberally to needy community members but not charging interest (Exod 22:14–15, 25–27; Lev 25:35–37; Deut 15:7–8; 23:19). Because people can have several bad harvests in a row, Israelites had also developed (God had commanded) other mechanisms of debt relief. Every seventh year creditors were supposed to cancel debts (Deut 15:1–2) and to release debt-slaves that debtor families had sent to their households to work off the debts (Deut 15:12–15; Lev 25:8–10, 41).

From Josephus we know that these covenantal mechanisms to protect people's livelihood and their ability to continue to live on their ancestral land were still operative in the first century CE. It had become officially recognized custom that every seven years debts were canceled. Ironically, scribal "legislation" to bypass the officially recognized laws protecting peasants provides an important bit of evidence that the cancellation of debts was practiced and expected in late second-temple times. The *prosbul* (literally, "to the council") promulgated supposedly by the learned scribe Hillel under Herod enabled creditors to avoid canceling people's debts by placing the debt document in the hands of a court, the effect of which was to allow people's debts to mount up. In the village communities, however, where people were subject to social pressure from others, these covenantal commandments and mechanisms provided guidelines for the constituent families to use in aiding one another and in co-operating within the community to keep each family viable.

What happened under the impact of Roman rule was that families who could not feed themselves after paying their taxes quickly exhausted their neighbors' ability to come to their aid. The families who at first helped their neighbors with loans ran into economic difficulty themselves and began to resent their poorer neighbors who could not pay them back. So families were forced to borrow from wealthy people outside the village, who charged high rates of interest, and fell into spiraling debt. The outside creditors gained control over land and/or the labor of family members, perhaps even evicted them from their ancestral land. In short, the new world disorder for Galileans and Judeans was not simply that some people had become impoverished and hungry. The fundamental forms of societal life, families and village communities, were disintegrating.

The Centrality of the Mosaic Covenant in Jesus's Mission

Interpreters of Jesus have been slow to entertain the possibility that Jesus was engaged in Mosaic covenantal teaching. This is partly a result of the focus on separate sayings. Probably more determinative has been the continuing influence of the Christian theological scheme in which Jesus was the revealer who proclaimed the "Gospel" (the center of "Christianity") that responded to and superseded the "Law" (the center of "Judaism"). Since the Mosaic covenant was so closely associated with "the Law/Torah" and interpreters were usually focused on individual sayings, it was difficult to discern covenantal references and the covenant patterns in the Gospels.

The discovery of the Dead Sea Scrolls has shown that covenantal teachings and covenantal patterns were still cultivated prominently in a scribal-priestly group in late second-temple times. Indeed, the Qumran community that left the Scrolls understood itself not only as a new exodus community but also as a renewed covenantal community, precisely in its rejection of the incumbent high priesthood in the temple and in its withdrawal into the Judean wilderness. Its own Community Rule and previously known Damascus Rule were renewed Mosaic covenants, patterned after the same structural components as the original Mosaic covenant (e.g., in Exod 20; Deut 5; Joshua 24).[18] Considering that Galilean and Judean villagers were also actively cultivating Israelite covenantal tradition, there is no reason why a popular prophet and renewal movement could not also adapt the Mosaic covenant central to the life of Israel.

Covenantal references, components, and patterns are prominent in the Gospel stories and speeches. They are most noticeable in Matthew but play important roles in the other Gospels as well as in the speeches of Jesus. It has often been recognized that the Sermon on the Mount is or includes a renewal of the Mosaic covenant: "you have heard that it was said of old . . ." followed by the recitation of many of the ten commandments, "but I say to you . . ." followed by Jesus's intensified covenantal demands. Comparison of the speech in Matthew 5–7 as a whole with the parallel speech in Luke 6:20–49 reveals that they have the same overall outline: they both begin with blessings, followed by new covenantal teaching, and end with the double parable of the houses on the rock and sand as motivation. The parallel materials in Matthew and Luke have been understood as derived from the source Q. Once we look for broader cultural patterns, however, it is evident that the parallel materials are the key components of the same covenant renewal speech. The first and by far the longest speech of Jesus in Q is a renewal of the Mosaic covenant.[19]

It has also gone largely unnoticed that Mark is equally concerned with renewal of the Mosaic covenant, which forms one of the story's most prominent themes.[20] It opens with the messenger of the covenant performing a baptism of repentance (for covenant breaking) and renewal, preparing the way, as prophesied. At the end of the first narrative step, in Mark 3:31–33, Jesus insists that the people "do the will of God," which is another way of saying that they should keep the covenantal commandments, as we know from the Lord's Prayer and the prophets and the whole book of Deuteronomy. At several key points in the story, Jesus refers explicitly to one or several of the covenantal commandments (e.g., Mark 7:9–13; 10:17–22). In the climax of the story, the last supper, a Passover meal celebrating the exodus, is also a renewal of the covenant. Jesus's words over the cup—"this is my blood of the covenant"—make direct reference to the blood that bound the people with God in the covenant-making ceremony on Mount Sinai (Exod 24). Most significant for this discussion is the series of dialogues in Mark 10:2–45 in which Jesus pointedly recites the covenant commandments and makes law- or commandment-like declarations. These dialogues constitute a covenant renewal speech parallel to that in Q/Luke 6:20–49, in effect, a covenantal charter for the communities of a movement.

Where the covenant renewal speeches come in the sequence of speeches or episodes in Q and in Mark is also significant. The covenant renewal speech is the first and the longest speech in the series of Q speeches, the beginning of Jesus's teaching and the basis for the following speeches (the same is true in both Matthew and Luke). In Mark's story the series of dialogues that constitute Jesus's covenantal teaching comes as he completes his mission in the villages of Galilee and nearby areas and heads up to Jerusalem. In both of the earliest

Gospel sources, Jesus's renewal of the Mosaic covenant is thus the center and the basis of his broader agenda of the renewal of Israel in opposition to the rulers of Israel.

Considering that in Israelite tradition the Mosaic covenant is concerned with the people's exclusive loyalty to their transcendent divine ruler and God's will for social-economic relations in Israel (that is, the rule/kingdom of God!), it should not be surprising that the covenant is also concerned with economic relations in the Gospel sources for Jesus's mission. It is remarkable that the covenant commandments, as criteria of political-economic relations, are operative at every level in Jesus's renewal of Israel in opposition to the rulers.

We start at the top of the new world order that meant disorder for the people. Caesar decreed that the people had to pay tribute and viewed refusal to pay as tantamount to rebellion. According to the first two commandments of the covenant, however, God was the exclusive ruler of Israel, and the people were prohibited from bowing down and serving other gods and lords. There was no separation of "church and state," of "spiritual and temporal kingdoms," in either the Roman imperial order or in the Mosaic covenantal tradition. Twenty-plus years before Jesus, some scribal teachers and Pharisees had organized people to refuse to pay the tribute, what Josephus calls the "fourth philosophy," which agreed with the teachings of the Pharisees. The Pharisees knew very well that it was against the covenant law to render tribute to Caesar when they attempted to entrap Jesus on this question. He replied in covenantal economic terms: "Give to Caesar the things that belong to Caesar, and give to God the things that belong to God" (Mark 12:13–17; author's trans.). Everyone listening in the temple courtyard in Mark's story, that is, at all levels of Judean and Galilean society, would have "gotten it," particularly the Passover crowds. Nothing from the people, especially from the piles of grain on the threshing floors at harvest time that were the subsistence villagers' livelihood, belonged to Caesar.

Moving down a step in the Roman imperial order to the client rulers in Jerusalem, the criteria on which Jesus pronounced God's judgment on the temple and high priests were the same as in the pronouncements of his prophetic predecessors. In the prophetic demonstration in the temple (in Mark 11:15–17) he quotes the focal metaphor from Jeremiah's well-known prophecy that God would destroy the temple, that stronghold of the bandits; that is, the increasingly wealthy high priests who headed the temple economy in Judea were acting like brigands who robbed the people of their goods and then took refuge in their sacred stronghold, the temple. In the prophetic parable of the tenants (Mark 12:2–9), Jesus draws on the familiar image from Isaiah

5 of the people as God's vineyard, for which the high priests are the tenants and caretakers. But they have not only exploited the people ("adding field to field, house to house"; Isa 5:8) but also killed God's messengers the prophets who called them to account on covenantal principles (cf. Q/Luke 13:34–35).

That the covenantal commandments are the criteria of God's judgment is even clearer in Jesus's declarations against the scribes and Pharisees, as representatives of the Jerusalem temple-state. As discussed earlier, the whole point of the covenant commandments against coveting and stealing and the covenantal mechanisms such as the sabbatical fallow year and the release from debts was to protect people's households, including lands, as the basis of their livelihood. Jesus's disputes with and pronouncements against the scribes and Pharisees include condemnations of their policies and actions that siphoned off people's resources in violation of the covenant commandments (to be discussed further in chapter 6). Like Jeremiah, Jesus is thus saying that the whole temple-state, which was the face of Roman rule in Judea, its high priestly rulers and its scribal and Pharisaic representatives, stands under God's judgment for exploiting the increasingly indebted and hungry people in violation of the Covenant.

Jesus's Renewal of Covenantal Community

Corresponding to Jesus's prophetic pronouncement of God's judgment of Israel's rulers on the criteria of Mosaic covenantal principles is his renewal of covenantal community at the center of the renewal of the people generally. The first long speech in Q/Luke 6:20–49 and the series of dialogues in Mark 10 are explicit statements of covenant renewal, focusing (like the Lord's Prayer) on the threatened livelihood of the people.

In addition to numerous allusions to traditional covenantal laws and teachings, Jesus's speech in Q 6:20–49 has the structure of the Mosaic covenant, as indicated earlier:

1. A statement of God's deliverance that evokes the peoples' gratitude and obligation
2. Principles of exclusive loyalty to God and principles of societal relations
3. Sanctions as motivation for observance

The new declaration of deliverance in Jesus's covenant renewal speech, however, is couched in terms of blessings and curses, which were part of the sanctions in the original covenant structure. The Community Rule from Qumran offers a scribal-priestly parallel. In the opening instruction for the covenant renewal ceremony at Qumran the blessings and curses are transformed into part of the statement of deliverance, now in the present and future rather than in the past. This continuation of the covenant pattern that includes the transformation of the blessings and curses from sanctions into a new declaration of deliverance, enables us to see the parallel transformation of covenant structure in Jesus's opening speech in Q:[21]

1. The blessings and woes have been transformed into new statements of deliverance in the present and/or imminent future, with which Jesus's renewed covenant begins.
2. The ensuing teachings not only allude to traditional covenantal teaching but constitute renewed covenantal principles, stated in the form of "focal instances."
3. Although the blessings and curses have been transformed into statements of new deliverance at the beginning of the speech, the third component, sanctions, is present, consisting of the double parable of building houses on rock and on sand with which the speech closes.

Like the other speeches in Q, this covenant renewal speech would have been regularly performed before communities with which it resonated on the basis of the villagers' Israelite cultural tradition. The speech took the form of "performative speech" that made something happen, as when a judge in court pronounces a defendant "Guilty as charged!" or a priest in church pronounces words of absolution: "Your sins are forgiven!" This speech, performed probably in village communities, thus *enacted* the renewal of the Mosaic covenant, which would have been the very basis for the renewal of Israel as an agrarian society whose fundamental social form was village communities.

That renewal, moreover, could happen only insofar as the speech addressed the symptoms of the disintegration of the people's communities. It opens with the bold declaration of new deliverance, following the standard form of the Mosaic covenant familiar from Israelite tradition: "Blessed are you poor, for yours is the kingdom of God," and so on (6:20–26). This series of parallel statements addresses the economic-social-psychological malaise of people who have become desperately poor, hungry, and downhearted. Indeed, insofar as the covenant blessings and curses promoted self-blame for misfortune and suffering, the people had been taught to blame themselves and had come to see their poverty, hunger, and illness as curses for their sinning, in violation of the covenant laws. This is what Jesus addresses in the episode where he declares forgiveness of sin in connection with his healings (Mark 2:1–12). Even more dramatically, evidently in full awareness of what had happened in the application of the covenant blessings and curses, Jesus begins the renewal speech by transforming the blessings and curses into a new declaration of God's deliverance for the poor and hungry, followed by condemnation of the wealthy, who are wealthy because they are exploiting the poor.

In the next step of the speech we can discern how the renewal of covenant community could happen concretely in social-economic relations if we attend to the social context of the "focal instances" in the component sayings. As noted in chapter 3, sayings such as "love your enemies" and "turn the other cheek," taken out of the speech context and seen through a misunderstanding of the historical context, were long assumed to apply to the Romans. It is now clear, however, that once the Roman legions had done their devastation through re- peated reconquests, they were withdrawn to distant bases, such as in Antioch in Syria, far to the north. The local "enemy," the one who might deliver an insult by a slap on the cheek or the one to whom one would lend or from whom one would borrow, was clearly a fellow member of the village community. Jesus's covenant renewal speech addresses these symptoms of local community disin- tegration, under the impact of the effects of Roman rule discussed earlier.

Thus, having just assured the people of God's new deliverance happen- ing now, Jesus calls them to put aside or overcome their debilitating local eco- nomic and social conflicts in a series of interrelated examples that are instances of a more general return to local cooperation (Q/Luke 6:27–42). That all of these sayings, these focal instances, make clear allusions to traditional Mosaic covenantal teaching—as we can readily detect from our handbooks that cross- reference laws and statements in the Covenant Code (Exod 21–23), the Purity Code (Lev 17–26), and Deuteronomy—indicates clearly that Jesus is summon- ing them to return to the time-honored principles of mutual sharing and coop- eration central to covenantal teaching.[22]

Jesus addresses such conflicts rooted the economic pressures with the principle "Love your enemies," followed by the interrelated examples. He briefly addresses debtors in the community in the command "If someone sues you for your cloak, let him take your shift as well" (Q/Luke 6:29). This command pointedly plays with a fundamental law in the covenant code that prohibits economic exploitation of the poor: "You shall not deal with others as a creditor. If you take your neighbor's cloak in pawn, you shall restore it before the sun goes down, since it is your neighbor's only covering at night" (Exod 22:25–27; Deut 24:10–13). Of course, if a debtor did as Jesus said and took off his shift too, he would have been standing there stark naked, embarrassing the credi- tor in front of the whole village, presumably so that he would back away from

claiming repayment of the debt (Jesus had a sense of humor!). Jesus mainly re-
states the traditional covenantal principle that Israelites should lend liberally to
their needy fellow villagers without charging interest (Deut 15:7–8; 23:19; Lev
25:35–37). He renews the covenantal command of sharing and generosity: "To
the one who asks from you give, and from the one who borrows do not ask back.
. . . But love your enemies, and do good and lend" (Q/Luke 6:30–35; author's
trans.). In allusion to another covenantal principle (Lev 19:2), "Be merciful as
your Father is merciful" (6:36), Jesus then patterns the command of generosity within the community on the divine generosity. "Love your enemies" and
the ensuing focal instances of Jesus's renewed commandments of lending and
borrowing here would have resonated with a wide range of Mosaic covenantal
teachings familiar to the villagers from Israelite tradition. The principles implicit in these focal instances bear a remarkable resemblance to the third petition
in the Lord's Prayer: "Your kingdom come . . . Cancel our debts, as we herewith
cancel the debts of our debtors" (Luke 11:2–4/Matt 6:9–12; author's trans.).

In the final section of the covenant renewal speech (Q/Luke 6:43–49)
the double parable of houses built on rock and on sand (6:46–49) provides the
clinching sanction on the whole series of covenantal admonitions.

In summary, in his first speech in Q, Jesus as a prophet like Moses in
performative speech enacts the renewal of the covenant. The speech enacts a renewal of the covenant in village communities where the fabric of
mutual sharing and cooperation that had traditionally held communities
together was disintegrating because of the pressures of Roman rule and rigorous taxation by client rulers. After God's new deliverance in the blessings
of the imminent kingdom that gives the people new hope, Jesus demands
that the people recommit themselves to active sharing of scarce resources
in a time when all are struggling. As in the Lord's Prayer, the people com-
mit themselves not only to extending loans to each other but also to canceling the debts of their debtors. What may not be evident at first glance is
that this recommitment to community cooperation and sharing would also
enable village communities better to resist the continuing attempts by the
wealthy creditors to exploit their debt and take control of their land and labor.
Renewing the cooperation and solidarity of covenant community as the basis
of renewal of the people enabled them also to resist the encroachment of their
rulers.

While the renewal of the covenant is prominent in Mark's overall story, as
noted earlier, it is most explicit and programmatic in the series of dialogues at
the close of Jesus's campaigns in villages in Galilee and beyond (Mark 10:2–45).

These dialogues are in effect a covenant renewal speech parallel to the covenant speech in Q.[23] The sequence of dialogues proceeds through the covenantal issues of marriage, membership, economic relations, and political leadership. In the first dialogue (10:2–12), which quotes the commandment against adultery, Jesus insists on the integrity of marriage, a key issue insofar as the family was the basic unit of production and reproduction. Considering how the elite used marriage and remarriage as a way of consolidating control of land, Jesus's concern in strictly prohibiting remarriage may have had to do with the disintegration of family units under the economic pressures of Roman rule.

The third step of the speech deals directly with covenant economics. The three short dialogues with "a man," the disciples, and Peter, respectively (in Mark 10:17–22, 23–27, 28–31), flow in sequence as a declaration of egalitarian economic relations. The man who asks how he can inherit "eternal life" gives himself away as wealthy. This is not the kind of question that would be asked by a peasant who is worried about where the next meal is coming from. Jesus immediately recites the last six covenant commandments that deal with social-economic relations. "You shall not defraud" seems to be a pointed paraphrase of "you shall not covet." Coveting someone else's goods would lead the coveter to defraud a vulnerable person desperate for work or for a loan to feed his children (cf. Deut 24:14–15). The man's insistence that he has kept these commandments is obviously phony. In Israelite society, like many other agrarian societies, the only way for someone to become rich was to take advantage of the vulnerable, that is, to defraud others by charging interest on loans (which was forbidden in covenant law, as just discussed), thereby gaining control of others' goods or resources (labor, fields, households). Of course, the man cannot respond to Jesus's command to sell his goods and give to the poor because he not only has great possessions but is deeply attached to them. The man thus provides a negative example, indicating to Jesus's follower what they should *not* do.

The next step in the dialogue reinforces and sanctions the covenantal teaching. The declaration about the camel going through the eye of the needle, which illustrates how impossible it is for a rich person to enter the kingdom of God, is peasant humor that only slightly veils the hostility. The preceding exchange between Jesus and the man keen on eternal life has just laid out the criteria for "entering the kingdom," that is, the economic principles of the Mosaic covenant commandments. And, as illustrated by the man who cannot give up his wealth, anyone who is rich has not kept the covenantal commandments.

We must listen with peasant ears to Jesus's statement in reply to Peter's self-interested query in the next exchange: "Truly I tell you, there is no one who has left house or brothers or sisters or mother or father or children or fields, for my sake . . . , who will not receive a hundredfold now in this age—houses, brothers and sisters, mothers and children, and fields, with persecutions—and in the age to come, eternal life" (10:29–31).

Often missed is the astoundingly concrete "this-worldly" character of Jesus's reassurance. The restoration is to occur "now in this age." Nor does the ensuing tag line "and in the age to come, eternal life," mitigate the concrete character of the fulfillment. This is a "throw-away line" referring back to the clearly rejected question of the rich man. That the renewal is to be "in this age" is reinforced and connected directly to the concrete situation of the members of the Jesus movement to whom the Gospel story is addressed by the addition of "with persecutions." Jesus is not referring to some fantasyland. He is talking, with wondrous exaggeration, about the renewal of village life in the presence of the kingdom of God that is happening now, "in this age" and in the face of (in spite of) persecutions. Lest we miss the covenantal pattern assumed and expressed in this series of dialogues, moreover, Jesus's final statement reinforces his renewed covenantal economic instruction with a clear allusion to the covenantal blessings. Adherence to covenantal economic principles, so that community members do not seek to become wealthy by taking advantage of others' vulnerability, will result in (unheard of) abundance for all in the community, albeit with no illusions about the political circumstances in which they are living.

In summary, the Romans and their client rulers simply assumed that they could use their power to extract resources from subject people. This not only impoverished the people but also undermined their traditional culture and social structure. Jesus launched a mission to revitalize not only the people's communal spirit but also their communal economic solidarity. In his renewal of covenant community, he called the people to mutual support and cooperative action to arrest the disintegration and restore the solidarity of their communities. As part of covenantal renewal, love refers not to a feeling or an attitude but to concrete economic practices in the village community, such as canceling debts and generous sharing of resources. In diametric opposition to the wealthy and powerful who were "growing their wealth" by "defrauding" the vulnerable people, Jesus insists that his followers share their resources in mutual assistance and communal solidarity.

Finally it is significant to note that it is in circumstances of relative powerlessness vis-à-vis the Roman imperial order that Jesus called for renewed commitment to covenantal economics. But it was precisely in those circumstances of poverty and powerlessness that Jesus and his followers found it essential to struggle to practice those values and principles of justice, cooperation, and solidarity. The imperial order was still in place. But Jesus was calling people to take control of and rebuild their own community life in the confidence that the imperial order stood under God's judgment.

6. Conflict with the Scribes and Pharisees

Interpretation of the conflict between Jesus and the Pharisees continues to be influenced by the standard older theological scheme of Christian origins. At the center of the parochial old religion of Judaism was the Law. As the precursors of the rabbis, the Pharisees were the authoritative teachers of the Law who emphasized scrupulous adherence to the minutiae of ritual observances and purity codes. In direct challenge to their legalism and restrictive casuistry, Jesus taught the Gospel of forgiveness, love, and responsive righteousness. Some interpretations even held that Jesus intentionally abrogated the Law in his disputes with the Pharisees in such matters as observance of the Sabbath.

In the aftermath of the Nazi Holocaust, both Christian and Jewish interpreters have been constrained to break through or mitigate this scheme, finding various ways to construct Judaism as less legalistic, the Pharisees as less of a straw man, and Jesus as a faithful Jew. Yet the influence of the old scheme persists in seeing Judaism as focused on "the politics of holiness," the Pharisees as dedicated to the maintenance of purity, and Jesus as having intensified (rather than abrogated) the Law.[1]

Especially important in moving beyond the Pharisees of the old scheme have been critical analyses of the sources, principally Josephus's histories, certain Qumran documents, the Gospels, and rabbinic references, that give very different pictures and at points even seem contradictory. None has been more important than the incisive analysis of rabbinic sources by Jacob Neusner, which has been particularly helpful to Christian interpreters of Jesus and the Gospels, who generally lack the training to work in rabbinic sources themselves. He has shown that the rabbinic traditions of the Pharisees are diverse and include layer upon layer of reshaping in the course of rabbinic debates.[2] He has also shown that the Pharisees were not the only and may not have been the principal precursors of the rabbis.

A hypothesis based on a supposed difference between Josephus's accounts in the *Jewish War* and the *Antiquities*, however, turns out to have been diversionary. In the later work, it was argued, Josephus was making a case to the Romans that they should appoint the Pharisees to fill the vacuum in the administration of Judaism in Palestine in the aftermath of the Roman destruction of the temple in 70 CE. This was a welcome hypothesis for interpreters of Jesus eager to lessen Jesus's conflict with Judaism. It enabled them to attribute the most severe clashes between Jesus and the Pharisees in the Gospel "controversy stories" to later development of the Gospel tradition by Jesus believers facing the (imminent) assumption of authority by the Pharisees. It turns out, however, that the Romans were not looking to appoint the Pharisees or any other figures as authorities over Judaism in Palestine.[3]

These analyses of sources and reconceptualizations, however, do not consider the political-economic-religious position and role of the Pharisees, which continue to be obscured by the synthetic construct of "Judaism." Research on several subjects directly pertinent to their role, moreover, is further undermining standard old assumptions about "Judaism" and "the Torah/Law."

The Position and Role of the Scribes and Pharisees in the Judean Temple-State

Instead of continuing to imagine that the Pharisees were some sort of ill-defined "group" or "sect" in "Judaism" (or one of several "Judaisms"), it would be more appropriate to the historical situation to discern the position and role of the scribes and Pharisees in the Judean temple-state.

Scholars devoted to "social-scientific" interpretation have applied sociological models to ancient Judean society, particularly the historical sociology of Gerhard Lenski.[4] This model, couched in terms of social stratification on the basis of study of modern industrial societies, does not appear to be generally applicable to Judea and other ancient Near Eastern societies or to the Roman Empire. As discussed in chapter 2, the sources for ancient Roman Palestine portray a deep division between the rulers, imperial and local, and the people they ruled and taxed. In one respect, however, some of the cross-cultural studies on which Lenski draws are adaptable for ancient Judea, and that is the relation between the priestly aristocracy of the Judean temple-state and the learned scribes who cultivated cultural traditions. Rather than apply a model, however, it may be more helpful to comb our sources for information that indicates the political-economic-religious position and role(s) of learned scribes in the temple-state and the implications for understanding the Pharisees.

The learned scribe Jesus ben Sira, active in the early second century BCE, provides a good deal of information about his own and other scribes' position and role in the temple-state, as mentioned in chapter 2. In contrast with the artisans and farmers whose manual labor supports the city, only the scribe has the leisure for the learning necessary "to serve the "great ones/rulers" (Sir 8:8; 38:24–39:11). As he mentions repeatedly, this meant serving as advisers to the collective rulership of the aristocracy (6:34; 7:14; 15:5; 21:17; 38:32–33), as members of courts that heard cases (for they had learned the decisions of courts and could expound judgments, 4:9; 11:7–9; 38:33; 42:2), and evidently as diplomatic envoys (39:4).[5]

Service in the temple-state was the purpose of the scribes' training, which was designed to instill the disciplined character necessary for service in the councils of "the great ones."[6] While it is common in biblical studies to imagine a cultural division of labor in which learned scribes specialized in (proverbial) wisdom, the priests taught torah, and the prophets pronounced oracles, ben Sira portrays wise scribes as learning of all of these segments of Judean tradition. The scribe "devotes himself to the study of the torah of the Most High, he seeks out the wisdom of all the ancients, and is concerned with prophecies" (38:34–39:1). Contrary to a common misreading of his wisdom in the book of Sirach, ben Sira does not (teach other scribes to) interpret the torah of the Most High (that is, he does not cite and comment on particular laws). He focuses rather on obedience to the commandments or the covenant of God.

Given the fundamental political-economic-religious division between rulers and ruled on the one hand and the emphasis in both torah and prophecy on nonexploitative social-economic relations on the other, a certain tension was inherent in the relation between the scribes and the aristocracy. As the professional intellectuals responsible for cultivation of torah and prophecies as well as wisdom, learned scribes developed a sense of their own authority as the custodians of divine revelation in the torah of God and prophecies. In order to have the leisure to devote themselves to learning and to the service of the temple-state, the scribes/sages were economically dependent on the priestly aristocracy. Yet in some of his instructional speeches ben Sira urges fledgling scribes to mitigate some of the effects of the great ones' exploitation of the poor (Sir 3:30–4:10; 13:15–24; 29:8–13; 34:27–34). He also warns them to be wary of the power of their aristocratic patrons (13:1–13; 31:12–32:13). In the relation between priestly rulers and the scribes who advised them, there was thus a potential for overt conflict.

It is not surprising, then, that when a dominant faction of the priestly aristocracy, in closer collaboration with their imperial patrons, re-formed the temple-state as the *polis* of Antioch-in-Jerusalem (in honor of the emperor Antiochus IV Epiphanes), several circles of scribes mounted significant resistance. Best known are the *maskilim*, producers of the ("apocalyptic") visions-and-interpretations in Daniel 7, 8, and 10–12, who suffered martyrdom for their steadfast (nonviolent) resistance. Then, when the Hasmoneans, who had led the Maccabean Revolt, set themselves up as the new high priestly rulers, a group of scribes and priests withdrew in protest in a new "exodus" into the wilderness and set up a renewed covenant community at Qumran.[7]

The Pharisees first make their appearance in Josephus's narratives of the upstart Hasmonean dynasty of high priests as a "faction" (*hairesis*) of scribes in the operation of the temple-state (*Ant.* 13:171–173, 288–298).[8] They evidently played a role similar to that of the scribes as represented by ben Sira. They "established regulations [*nomima*] for the people . . . , from the tradition of the ancestors, that were not written down in the laws of Moses" (*Ant.* 13:288–298, 296–98). The high priest Hyrcanus broke with the Pharisees, rescinded the regulations (*nomima*) they had established for the people, and went over to the party of the Sadducees, who recognized only the regulations that were written down. The Pharisees were then evidently active in the resistance to the continued expansionist wars of Alexander Yannai (103–76 BCE), who retaliated brutally (*Ant.* 13:372–383).[9] But his widow and successor as ruler, Alexandra Salome (76–67 BCE), restored the Pharisees to their role in the operations of the temple-state and reestablished their regulations as official laws of the temple-state (13.401–32).

Because Josephus makes few and only brief references to the Pharisees under Herod's rule and that of the high priesthood in the first century CE, Neusner concluded that the Pharisees withdrew from politics and devoted themselves to piety, particularly in their own scrupulous observance of priestly rules of purity in eating.[10] While they surely lost much of their influence when Herod consolidated power in his own administration, however, the Pharisees evidently continued to play a role in political affairs. Judging precisely from Josephus's brief references, "Pollion the Pharisee" and/or "his disciple Samaias" had spoken out against the arrogant young military strong man Herod for murdering the Galilean brigand-chief and hero, Hezekias (*Ant.* 14.172–76; 15.3–4). They and their Pharisaic disciples ("over 6000 in number") then refused to take the loyalty oath to Caesar and his own rule that Herod had imposed on the populace (*Ant.* 15.368–370; 17.41–45). That Herod, uncharacteristically, did not retaliate for such blatant insubordination suggests not that they had withdrawn from politics but rather that they were still active in the service of the temple-state that Herod had retained. Josephus asserts further (*Ant.* 17.41–45) that this "faction of the Judeans who claim strict observance to the ancestral laws" was influential at Herod's court through the women, particularly his brother Pheroras's wife. But when they prophesied that Herod would be succeeded by Pheroras and his children, Herod executed the Pharisees most implicated.

After the Romans replaced Herodian rule of Judea with the high priestly aristocracy under the oversight of a Roman governor, the Pharisees appear to have regained prominence in the temple-state. This is presupposed in Josephus's references to leading Pharisees playing a significant role in the "provisional government" that attempted to maintain control of Judea and Galilee while pretending to be leading the revolt against the Romans. In his account of events of the revolt in the summer of 66 (*Life* 21–23; *War* 2.411), the phrase "the high priests and the leading Pharisees" appears to be a standing term for the priestly aristocrats and their Pharisaic "retainers" who remained in Jerusalem and were attempting to take control of the situation again. Simon son of Gamaliel, from an illustrious family in Jerusalem and of the Pharisaic party, was evidently very politically adept, such that he could supposedly persuade the council (*koinon*) of Jerusalemites to take a particular course of action (*Life* 190–191).[11] Josephus also mentions several other particular Pharisees who were appointed as envoys dispatched by the high priests Ananus and Jesus, heads of the "provisional government," to deal with affairs in Galilee (*Life* 195–199). Insofar as these Pharisees evidently already had a close working relationship with the leading high priests at the beginning of great revolt in 66, it is clear that the Pharisees had continued in their traditional role as advisers and assistants of the high priestly aristocracy in the governance of Judea during the first century CE.

As with earlier generations of scribes and Pharisees, however, not all were happy with the politics of their high priestly patrons, particularly when they collaborated too closely with the imperial rulers. At the beginning of Roman rule through the high priesthood in 6 CE, the Pharisee Saddok and probably others joined with the scribal teacher (*sophistes*) Judas of Gamla and others in "the fourth philosophy" that organized resistance to the Roman tribute (*Ant.* 18.4–6, 23). There is no justification, however, in collapsing Josephus's distinction between the Pharisees and other scribal teachers who protested or resisted Roman, Herodian, and/or high priestly rule.[12] Judas and others in the "fourth philosophy" agreed in all other respects with the views of the Pharisees, *except* that they had an intense passion for freedom rooted in their devotion to God as their exclusive ruler and master (*Ant.* 18.23). And it accords with Josephus's accounts and other sources, such as rabbinic debates and the Gospel stories, that there were scribes and teachers who did not belong to the faction of Pharisees. Among them were the pious and politically concerned scribes who produced the Psalms of Solomon, who condemned both Hasmonean rule and the Roman domination that ended it. Similarly, at the end of Herod's rule, two of the most renowned and respected teachers inspired their students to cut down the Roman eagle that Herod had erected over the gate of the temple; Herod had them all burned alive for their efforts (*Ant.* 17.149–167; *War* 1.648–655).

In sum, while the Pharisees appear to have been a faction among the scribes who served in the temple-state, there were other learned scribes as well. And among both the Pharisees and other scribes there was a range of stances vis-à-vis the high priestly rulers; some played influential roles in the temple-state, and some mounted protests at key junctures. The scribes and Pharisees would thus have constituted the intellectual-legal-clerical "retainers" who assisted the "governing class" in Lenski's model of "stratification." But this classification does not indicate their particular cultural function, their mediating position between the rulers and Israelite cultural traditions, the inherent tensions between these "retainers" and their high priestly patrons, and the potential conflict between the Judean rulers and their scribal retainers in the overarching imperial situation.[13]

It is important also not to lose sight of what was evidently still the principal function of the Pharisees and other scribes in their service of the temple-state in Roman Palestine. In this case the other sources for the Pharisees and scribes confirm what Josephus says repeatedly, that the Pharisees were viewed generally as the most accurate in knowledge and recitation of the laws.

> [sharing power with Alexandra Salome] the Pharisees, a corps of the Judeans were considered to have greater piety than the others and to be more accurate [*akribesteron*] in reciting [*aphegeisthai,* expounding] the laws [*tous nomous*]. (*War* 1.110)
>
> The Pharisees are considered most accurate in expounding the regulations [*akribeias exegeisthai ta nomina*] and [are] the leading faction/party. (*War* 2.162–163)
>
> The faction/party of the Pharisees differ from the others in the accuracy concerning the ancestral regulations [*ta patria nomima . . . akribeia*]. (*Life* 191)

In these passages Josephus was referring not specifically to the Pharisees' own distinctive "regulations" derived from "the tradition of the ancestors" but more generally to "the laws of the Judeans" ("the laws," in Hellenistic Greek, often being a standing term for the ancestral laws and customs that functioned, in effect, as the polity or "constitution" of a particular state and/or its people). The Pharisees' "accuracy" about the laws should not be construed as reflecting an obsession with purity or other "strict construction" of ancestral regulations. This is the impression that Christian interpreters have taken away from the controversies between Jesus and the Pharisees in the Gospels (to be discussed). As we now know from several of the Dead Sea Scrolls, the priests and scribes of the Qumran community were far more rigorous and strict, and they rejected the Pharisees as "smooth interpreters," that is, as overly lax in their understanding. The rabbinic traditions of the Pharisees similarly represent them as precise but adaptable in their knowledge and application of the ancestral regulations.[14]

The "accuracy" of the Pharisees concerning the laws, moreover, was no mere academic matter but was operative in the politics of the temple-state. As Josephus observed in his summary of the factions/parties of the Judeans at the beginning his history of Judea under the high priestly aristocracy, "The Pharisees . . . are very influential among the city people [*tois demois*, that is, the Jerusalemites] and all prayers and sacred rites are done according to their exposition" (*Ant.* 18.15). Indeed, so influential were the Pharisees at mid-first century that Josephus himself, although he never joined the Pharisees, "practiced politics" according to the party of the Pharisees (*Life* 12).[15] The high priests and other wealthy and powerful figures wielded power in Jerusalem. But their operation of the temple-state, whether in sacred rites or in more "political" matters, proceeded according to the views and rulings of the Pharisees and other scribes that were rooted in ancestral traditions.

Complications from Recent Research

Our understanding of the social location and role of the scribes and Pharisees is now being complicated by the same largely separate lines of recent research that are challenging the previous focus on separate saying as the sources for the historical Jesus, as discussed in chapter 1. The research in these areas is recent enough that interpretation of Jesus, the Pharisees, and the conflict between them in the Gospels has not yet dealt with the implications.

Literacy was severely limited in Roman Palestine, confined basically to scribal circles and the Herodian administrations, and writing was used primarily as an instrument of power by the elite.[16] Even though their professional training in reading and writing is what made them distinctive as scribes, they learned and cultivated texts as well as still-developing (oral) tradition by oral recitation, as recent studies of ancient scribal practice are showing.[17]

This oral cultivation even of texts that were also written on scrolls should help explain some of the key findings from study of the Dead Sea Scrolls. Close examination of the manuscripts of the books of torah and the prophets that were later included in the Hebrew Bible has found not only that multiple textual traditions (in fact, different version) of those books coexisted but that those different versions were all still developing.[18] Moreover, with the notable exception of the *pesherim* of several prophetic books in which the Qumranites applied phrases and figures from the texts to their own historical situation, it is difficult to find interpretation of established scriptural texts in Qumran texts or in other, contemporary Judean texts. The Community Rule and the Damascus Rule, for example, make references to phrases and statements that we recognize from already existing texts but do not then interpret them. Contrary to what has previously been asserted, the rulings and regulations of the Qumran community that appear in their compositions are not derived by interpretation of already authoritative texts of torah. What was found at Qumran instead are alternative texts of torah, such as the Temple Scroll from Qumran or the book of Jubilees. Contrary to the mislabeling by some scholars, moreover, these were not *rewritings* of already existing books such as Genesis, Exodus, Numbers, or Deuteronomy but were *alternative* texts of torah, some of which overlap with the torah found in the books that were later included in the Hebrew Bible.

The combination of these findings of recent researches means not only that the books of Genesis through Deuteronomy (what we have come to think of as "The Torah") had not yet achieved the prominent or exclusive authority they later enjoyed but also that scribes were cultivating torah orally, a repertoire that they then drew upon in composing new texts of Mosaic torah. This means that the Pharisees were not the only scribal group to have cultivated "regulations" (their "tradition of the ancestors") not written in the laws of Moses. The regulations for the conduct of community affairs in the Community Rule and the Damascus Rule from Qumran are parallel. All of these versions of torah—the books later included in the Hebrew Bible, alternative texts of torah, and the regulations promulgated by the Qumran community or "the regulations derived from the ancestors" of the Pharisees—held relative authority for the scribal groups that cultivated them.[19]

All of this information makes for a suggestive comparison with the way Josephus, rarely mentioning "the (written) laws of Moses," refers very generally to "the laws of the Judeans" and "the (ancestral) regulations" or "the laws"—which the Pharisees were understood to know most accurately. Texts of torah written on scrolls, including the Pentateuchal books that were later included in the Hebrew Bible, were indeed laid up in the temple and kept in scribal circles, such as Qumran. But the laws of the Judeans were remembered, recited, and applied in the operation of the temple-state by the scribes, including Pharisees, as a fundamental part of their role in the Judean temple-state.

It is important to note that the scribes' and Pharisees' memorial knowledge and oral recitation of "the laws" are not to be mistaken for the "oral law" in the dichotomy between the "oral" and "written" law that modern scholars have generally applied to the Pharisees' traditions of the elders as opposed to "the laws of Moses" that were written. The concept of "torah-in-the-mouth" was only gradually developed in rabbinic circles, becoming clearly articulated only in Amoraic times, as Martin Jaffee has convincingly argued.[20]

Given the limited literacy and production and cultivation of texts in scribal circles, it seems doubtful that the vast majority of the people who lived in village communities would have had direct contact with the (still developing) texts of torah and prophets. They almost certainly knew of the existence of the authoritative texts laid up in the temple and may well have held them in awe, as happens in societies where writing is rare. That they were nonliterate and had little or no direct contact with written texts, however, does not mean that villagers were ignorant of Israelite traditions. They cultivated their own popular Israelite tradition orally in families and in village communities, as noted in chapter 5. Covenantal commandments and customs constituted the basis for family and community life. Previous scholarly arguments that the (written) Torah was known in Galilee have focused on matters such as observance of the Sabbath and the practice of circumcision. But Galilean villagers hardly needed to be literate to know about and observe the Sabbath, to circumcise their male infants, to honor their fathers and mothers, to refrain from stealing from their neighbors, to leave their fields fallow on the seventh year for the sake of the poor, to celebrate Passover, or to recite stories of Elijah and Elisha.

That Judean and Galilean villagers cultivated their own popular Israelite tradition that differed in various ways from the more "official" Judean (Israelite) tradition cultivated mainly in scribal circles in Jerusalem has particular importance for approaching the conflict between Jesus and the scribes and Pharisees portrayed in the Gospels.[21] These "traditions," both popular and official, were not simply free-floating culture but were the customs, laws, commandments, and stories by which people lived or by which the Jerusalem aristocracy and scribes operated the temple-state and governed the society. They probably had a good deal of parallel "content," and historically there had been regular interaction between them, as when scribes included popular customs and practices, stories, and even dissident figures in their texts. But there would have been differences in emphasis, which may have led to seemingly different patterns of belief and practice. An obvious example might be stories of Elijah and Elisha that would have originated in northern Israel. The stories of these prophets leading the opposition to the Omride kings of the northern kingdom of Israel had been taken up into the (proto-)Deuteronomistic history by the scribes who produced it, which was clearly useful in the court of the Davidic monarchy in Judah as propaganda against the rival monarchy (1 Kgs 17–21; 2 Kgs 1–9). But presumably the northern Israelites continued to tell and retell these stories.

That the Galileans had come under Jerusalem rule only a century before the lifetime of Jesus would have compounded the differences between the "great tradition" cultivated by the scribes and Pharisees in Jerusalem and the Israelite popular tradition of Galilean villagers. Judeans had lived under Jerusalem rule for centuries and under the laws of the temple-state since it was established under the Persian empire. Galileans, on the other hand, who were evidently descendants of the northern Israelites,[22] had been under separate rulers for centuries until they were brought under Jerusalem rule and subjected to "the laws of the Judeans" in 104 BCE. They then lived under Jerusalem rule for just a century before the Romans placed them under Antipas, after the death of Herod, so that the high priesthood in Jerusalem no longer had direct jurisdiction.

Even though Josephus's histories and other sources refer to the inhabitants of Galilee as "the Galileans," as distinguished from "the Judeans," it is often claimed or simply assumed that the Galileans were "Jews." To control the area following the Jerusalem takeover, the Hasmonean high priests and then Herod sent officers and garrisons of Judean soldiers to the fortresses they established in Galilee. Such officers or their descendants may well have been the "gentry" of the area that "the Galileans" drowned in the Sea of Galilee as Herod was conquering his subjects in Galilee (*Ant.* 14.421–430, 432–433, 450; *War* 1.315–316, 326). Antipas also presumably brought Judeans with him into his regime and to the capital cities he (re)built at Sepphoris and Tiberias. There would thus have been at least some Judeans in Galilee during the lifetime of Jesus.

There is no evidence, however, of mass migration of Judeans northward into Galilee during the chaotic last decades of the Hasmoneans and the reign of Herod. Previous claims that prominent priestly families resided in Sepphoris during the first century CE appear to be projections from later sources.[23] The consensus among Jewish historians is that the migration of sages northward to Galilee happened well after the destruction wrought by the Romans in 67–70

CE and probably primarily after the further Roman devastation of Judea in suppressing the Bar Kokhba Revolt of 132–135 CE. In late second-temple times, therefore, community life in the villages of Galilee would have been based on Israelite popular tradition similar to that of the villagers in Judea.

That conclusion does not contradict Josephus's statement that the Hasmoneans required the Galileans to live according to "the laws of the Judeans." The claim that this meant that the Hasmoneans forcibly "converted" the Galileans is another scholarly projection of the construct "Judaism" that obscures historical political-economic-religious relations.[24] It is also utterly unrealistic to imagine that the Hasmoneans were attempting to replace the local and regional (Israelite) customs according to which community life was conducted with "the laws" and "the regulations" and the texts of torah that scribal circles in Jerusalem cultivated. Hasmonean rule of the Galileans was a matter of the relations between the temple-state in Jerusalem and the people of Galilee. "The laws of the Judeans" probably refers to the polity of the Judean temple-state, to which the Galileans were to submit. The implications, probably, would have been primarily about tithes, offerings, and other relations between the villagers and the temple and high priesthood in Jerusalem.

The different history of Galilee raises the question of the Pharisees' role in Galilee. The Synoptic Gospels are the only sources that represent the (scribes and) Pharisees as active in Galilee. By contrast, Josephus portrays them as active in temple-state politics in Jerusalem, the only foray of Pharisees into Galilee being by that undertaken by three members of a delegation from the provisional government in 66–67 CE (*Life* 191–198). It is difficult, from what we know of Hasmonean and Herodian rule in the first century BCE, to imagine historical circumstances in which the Pharisees might have played a role in Galilee that would provide a possible historical basis for the emergence of the controversies between the Pharisees and Jesus that appear in Mark, Matthew, and Luke. The sixty-some years during which the Hasmoneans ruled Galilee were filled with turmoil that preoccupied the regime, which had little energy left to put to consolidating its rule in Galilee. In the three decades after the takeover of Galilee, Alexander Yannai fell into virtual civil war with the scribes (including Pharisees) and others who opposed his perpetual wars of conquest. After the Pharisees were restored to power by Alexandra Salome, civil war erupted between rival Hasmoneans, the Romans conquered Palestine, and again rival Hasmoneans battled for control, with destructive effects on villages and their resources. Herod then established his own administration and subordinated the temple and the high priesthood to it. While the Pharisees evidently still played some role in the affairs of the temple (and even the royal court), it seems highly unlikely that Herod deployed them as representatives of Jerusalem rule in Galilee.

Once the Romans appointed Antipas as ruler of Galilee, the high priesthood in Jerusalem no longer had (direct) jurisdiction over the Galileans. Antipas, concerned about his own revenue base in Galilee, would presumably not have looked favorably on activities by representatives of the Jerusalem temple-state to keep revenues flowing from Galileans to the temple and priests. In building Tiberias, moreover, or at least his palace, which featured Hellenistic-Roman-style décor, he virtually thumbed his nose at the Jerusalem-based guardians of Judean tradition (*Ant.* 18.36–38).

It is nevertheless at least conceivable that, with or without Antipas's tacit permission, the Jerusalem high priesthood delegated Pharisees to devise ways of continuing the flow of revenues to the temple from Galilee, whether in tithes and offerings or in other forms. The device of *qorban*, by which villagers could "dedicate" a portion of their crops (as revenues) to the temple, mentioned in Mark 7:9–13, may have been just such a means by which the Pharisees attempted to secure support for the temple.[25] That the provisional government in Jerusalem, led by the high priests, in the summer of 66 CE immediately sent envoys (initially Josephus) to take charge of affairs in Galilee and that the priests among them thought they were entitled to collect tithes from the Galileans suggests that the Jerusalem high priesthood believed that it had a rightful claim to jurisdiction over Galileans as well as Judeans (*Life* 63, 80; *War* 2.562–569). The Pharisees' work in the temple-state could thus have continued to affect Galileans even after Jerusalem no longer ruled the area, during the lifetime of Jesus and the first few decades during which Jesus traditions developed.

Yet we should not imagine that the Pharisees were regularly active *in* Galilee, much less resident there. Even in the Gospel of Mark, the scribes and Pharisees "come down from Jerusalem" to Galilee (3:22; 7:1) and are assumed to be Judeans resident in Judea in the parenthetical regional reference to "the Pharisees and all the Judeans" (7:3). In John's Gospel as well as in Mark, the Pharisees are assumed to belong in Jerusalem, where they are closely associated with the high priests. The Pharisees were thus not members of village communities in Galilee (or in Judea) on the basis of which they could have been leaders of village assemblies (*synagogai*), whether before, during, or after the mission of Jesus. The Pharisees could thus not have been connected with some sort of "synagogue reform movement," nor could they have been competitors of Galilean leaders such as Jesus.[26]

Nor, solely on the basis of representations in the Synoptic Gospels, can we credibly imagine that the (scribes and) Pharisees visited villages in Galilee (or Judea) when they "came down from Jerusalem" and that they just happened to be present in the house where Jesus healed the paralytic, just happened to see him eating with toll collectors and sinners in Levi's house, and just happened to see him heal a man's withered hand in a village assembly (Mark 2:1–12, 15–17; 3:1–6). The stories of the Pharisees eating with Jesus in Luke are stage settings for debates. The Pharisees' having Jesus under surveillance in Mark lacks historical credibility. Even the references to the (scribes and) Pharisees being "greeted with respect in the *agorai* [city-squares, usually translated as "marketplaces"] and having the best seats in the assemblies and places of honor at banquets" (Mark 12:38–39; Q/Luke 11:43) do not place them in villages. It seems doubtful (e.g., from archaeological excavations) that many villages would have had "city-squares" or banquets. Similarly, the "assemblies" would more likely have been those of the (high) priests and scribes/Pharisees in Jerusalem (as in ben Sira's references).

In sum, it is extremely difficult to tell how much and what kind of influence the (scribes and) Pharisees may have exercised in Galilean (or Judean) village communities. They had some, or they would not be subject to attack in the Gospel materials that presumably derive from Galilean origins. But they cannot be said to have had direct power or authority over Galileans. If we assume that their prominent role in the temple-state resulted in their having some influence on life in Galilee, they would still not have been a leading political or religious force there. They would have been outsiders, representatives of the Jerusalem temple-state. The combination of those factors could have been enough to account for the hostility to them in the Gospels.

Jesus in Conflict with the Pharisees

Again, what are considered the earliest Gospel sources, the Gospel of Mark and the Q speeches, offer somewhat similar representations of the conflict between Jesus and the scribes and Pharisees. While in very different forms, one a sustained story and the other a series of speeches, these two sources both portray Jesus as engaged in the renewal of Israel in opposition to the rulers. And both present the scribes and Pharisees as representatives of the high priestly rulers in Jerusalem. The Gospel of Mark presents the (scribes and) Pharisees as the principal opponents of Jesus and his renewal of Israel in Galilee and beyond before he marches up to Jerusalem, where they play a relatively lesser role. In "coming down from Jerusalem" and later attempting to entrap him in the temple, they are clearly acting as representatives of the high priests. In a series of brief conflicts on various issues, they criticize or challenge Jesus's (or his disciples') actions, setting up his criticisms and/or declarations of principle and even his condemnation in response (Mark 2:[1-] 6–11, 15–17, 18–22, 23–28; 3:22–27; 7:1–13; 10:2–9; 12:13–17). The Q series of speeches includes a set of woes against the scribes (lawyers) and Pharisees, prophetic indictments on various counts that also mock them, and toward the end a pronouncement of judgment against them. It is clear particularly from the latter that they are representatives of the high priesthood and of the temple in Jerusalem. These two sources thus offer very different kinds of Jesus traditions that developed independently into two very different kinds of texts in the Mark story and the Q speeches.

The common features of the two presentations of Jesus's conflict with the Pharisees are thus all the more striking. In both the Markan controversy episodes and the Q series of woes Jesus speaks in the role of a prophet pronouncing principles and/or condemnation. In both he appeals implicitly or explicitly to the commandments of the Mosaic covenant or makes commandment-like pronouncements. In both he presupposes, argues on the basis of, or insists on the practices of the Israelite popular tradition in opposition to the Pharisees, who represent the official position. Jesus is the spokesperson for the Israelite popular tradition against the scribes and Pharisees as representatives or promulgators of the official tradition. In both sources issues of purity are present, but Jesus shifts the focus to political-economic issues, the same issues in both sources. But the controversy episodes and the woes are not just about the difference between the "great" and "little" cultural traditions. Nor are they about keeping purity laws or strict Sabbath observance. They are rather about fundamental political-economic-religious matters such as adequate food, the disintegration of family, and the drain of economic resources to support the temple and the empire at the expense of local needs. We thus have two sources with very different forms both representing Jesus as focusing on the same issues in conflict with the scribes and Pharisees.

Controversies between Jesus and the Pharisees in Mark

The point of the controversy between Jesus and the Pharisees in Mark 2:23–28 is Jesus's strong positive declaration that the Sabbath was made for humankind. This is "set up" by the disciples plucking (and snacking on) heads of grain as they pass through the fields and by the Pharisees' accusation that this "is not lawful on the Sabbath." The first step in Jesus's response seems to broaden the issue and shifts the focus to the conflict between people's hunger and the sacrality of the temple.

Observance of the Sabbath was God's commandment in the Mosaic covenant (Exod 20:8–11; Deut 5:12–15). As with aspects of community life

protected by the other commandments, it was an economic matter, a sev-
enth-day rest from the labor necessary to eke out a subsistence living for each
household. The observance was instituted as a deliberate measure in reaction
against the heavy demands placed on the people's productive labor by ancient
Near Eastern rulers. This is indicated both by the grounding of the observance of the Sabbath rest in memory of the people's hard labor in Egypt (in the
Deuteronomic version, 5:15) and in the second commandment, against serving
other gods (with portions of one's crops taken as offerings and tribute, Exod
20:4–5; Deut 5:8–9). Over the centuries Israelite villagers would have developed certain customs that guided observance of the Sabbath and that became
part of the "common law" of Israelite popular tradition. Some of those customs
were included and adapted in collections of laws made by professional scribes,
as in Exod 34:21 and Deut 23:24–25. Later scribal texts include more extensive
rulings about kinds of labor that are not permitted on the Sabbath.

It may be helpful to examine some of the Israelite customs, scribal
(Deuteronomic or Levitical) adaptations, and later scribal regulations about
working on the Sabbath, particularly those pertaining to plucking grain.[27]
Although it now stands in a scribal collection, Deut 23:24–25 may offer a clue
about what may have been a custom that permitted snacking on one's neighbor's grain or grapes when walking by fields but not harvesting and carrying
away grain or grapes, which would presumably have been a violation of the
commandment against stealing. Found among the Dead Sea Scrolls was a text
fragment containing a Judean scribal ruling from close to the time of Jesus:

> Any destitute [Israelite] who goes into a threshing floor may eat there
> and gather for himself and for [his] hou[sehold. But should he walk
> among grain standing in] the field, he may eat but may not bring it to
> his house to store it. (4Q159 Vermes trans.)

The disciples in the episode about the Sabbath may thus have been following a
custom that permitted plucking/snacking from standing grain.

The Pharisees in the story, however, state that this was not permitted
on the Sabbath and that it is to this objection that Jesus replies. As on most
matters, we have no information about popular customs on this question. But
we do have more wide-ranging scribal rulings regarding work prohibited on
the Sabbath. Following the story of the creation, in which observation of the
Sabbath was grounded (cf. Exod 20:8–11), the second-century BCE book of
Jubilees (2:17–33) prohibits twenty-two kinds of labor. An early rabbinic discussion more than three hundred years later prohibits thirty-nine kinds of labor on the Sabbath (m. Sabb. 7:2, where no text of torah such as Exod 34:21

is cited). The list, however, while it includes agricultural labor such as sowing, reaping, and threshing and preparation of food such as grinding and kneading, does not include plucking of fruit or grain. Would the distinction in Deut 23:25 between plucking a few ears and cutting the grain with a sickle have suggested that in contrast to reaping (and food preparation, which was supposed to be done on the previous day, Jub. 2:29–30), plucking would not have been viewed as work prohibited on the Sabbath? While walking a thousand yards or so was generally allowed, the rigorist scribal-priestly community at Qumran was more restrictive: "No man shall walk in the field to do business on the sabbath" (CD 10:19–20). The Pharisees, however, whom the Qumranites criticized as "smooth interpreters," were presumably not so restrictive. Thus it seems likely that this controversy story in Mark is presenting a caricature of the Pharisees as prohibiting even simple snacks on the Sabbath as a foil for Jesus's declaration about the Sabbath.

In the first step of his response, Jesus challenges or perhaps rather mocks the Pharisees as the professional experts who possess authoritative knowledge of the scriptures, the sacred written texts of the official Jerusalem tradition. Ostensibly astonished by their question, the nonliterate prophet then asks them, "Have you never *read* . . . ?," appealing to one of the stories in the authoritative scripture with which they would presumably be familiar.[28] But the story to which Jesus refers must also have been one of the stories about the brash, young, popularly acclaimed King David that were still told among Galilean and Judean villagers (judging from the several popular messianic movements based on them). The version of the story of David and his men is not the one that the scripturally knowledgeable Pharisees would have known, which was presumably the textual ancestor of the one we know from our critically established text of 1 Samuel.

The text of 1 Samuel in which this story ostensibly occurs (21:1–6) was notoriously "unstable" in antiquity, as suggested by the variations between the received Hebrew text and the standard Greek translation (the Septuagint). As measured by the standard written texts even in their variations, however, Jesus's version of the story is distinctive.[29] Most striking is the displacement of Ahimelech as priest at Nob, when David was a fugitive, by his son Abiathar, who was one of the head priests after David had consolidated his power as king in Jerusalem (compare 1 Sam 21:1–2; 2 Sam 15:35; 20:25; what stands behind 1 Sam 23:6–11 may help explain the confusion of the father and the son). "Jesus's" version in the Markan episode has details that do not appear in the scriptural story (as known from 1 Sam 21:1–6, even with textual variants).

David is accompanied by companions who are hungry; he does not simply ask for bread but presumes to enter the house of God; and he actually eats the bread. Mark's Jesus is not quoting from knowledge of the official written text but taking what he needs from this story of David as known from popular Israelite tradition, in which Jesus, his followers, and Mark's story were all rooted.

"Jesus" also makes the story (that he assumes is also contained in the Pharisees' scripture that they would have "read") fit the situation he is addressing, the relation between the temple and the high priesthood that the Pharisees represent and his own popular movement, which they are attempting to check. He implies that "the house of God" is the temple in Jerusalem, which also fits and is confirmed by the identification of Abiathar as "high priest." Appealing to David's behavior as a precedent that justifies his disciples' action, Jesus has David boldly enter "the house of God" and help himself to "the bread of the Presence." Even a rustic prophet from Galilee would presumably know that this would have been an outrageous violation of the purity regulations that prohibited access to the sanctuary and protected the bread of the Presence. The latter reserved the loaves of the bread of the Presence, placed fresh upon the altar every Sabbath, for the (high) priests: "They shall be for Aaron and his descendants, who shall eat them in a holy place, for they are most holy portions for him from the offerings by fire to the LORD, a perpetual due" (Lev 24:9). David's and his companions' egregious violation of the sacred precincts and their eating of the sacred bread that was "not lawful for any but the priests to eat," moreover, was justified because they "were hungry and in need of food."

Rhetorically, at least, the first step of Jesus's response escalates the issue of observation of the Sabbath in village communities to the level of the sacral economics of the temple-state. The people's need for food is most important, and obtaining food for hungry people justifies even violating the sacrality of the altar. Keeping in mind that the representation of the Pharisees' objection to the snacking here may be somewhat of a caricature, their latter-day successors the rabbis humanely allowed that anyone suffering from ravenous hunger was to be fed on the Sabbath, even with unclean things, "until his eyes brightened" (m. Yoma 8:6).

In Jesus's declaration about the purpose and use of the Sabbath he builds on what presumably stood in the Judean scripture as well as popular tradition, that the Sabbath was grounded in the people's need for rest from heavy labor as well as grounded in God's rest from the labor of the creation (see again Exod 20:4–5; Deut 5:8–9). And perhaps Mark's Jesus knows of scribal positions that would serve the people's interest. The formulation of Jesus's declaration that "the sabbath was created for humankind, not humankind for the sabbath," closely parallels a later scribal statement rooted in the same understanding of the creation: "humankind was not created for the world, but the world for humankind" (2 Bar. 14:18). A saying in later rabbinic literature is similar in substance: "the sabbath is delivered to you, you are not delivered to the sabbath" (Mekilta 109b on Exod 31:14). Jesus's parallel second statement, "so the human one is lord also of the sabbath," draws the conclusion implicit in the first. In synonymous parallelism with "humankind" in the first statement, the idiomatic phrase "the son of man" here evidently means "the human one," as in Mark 2:10. In Mark's story and in the Jesus tradition behind it, these statements of Jesus about the Sabbath are not "Christian" declarations about the Sabbath or of Christology. They are rather renewals of common Israelite tradition, part of Jesus's more programmatic renewal of Israel against the rulers.

In this Markan controversy, Jesus states, in opposition to (what may be a caricature of) the Pharisees as representatives of the official emphasis on the sacrality of the Sabbath as part of the holiness of the temple and priesthood, that people can violate restrictive rules for the sake of human needs such as hunger. Subsistence needs of the people take precedence over the elite's concerns for the protection of the sacred. As a prophet speaking from the Israelite popular tradition, Jesus defends the satisfaction of the most basic needs, such as hunger on the Sabbath, which was created for the restoration of the people's life and labor in the first place.

Again in the controversy in Mark 7:1–13 the Pharisees' and scribes' challenge to Jesus and his disciples (that they eat with "common," that is, "unwashed" hands) is a foil for Jesus's declaration, now about the basic commandment of God. The further discussion of their insistence on following purity regulations in eating adds to the "set-up" for Jesus's response. The opening statement that "the Pharisees and some of the scribes had come from Jerusalem" defines the conflict as one involving the broad divide between the Jerusalem rulers and the villagers, compounded by the fact that Galilee was no longer under their direct jurisdiction. Jesus again speaks as the representative of popular practices and the Israelite popular tradition. That the Pharisees apply and Jesus attacks the "traditions of the elders" makes explicit the divide between the official tradition based in Jerusalem and the popular tradition in which people are embedded. Just that division and the respective interests expressed in the official and the popular traditions are played out in this controversy.

Part of the set-up is an explanation of the purity practices of "the Pharisees and all the Judeans" for the hearers of Mark's story who would not have been familiar with them (perhaps Galileans but certainly Greek speakers in Syria and elsewhere beyond Galilee who had joined the Jesus movement). That the Pharisees and other "Judeans" are buying food in the marketplace (*agora*, city-square) indicates that they are residents of Jerusalem, not Judean villagers who would have been eating food they had raised themselves. And Jerusalem was where the scribes and Pharisees were based, lived, learned, and carried out their service of the temple-state.

Recent analysis of the rabbinic traditions of the Pharisees active before the Roman destruction of Jerusalem and the temple has appreciably clarified their practices in comparison with those of the priests on the one hand and ordinary people on the other.[30] Priests, who served in the temple, were expected to maintain purity rules for the handling and eating of food. But there would have been no reason for ordinary people to be concerned about purity, except when they went to the temple for Passover or one of the other festivals. There is no evidence that ordinary Judeans other than Pharisees or Qumranites were concerned about observing purity regulations in eating or in other matters. In an early rabbinic discussion of washings of hands, foods, and utensils, the Pharisees are lower in the purity hierarchy than priests and their families who eat priestly rations and heave-offerings, and especially the officiating priests who eat holy things from the altar (m. Hag. 2:7). Critically analyzed rabbinic discussions thus suggest that the Pharisees were not rigorists to the same degree as were priests and Qumranites, contrary to older Christian constructions, and that they did not attempt to impose their own practices on the people in general.[31] The statement at the opening of the controversy in Mark 7 that the Pharisees were trying to enforce purity practices on Jesus's disciples may thus be an exaggeration intended to set up Jesus's statement about God's commandment.

The washings and other purity practices of the Pharisees are part of the broader "traditions of the elders" that they accuse Jesus's disciples of failing to observe. These must be more or less the same as "the tradition of the ancestors" mentioned by Josephus, the regulations that the Pharisees had established that were not in the written laws of Moses (*Ant.* 13.296–297, 408; cf. Paul's former zeal for "the traditions of my ancestors," Gal 1:14; Phil 3:5–6).[32] Given that Josephus presents the Pharisees' "traditions of the ancestors" as included in Hasmonean state law and comments that affairs in Jerusalem were conducted according to the views of the Pharisees, the suggestions that "the Pharisees and all the Judeans" observe them in Mark 7:3–5 has a certain degree of credibility. The caricature comes in the focus on purity practices. With this broadening to the more inclusive "traditions of the elders," however, the set-up is complete.

In response, Jesus first attacks "the traditions of the elders" in general. This has been mistaken as an attack on the "Jewish Law" more broadly. But Mark's Jesus is being more precise. He quotes a prophecy of Isaiah, appealing to its authority has having been "written," to set up a contrast between such teaching as the mere tradition of humans and the basic commandment of God. In ancient manuscripts of Mark the text of the lament he quotes (in Mark 7:6–7) is closer to the Septuagint (Jewish Bible in Greek) than to the Hebrew text of Isa 29:13, yet still displays some significant differences.[33] This suggests that the quotation was from memory. Mark's Jesus makes "this people" of the prophetic lament a reference to the Pharisees and scribes. The first lines lend (written!) prophetic authority to the charge that they are "hypocrites." The last line sets up Jesus's accusation that they "abandon the commandment of God and hold to human tradition." Jesus has just shifted the subject from purity practices to the Pharisees' broader "tradition of the elders" in contrast with the commandment of God.

Jesus then intensifies the accusation against the Pharisees and scribes, focusing on one of the most fundamental duties in any society, people's care for their aging parents (7:9–13). This changes the subject again, refocusing the conflict on the use of scarce economic resources. He begins in a sarcastic tone: "You have a fine way of rejecting the commandment of God in order to keep your tradition!" (7:9). He quotes one of the covenantal commandments that Moses had received from God on Sinai, "Honor your father and mother," and adds, from the oldest, most venerable law code in Israelite tradition ("the Covenant Code," known to us in Exod 21–23), "Whoever speaks evil of father or mother must surely die" (7:10; cf. Exod 21:17). In the next two sentences Jesus indicates clearly that this refers to economic support of parents. He further accuses the Pharisees of not allowing people "to do anything for" a parent by siphoning off "whatever support [the parents] might have had from [their children]." The Pharisees are thus "making void" the fundamental "commandment of God" precisely through their "tradition of the elders." And, Jesus asserts, widening the focus to the broader effect of their "tradition of the elders," they are doing many such things.

The way by which the Pharisees are denying economic support to the parents is the device in their tradition of the elders called *qorban*. Used in an oath formula, it meant a dedication to God. According to Josephus, people who had been dedicated to God had to pay large sums to the priests to be relieved of their obligatory service (*Ant.* 4.73; cf. Lev 27:1–8; had creditors so dedicated their debtors?). This reference indicates that the practice was current at the time.[34] For the device to have deprived parents of needed support from their children, the latter must have dedicated part of the family land or its produce to God (for the temple). The Pharisees must have been encouraging the dedication to God/the temple of resources needed locally for the support of family (Jesus purposely focuses on support of parents).

This reconstruction would fit the historical context. After Herod's death the Romans had installed Antipas (not the Jerusalem high priesthood) as ruler over Galilee. This would presumably have severely limited the ability of the high priests and their representatives to demand payment of tithes and offerings from what was now Antipas's tax base. But an alternative way of seeking support that seemed particularly appropriate to the temple would be to encourage *dedication* of a portion of land or its produce. Focusing on the Pharisees' encouraging people to *dedicate* part of their land or produce, Jesus condemned how their advocacy for the temple drained away economic resources needed for the support of families already in economic difficulties.[35]

As the last statement in the controversy indicates, Jesus is condemning the general effect of the scribes and Pharisees—that, in their cultivation and application of the laws, including their "traditions of the elders," they are in effect adding to the exploitation of the people, making void and violating the basic commandment(s) of God that were given to protect the people's economic viability and just social relations.

Other controversies in Mark's stories do not focus so pointedly on economic issues. But in all of them Jesus criticizes the restraining effects of the Pharisees' activities on the people's lives. In the final episode in Jesus's confrontation of the rulers in Jerusalem, however, he again sharply condemns the scribes for "devouring widows' households" (their whole livings), as illustrated in the ensuing poor widow's last penny, for the support of the temple. In Mark Jesus attacks the scribes and Pharisees for the oppressive effect on the people of their role in the temple-state.

Jesus's Woes against the Pharisees and Scribes in Q/Luke 11:39–52

The Q speeches include a series of woes against the scribes (or lawyers) and Pharisees. The sequence and wording of the woes in Matthew and Luke are sufficiently different that it may be impossible to reconstruct the text of the woes with much confidence. Attending to the differences of wording between Matthew 23 and Luke 11:39–52 will thus be helpful in allowing us to sense the possible range of rhetoric and meaning in these accusations.

Interpreters of the "sayings" of Jesus in Q have continued to work within the standard Christian theological scheme of the origins of "Christianity" from "Judaism," which thus determines their readings. Taking the Pharisees (and scribes) as the principal spokesmen for (normative) Judaism, they view "Jesus's" condemnation of the Pharisees as a rejection of Judaism generally. Since the woes include condemnation of "this generation" and "Jerusalem" as well, the condemnation must be of "all Israel."[36] Assuming that "the Law," of which the Pharisees (and scribes) were the official interpreters, was central in Judaism, they find the struggle over "the Law" in Q, especially in the woes, whether or not it is referred to.[37]

Particularly important for those reading the woes through the lens of the standard scheme of Christian origins are the woes against cleansing the outside of the cup and against the tithing of mint, dill, and cumin (Q/Luke 11:39–41, 42). On the assumption that these issues lay at the heart of Pharisaic concerns and focusing particularly on the phrase (in 11:42) "these [i.e., justice and mercy] you ought to have done, without neglecting the others [i.e., tithing the herbs]," some have argued recently that cultic laws such as those concerned with purity and tithing were not being rejected but were being set within a broader context of divine demands.[38] In contrast to the case in Paul, the woes in Q did not break or reject "the Torah" but radicalized it. The Jesus followers who produced Q were thus in effect another Jewish "sect" in competition with the Pharisees.

Another reading through the same standard lens (of Judaism) finds a three-stage development behind the woes against the Pharisees.[39] In the first stage, reflected in Q/Luke 11:39–41, the Q community is still "Torah-observant." But in Q/Luke 11:46, where "loading people within heavy burdens" is understood as referring to the practice of scribal interpretation that multiplies rules, the Q community is rejecting Pharisaic legalism and leadership of the synagogues. Finally, in the more vituperative woes (Q/Luke 11:44, 47–48, 52) the Pharisees are condemned as the very enemies of God's purpose. Yet another reading according to the standard scheme notes that in Q/Luke 11:39–41 the vessels are understood as metaphors for ethical, not ritual, purity, and calling the Pharisees "unmarked graves" uses corpse pollution as a metaphor for moral failing. This suggests that purity is indeed important for the Q community but that it is redefined in ethical terms.

Once we move out of the old scheme of Christian origins and into the ever more complex and precise knowledge of the role of the Pharisees in Roman Palestine that is increasingly available from recent research, a different set of issues emerges in Jesus's woes against the (scribes and) Pharisees. The woes, moreover, like the other teachings of Jesus in the "Source" used by

Matthew and Luke, can now be seen to have been a connected series in one of Jesus's speeches on various issues of concern to communities of Jesus followers. The series of woes in Q/Luke 11:39–52, moreover (even in the different orders in Matthew 23 and Luke 11), can now be seen to have been a string of prophetic indictments followed by a pronouncement of sentence (punishment) in a distinctively Israelite prophetic tradition of such woes.[40] Most of the examples of prophetic woes occur in the earliest layers of the prophetic books of Amos, Micah, Isaiah, and Habakkuk, perhaps coming from oral tradition of the prophets themselves. The form of oracle couples an indictment or series of indictments of rulers or their officers for oppression of villagers in violation of a covenant commandment with a statement of punishment. Some woes are single indictments with statement of sentence, but many come in sets of two, three, or four, followed by a statement of sentence (Amos 6:1–3, 4–6 +7; Isa 5:18–19, 20, 21, 22–23 +24; Hab 2:9–11, 12, 15 +16–17, followed by another woe in 19). That this prophetic form continued in use is indicated closer to the time of Jesus by its appearance in the Epistle of Enoch (1 Enoch 94–102), where the woes against the wealthy and powerful (rulers) appear in sets of three to eight, followed by statements of sentence.[41] Rooted in this tradition of sets of woes, Jesus's woes in Q/Luke 11:39–52 must be taken as a series of related indictments of the scribes and Pharisees, climaxed by a statement of sentence.

Upon close critical examination of the woes, it seems highly questionable that they are about the law/torah at all or about the supposed Pharisaic obsession with purity. Only one of the woes, in the Matthean version (Matt 23:23/ Luke 11:42) even refers to (the weightier matters of) the law (as what the Pharisees have neglected). Only two others mention issues of purity (Q/Luke 11:39, 44), and then in a rhetorical mocking of the Pharisees rather than as the main issue of indictment. The woe in Q/Luke 11:42 begins with reference to tithes, which were a matter not of ceremonial law but of taxes. The reference to "mint, dill, and cumin/every herb" is hyperbole and caricature, seemingly mocking or ridiculing the Pharisees. The focus, however, quickly shifts to an exhortation about justice and compassion. The woe in Luke 11:39–41/Matt 23:25–26 does indeed refer to the Pharisees' concern about ritual purity[42] but quickly makes the vessels into metaphors, explicitly in Luke's version, implicitly in Matthew's. With that shift, however, the issue is no longer purity. That the Pharisees are like "unmarked graves/whitewashed tombs" in Luke 11:44/ Matt 23:27–28 alludes to the Pharisees' concerns about purity. But again purity functions metaphorically, indicting those who are supposedly concerned about it for being themselves a danger to the people. In the only three woes that mention either the law/torah or issues of purity, the focus is on something else—suggesting the need for a closer examination of this series of prophetic indictments.

The rhetorical charge in Luke 11:42/Matt 23:23 that the Pharisees were concerned with even the minor items, which were perhaps not deliberately cultivated, such as mint and herbs, serves to indicate how rigorous they were about the principal cultivated products subject to tithes and taxes, such as grain, on which the very survival of subsistence producers themselves depended. If the scribes and Pharisees, in their service of the temple-state, were still insisting on payment of tithes in addition to the taxes that Galilean villagers were paying to Antipas (or, later, Agrippa I and II), they would indeed have been neglecting compassion and justice in the eyes of hungry villagers. The indictment in this woe alludes to traditional prophetic covenantal exhortation demanding *mispat, hesed, sedeq, 'emet*, known in the "great tradition" from such texts as Hos 4:1; 12:7; Mic 6:8; and Zech 7:9–10: "Thus says the LORD of hosts, 'Render true judgment, show kindness and mercy each to his brother, do not oppress the widow, the orphan, the alien, or the poor'" (Zech 7:9–10). Presumably villagers would have been familiar with this tradition of prophetic call for economic justice, even though they probably had no direct contact with the written texts of the prophets. The charge that the Pharisees neglect justice and compassion, with its allusion to the tradition of prophetic exhortation, following upon the rhetorical mocking of how rigorous they are in advocacy of tithing laws, makes this woe not a dispute about the laws but an indictment of the Pharisees for merciless injustice in their role as legal retainers of the temple-state.

The two woes that appeared to earlier interpreters most clearly to focus on purity rather use the Pharisees' concern about purity in a metaphorical way. How the metaphor works is simplest and clearest in Luke 11:44, while the version in Matt 23:27–28 spells the analogy out explicitly. Alluding to the Pharisees' concern about purity, this woe compares them to unmarked graves, which people do not see, meaning that they are dangerous in ways the people cannot see or detect. The simple simile in Luke 11:44 then aids us in discerning what may have been intended in the woe in Luke 11:39–41/Matt 23:25–26. Again mocking their concern about purity, which villagers would hardly have shared, this woe charges the Pharisees with nothing less than "extortion and rapacity." This ominous indictment, like the one about tithing, evidently pertains to how they operated in their political-economic role as legal retainers of the temple-state.

The remaining woes, which do not allude to the law or purity, focus on yet other aspects of the scribes/lawyers' and Pharisees' role as retainers of the temple-state in Jerusalem. It would have been irritating to villagers that the scribes and Pharisees who advocated rigorous payment of tithes, thus in effect pressing them to the limits of subsistence, then presumed to expect honor and deference in public places, the indictment in Luke 11:43/Matt 23:6 (similarly Mark 12:41–44).

The "heavy burdens" in Luke 11:46/Matt 23:4 were not the multiplication of rules by legalistic Pharisees but rather the burdens of tithing and other dues. As discussed earlier, one of the functions of the scribes and Pharisees was knowledge and application of "the laws of the Judeans" that governed the relations between the villagers and the temple-state, including tithes and offerings. The reference to the Pharisees/lawyers' not touching those burdens with one of their fingers is thus an allusion to how the scribal retainers could alleviate the burdens of the peasant producers, if only they would, with a flick of the scribal pen in their fingers.

To interpreters who based their knowledge of Israelite tradition and life in Palestine under Roman rule mostly on the books later included in the Hebrew Bible, the woe in Luke 11:47–48/Matt 23:29–32 may have appeared to be rhetorical exaggeration. Few of the "canonical" prophets as known in the Hebrew Bible were persecuted and none killed. As noted, however, in late second-temple times both the "great tradition" cultivated in Jerusalem and the popular tradition cultivated in village communities were still developing and were far more diverse than what was delimited in the later "canonization." It is clear from such texts as the Martyrdom of Isaiah and the Lives of the Prophets that legends of the prophets' persecution and martyrdom were being actively cultivated.[43] Of the five prophets said to have been martyred under kings, the three said to have been in Jerusalem were Isaiah, Amos, and Zechariah son of Jehoiadas, who is the last prophet to appear in the Lives. According to the legend, moreover, he was supposedly killed "near the altar" (23:1).[44]

Memory of the prophets, moreover, was being cultivated in monuments as well as in legends. Contemporaries claimed to know the burial places of the prophets. It is not hard to imagine that the building of memorials to the prophets was part of the wider program of building under Herod and his successors. The ostentatious religious-cultural renaissance of buildings and monuments inaugurated by Herod, such as the entrance to David's tomb (*Ant.* 7.392–394; 16:179–188), was sustained by wealthy diaspora Jews and prominent proselytes from abroad (*Ant.* 20:95; *War* 5:55, 119, 147).[45] Assuming that the temple-state supervised the monuments to patriarchs and matriarchs and prophets, responsibility for their maintenance very likely fell to the scribal retainers. A latter-day popular prophet such as Jesus and his hearers, however, would have been understandably resentful at such ideological mystification. In the social memory of villagers it would have seemed ironic and hypocritical for the representatives of the current rulers to be cultivating the memorials of the prophets who had been persecuted and martyred by earlier rulers.

The woe that prefaces most of the others in Matthew's version (23:13) and concludes them in Luke's version (11:52) is a comprehensive indictment that sums them up. The phrase "shutting the kingdom of heaven" and "taking away the keys of knowledge" are parallel, equivalent expressions. As in key prophetic phrases (e.g., Isa 1:2–3), "knowledge" here refers to covenant keeping, which would be synonymous with living under or according to the kingdom of God/heaven. The woe indicts the Pharisees for blocking the way in their role as retainers so that the people cannot enter the kingdom (now being proclaimed and manifested in Jesus's mission).

The whole set of woes thus constitutes a series of prophetic indictments of the scribes and Pharisees, deeply rooted in Israelite prophetic tradition, for the ways in which they contributed to the exploitation of the people, only some of which are related to their special function of knowing the laws most accurately.

The declaration of sentence with which the woes climax in Luke 11:49–51/Matt 23:34–36 is, similarly, no mere dispute about the laws but a prophetic pronouncement of judgment. The judgment is harsh in tone, like those in the Israelite prophetic tradition in which it is rooted. Its repetition from the immediately preceding woe of the charge of killing the prophets provides the link between indictments and sentence. Jesus's prophetic lament over the Jerusalem ruling house in Q/Luke 13:34–35 refers to the same charge. It is evident elsewhere in the speeches (e.g., Q/Luke 7:18–35) that John the Baptist and Jesus were understood as the final ones in the long line of martyred Israelite prophets (Q/Luke 6:22–23).

That the blood of the martyred prophets is required of "this generation" has led some interpreters to imagine that the sentence condemns "all Israel" or "Judaism." But this is only another reading that results from the synthetic construct of "Judaism." "This generation" (or "this kind," *taute genea*) appears to have been a contemporary idiomatic expression the meaning of which must be determined from the immediate context and other contexts in Q speeches and the other Gospels. The term has a broad general reference in Mark 8:38 (pejorative) and 13:30 (neutral). It refers to the disciples in Mark 9:19 and to the Pharisees in "this generation's" request for a sign in Mark 8:12, which has a parallel in the Q speeches in Q/Luke 11:29–32. If Matt 12:38 represents the order of Q as preface to the Q version of the request for a sign,[46] then the Q speech focused on the request for a sign also uses "this generation" in reference to the Pharisees in that connection. Significantly, the only other use of "this generation" in the Q speeches occurs in a court context of adversarial address, suggesting figures such as scribes and Pharisees (Q/Luke 7:31–35). The Q speeches thus appear to be fairly consistent in using "this generation" to refer directly or indirectly to scribes and Pharisees.[47] "All Israel" is not implicated. As in earlier prophetic woes and sentences, so in Jesus's woes and sentence, the indictments and punishment are against the rulers and/or their representatives. The sentence in Q/Luke 11:49–51 appears to include the Jerusalem rulers along with the scribes and Pharisees.

Jesus's Conflict with the Scribes and Pharisees

Critical attention to the overarching political-economic-religious structure of life in Palestine under Hellenistic and Roman imperial rule has led to an appreciation both of the fundamental divide between the urban-based rulers and the villagers they ruled and of the conflictual dynamics this set up (discussed in chapter 2). This opened into a more historically appropriate understanding of the broader historical context and the political-economic-religious structure in which the sources for the scribes and Pharisees can be read with new eyes. It is increasingly clear that the Pharisees and other learned scribes functioned as intellectual-legal "retainers" of the Judean rulers, as advisers and representatives of the priestly aristocracy thoroughly trained in the cultural heritage for service in the temple-state. Josephus's accounts of the Pharisees present them in just such a role, not just under the Hasmoneans but also under Herod and the high priestly aristocracy in the first century CE. Finally, taking into account important research in the limited literacy, the uses of writing, and scribal practices, we can understand the political as well as the cultural-religious importance of the scribes' knowledge and application of "the laws of the Judeans" for the operation of the temple-state.

The scribes and Pharisees played an important, sometimes mediating role in the politics of Roman Palestine, as indicated in chapter 2. On the one hand they assisted the high priestly rulers of Judea put in place by the imperial rulers. As the professional guardians of the ancestral Judean laws and traditions on the other hand, they probably were a source of some restraint on their high priestly patrons, even engaging in active resistance at key points. As mentioned earlier, most of the Judean (scribal) texts produced in late second-temple times, particularly "apocalyptic" texts, are sharply critical of the high priesthood. At key junctures, when the high priests collaborated too closely with the imperial rulers, at least a few scribal teachers and even some Pharisees mounted resistance. Generally, however, scribes and Pharisees served the temple-state and in that role were suspect and evidently were resented by the people. The most dramatic illustration of this came at the beginning of the revolt against the high priestly rulers and Roman rule in the summer of 66 CE. According to Josephus's account of the revolt, some of the dissident scribal teachers who had formed the group known as the Sicarii made a bid to lead the revolt. The ordinary people, however, attacked them and drove them out of Jerusalem, at which point they withdrew to the fortress of Masada and sat out the rest of the revolt. It seems that the scribes and Pharisees, who were based in Jerusalem, had little or no rapport with villagers and ordinary Jerusalemites, despite Josephus's statements that they were (at times) allied with the "people" of Jerusalem.

Jesus's conflict with the scribes and Pharisees fits just this picture of Roman Palestine. Mark's story and the series of speeches in Q provide very different kinds of Jesus traditions attesting his sharp conflict with the (scribes and) Pharisees. Contrary to the previous reading of these sources as focused on purity laws and other legalisms, these two different kinds of Jesus traditions exhibit parallel challenges to the scribes and Pharisees. They both rhetorically mock or caricature the Pharisees' concern about ritual observance and the practice of purity—which was misunderstood as conflict over the Law of Judaism by modern scholars. Both the controversies in Mark and the series of woes in Q focus, however, on Jesus's sharp criticism and condemnation of the effect that the scribes' and Pharisees' role as representatives of the temple-state has on the people.

If, as historians, we then "triangulate" from these two sources that offer similar portrayals of Jesus's conflict with the Pharisees, we can project a somewhat similar general picture. Jesus, the Israelite prophet in Galilee, deeply rooted in and a spokesperson for the Israelite popular tradition and particularly for the Mosaic covenantal principles that protected villagers' interests, uttered prophetic woes and other prophetic statements that condemned the scribes and Pharisees for the restrictive and debilitating effects on the people of their service to the temple-state. Especially in the Markan controversies, Jesus's criticism of the scribes and Pharisees is based on Mosaic covenantal commandments, and he reasserts those commandments or makes commandment-like pronouncements. Jesus's conflict with the scribes and Pharisees is thus closely linked to his renewal of the Mosaic covenant at the center of his renewal of Israel against the rulers of Israel. The "flip side" of his renewal of the Mosaic covenant in village communities was his condemnation of the Pharisees and scribes for enabling the expropriation of resources needed by families and village communities to support their subsistence living. Ironically, the learned scribes and Pharisees who served as the established guardians of the laws of the Judeans that were supposedly rooted in Mosaic covenantal torah were facilitating the rulers' exploitation of the people whose life was guided by that same Mosaic covenantal torah in its popular version.

7. The Crucifixion as Breakthrough

At the end we come back around to what seems most certain about the historical Jesus: he was crucified by order of the Roman governor, Pontius Pilate. Recent interpretations of Jesus, particularly those focused on his sayings, have difficulty explaining the crucifixion, especially relating it to Jesus's teaching. Given the prevailing depoliticization, many interpreters ignore or deemphasize or reject as secondary Gospel traditions of Jesus's condemnation of the rulers. Neither of the two most prominent lines of recent American interpretation of Jesus, for example, can explain why Jesus would have been crucified. Judging from what we know about the Roman practice of crucifixion, the governors of Judea would not have crucified either a sage who taught an itinerant individual lifestyle or an apocalyptic visionary who preached the "end of the world." Interpreters can thus discern no direct relation between Jesus's "ministry" and his crucifixion and the formation and expansion of his movement(s).

The Gospel sources, on the other hand, Mark and the other narrative Gospels and the Q speeches present Jesus's death as the integral result of his mission of renewal of the people in opposition to the rulers. Further analysis of the Gospels' presentations, following the relational approach being developed in these chapters, suggests that Jesus's "speaking truth to power" and his crucifixion not only were the climax of his mission but also constituted the "breakthrough" that energized the rapid expansion of the movement of renewal that Jesus had begun. Discerning this integral relation of Jesus's prophetic condemnation, his crucifixion, and the expansion of his movement requires appreciation of three relational realities not usually considered: the purpose of crucifixion in a charged situation of conflict, the effects of coercive power (exemplified by the dehumanizing crucifixion) on subject peoples, and the role of a leader in articulating the people's resentment and desire for dignity in the face of power. As a concluding step in a more relational and contextual approach to the historical Jesus, we again read the Gospels as sustained narratives, critically considering their obvious embellishments and critically comparing the representations in the different early sources (as discussed in chapter 1). And again we analyze the portrayals in the Gospel sources in the context of the historical crisis of the Galilean and Judean people and the Judean temple-state that resulted from the Roman conquest and imperial rule of Palestine.

Clearing the Way

The failure to discern the relation between Jesus's mission and his crucifixion and his movement is partly a result of the individualism that dominates most interpretation of Jesus. It is also a result of the continuing influence of the standard theological scheme of Christian origins, in which the crucifixion is understood as a debilitating defeat for the disciples, followed by the resurrection of Jesus that inspired them to start a movement (the birth of the "church"). It is thus important to note that the Gospel sources do not suggest either that the disciples felt defeated by the crucifixion or that "the resurrection" was what inspired them to form "the church."

A few text fragments have appeared to suggest that the disciples felt defeated prior to "the resurrection" only because they were taken out of literary context. At the last supper in Mark's narrative Jesus predicts that the disciples will all become deserters after he is arrested, which indeed they do (14:27, 50). Mark's story, however, clearly presents their desertion as a response to his arrest, not to his crucifixion, and the motif may have been influenced by a prophecy (that we recognize as from Zech 13:7). In the broader context of Mark's story, moreover, the disciples' desertion, preceded by their failure to watch with Jesus in Gethsemane and followed by Peter's denial, is the climax of the Gospel's subplot of the disciples' failure to understand and follow Jesus that gradually unfolds through the narrative. It thus cannot be attributed to a memory of the disciples' desertion, as if it were rooted in a feeling of defeat in anticipation of the crucifixion. Matthew's Gospel more or less follows Mark's narrative.

In the "Emmaus road" legend in Luke (24:13–35) two followers of Jesus express disappointment that this "prophet mighty in deed and word," who they believed "was the one to liberate Israel," was crucified (24:19–21). This episode, however, *follows* the announcement by the two men "in dazzling robes" at the empty tomb that Jesus is alive; the two followers have already heard the women's report that Jesus is indeed alive. Only when "the stranger" breaks bread with them do they recognize him. This episode thus seems to be less a memory of the discouragement of the disciples in general than a story meant to strengthen subsequent believers' recognition of the risen Jesus in the celebration of the Lord's Supper.

Another legend taken to suggest that the disciples were downcast following the crucifixion is the episode in John's story in which the disciples meet in a house behind locked doors (20:19–23). But in the Gospel of John this meeting *follows* the episode of the empty tomb, in which "the other disciple . . . saw and believed" and, after Mary Magdalene encountered the risen Jesus, she told (the rest of) the disciples. John's narrative, moreover, says explicitly that "the doors were locked for fear of the Judeans" (the high priests and Pharisees, who are hostile to Jesus and his movement throughout the Gospel), not because the disciples were downhearted following the crucifixion. It is thus difficult to find any support in the Gospel sources for the previously standard interpretation that crucifixion left the disciples feeling defeated.

Nor do the Gospel sources provide support for the previously standard view that it was the "resurrection" of Jesus that motivated the formation of a movement. Given the variety of references in the Gospels and other texts to the "empty tomb" or the "exaltation" or "enthronement" or "appearances of the (exalted) Lord," it is by no means clear that there was a common understanding of "the resurrection" in general or of "the resurrection" of Jesus in particular. The Q speeches make no mention of any sort of resurrection of Jesus. In the Gospel of Mark, after multiple episodes in which Jesus confronts the high priests and their representatives in the temple and a lengthy narrative of his arrest, trials, mocking, and crucifixion, the story ends with a brief episode at the empty tomb. The point emphasized in the episode, moreover, is that Jesus is going ahead of the disciples to Galilee— where they would presumably continue the movement of renewal that he and they had already started (Mark 16:1–8).

The Gospel of Matthew makes Jesus's renewal-of-Israel movement more programmatic with the five major speeches. To the empty-tomb scene the Gospel adds merely that "Jesus met them," that is, the disciples (28:9), and ends with Jesus's brief commission to expand the movement by making "disciples of all peoples." In the visionary appearances of Jesus that the Gospel of Luke adds to the empty-tomb story (24:13–35) Jesus gives instruction for a movement of renewal already under way and about to expand (in the book of Acts). After Jesus ascends into heaven at the beginning of Acts, the movement receives further inspiration, but from the outpouring of the Holy Spirit, not from "the resurrection." In John, the only Gospel with clearly bodily resurrection appearances, Jesus's appearance to the disciples behind locked doors is to transmit the Holy Spirit by breathing on them (20:19–23). As in the other Gospels, however, the movement is already well under way, specially instructed by the "farewell discourses" (John 13–17). In fact, all of these Gospel sources portray Jesus as generating a movement that continues on through the crucifixion, not one inspired by "the resurrection."

The Purpose of Crucifixion

Crucifixion, a distinctively Roman form of execution, was designed to terrorize subject peoples into submission. It was the most brutal mode of execution in antiquity, "the most wretched of deaths" (Josephus, *War* 7.203). Roman officers had the victim beaten beforehand, then forced him to carry the cross or the crossbeam to the public site of execution. They then nailed or bound the victim by his arms to the beam, which was raised up and affixed to the stake. With the victim's body partly supported by a peg on the upright, the soldier-executioners then bound or nailed the victim to the stake with an iron nail through the heels. Only after several days of excruciating pain and asphyxiation would the victims finally die. The asphyxiation could be hastened by a severe blow that broke the lower legs. While hung on crosses, the victims might well become carrion for birds and animals of prey. As Seneca commented, being "fastened to the accursed tree" meant "wasting away in pain, dying limb by limb, letting out life drop by drop, . . . swelling with ugly weals on shoulders and chest, and drawing the breath of life amid long-drawn-out agony" (*Ep.* 101). Crucifixion, "that most cruel and disgusting penalty" (Cicero, *Verr.* 2.5.165), was thus a method of slowly torturing the victims to death.[1]

The Romans' purpose in using this utterly dehumanizing form of execution was to intimidate their slaves and subjugated provincials into submission. After the slave revolts in Italy the elite Romans carried out mass crucifixions for their "demonstration effect" in deterring further revolts by the ever larger gangs of slaves on the expanding estates of the Roman patricians (Livy, 22.33.2; 33.36.3). They crucified 450 slaves after the first revolt in Sicily and 6,000 more along the Appian Way from Capua to Rome following the Romans' defeat of the revolt led by Spartacus. As Quintilian (c. 35–95 CE) commented, "Whenever we crucify the guilty, the most crowded roads are chosen, where the most people can see and be moved by this fear. For penalties relate not so much to retribution as to their exemplary effect" (*Decl.* 274). More than a century later, under Nero, the Senate revived the custom of executing all the slaves of a household (which might number in the hundreds) if a slave killed the master (Tacitus, *Ann.* 13.32.1).

In the provinces the Romans used crucifixion, along with slaughter and enslavement, to terrorize conquered peoples into submission. In the generations before, during, and after the lifetime of Jesus, Galileans and Judeans knew very well what would happen to those who resisted Roman rule. In retaliation against the revolt in 4 BCE, the Roman general Varus crucified about two thousand people, after destroying villages and killing the inhabitants, as noted in chapter 3 (*War* 2.75; *Ant.* 17.295; cf. T. Mos. 6:9). Roman governors periodically staged crucifixion of insurgents to deter further resistance. In the 40s CE the governor Tiberius Alexander crucified James and Simon, sons of Judas of Gamla, who had led the refusal to pay the Roman tribute in 6 CE (*Ant.* 20.102). In the 50s, after capturing the brigand-chief Eleazar (who had led an insurgency), Felix crucified many other "brigands" (the Roman term for insurgents as well as brigands; *War* 2.253; *Ant.* 20.160–161). During the siege of Jerusalem in 70 CE, the Roman general Titus had fugitive Jerusalemites "scourged and subjected to torture of every description, before being crucified opposite the walls . . . in the hope that the spectacle might induce the Judeans to surrender" (*War* 5.446–451).

The Crucifixion of Jesus

While Jesus was crucified by the Roman governor evidently for serious disruption of the imperial order, key aspects of the Gospels' portrayal are quite incredible, embellishments that added to the expanding significance of the traumatic event for Jesus movements.[2] It would thus be pointless to critically analyze each episode for the residue of "what really happened." Yet it may be helpful to separate embellishments from the features of the Gospels' portrayals that do have some historical verisimilitude in order then to focus on how the crucifixion of Jesus may have been the key event in Jesus's mission and movement.[3]

Most historically diversionary—and later historically tragic in their effects—are the Barabbas episode and the related motifs of Pilate's washing of hands and "the Jews'" guilt for Jesus's crucifixion. There is no evidence other than the Gospels narratives for Pilate's or any other Roman governor's custom of releasing a prisoner at Passover. No Roman governor would have released "a rebel who had committed murder during the insurrection" any more than he would have released an agitator who had just disrupted temple business.

As often noted, moreover, the Gospels' portrayal of Pontius Pilate's actions cannot be squared with what is known of him from other sources. Josephus supplies accounts of a tough, almost impulsive, hard-bitten governor. In a series of provocative actions, he sent his troops into Jerusalem bearing their standards with images offensive to the Judeans, he funded construction of an aqueduct by expropriating funds from the temple treasury, and he resorted to deception for brutal crowd control (*War* 2.169–177; *Ant.* 18.55–62). The Gospels' representations of Pilate have thus seemed apologetic, even a white-wash. It seems unlikely that Pilate would have "wished to satisfy the crowd" (Mark 15:15) or found Jesus innocent (Luke 23:13–22) or "washed his hands" of the matter (Matt 27:24).

From what we know of the collaboration between the high priests and the Romans who maintained them in power, it seems likely that the high priests may have attempted to influence Pilate. But it is unlikely that a crowd in Jerusalem at Passover to celebrate the people's exodus deliverance would clamor for the execution of a prophet who had pronounced God's judgment against the injustices of the highly unpopular high priests. The portrayal of the crowd's role in the trial of Jesus, moreover, stands in tension with their portrayal as be-ing "spellbound by his teaching" and the high priests being afraid of the crowd in the preceding episodes of confrontation (11:18, 32; 12:12, 37).

Pilate's verdict of Jesus's innocence, his own innocence of Jesus's death, and his placing the blame instead on "the Jews," like the whole Barabbas epi-sode, were the inventions of the movements of Jesus's followers. It seems like-ly that these were defensive reactions by Jesus movements (some now called "Christians") following the great revolt against Roman rule in 66–70 CE. Uneasy about their own loyalty to one who had been crucified as an insurgent against Roman rule, they were probably eager to dissociate themselves from the rebellious Judeans in Palestine after the Roman destruction of Jerusalem. Tragically, these features of the Gospel narratives became a principal basis for later Christian doctrine that the Jews were guilty of deicide and for centuries of Christian anti-Judaism that eventually led to the Nazi Holocaust.

From what we know about Roman crucifixions in general and Roman rule in Judea, however, some features of the Gospels' portrayal of Jesus cruci-fixion have some measure of historical verisimilitude. It is significant that two (other) "brigands" (not "thieves") were crucified at the same time. Insofar as the Romans routinely used the term "brigands" for rebels or agitators against their rule, these "brigands" may actually have been insurgents or brigands-turned-insurgents, such as Eleazar ben Dinai. Moreover, since Roman soldiers com-monly broke the legs of the crucified, it may have been memorable that Jesus's legs were not broken, for whatever reason (cf. Gospel of Peter 4:13–14; distinc-tive twist in John 19:31–37).

It also seems likely that the high priests would have collaborated in some way in the arrest of Jesus. Josephus's account of Jesus suggests as much: "Pilate, upon hearing him accused by men of the highest standing among us, condemned him to be crucified" (*Ant.* 18.63). Caiaphas in particular seems to have worked well in tandem with Pontius Pilate. While Roman governors of Judea usually appointed a new high priest shortly after they took office, Pilate left Caiaphas in his position for another ten years, throughout his own tenure as governor, despite his own repeated trampling on Judean sensibilities (see Philo, *ad Gaium* 302). In Josephus's account of another rustic prophet a generation later, Jesus son of Hananiah, who was pronouncing woes against Jerusalem, the high priests arrested and beat the prophet and then handed him over to the governor Albinus (62–64 CE; *War* 6.302–305). This provides a parallel to the Gospel accounts that the high priests were involved in the arrest of Jesus and handed him over to the Roman governor.

Josephus's account of Jesus son of Hananiah also suggests that the Gospel accounts of Jesus's hearing before Pilate have at least general historical verisimilitude. After Jesus son of Hananiah was handed over by the high priests, the governor Albinus interrogated him but, in his case, decided not to execute him since he seemed to be merely a maniac who was prophesying doom. If this case was typical of the handling of prophets that seemed dangerous, it seems likely that Jesus of Nazareth would have been beaten (by order of Pilate). Whether he underwent a trial before a high priestly council is not clear. He may well have been interrogated by Pilate. That he was crucified, not stoned, of course, means that he was executed by the Romans and not by "the Jews."

Why Jesus Was Crucified

Perhaps the most prominent interpretation of Jesus's death is that he was crucified because he claimed to be or was acclaimed by his followers as "Messiah" ("Christ," in Greek).[4] That Jesus was the Christ/Messiah was one of the "Christologies" of nascent "Christianity." The apostle Paul refers to Jesus as "Jesus Christ," almost as if "Christ" is part of his name (although Paul uses "Lord" as his title). The Gospels of Matthew, Luke, and John all portray Jesus as a/the messiah, as well as a prophet, and locate him in the lineage of David, the prototypical king of Judah and Israel. That Pilate reportedly crucified Jesus as "king of the Judeans" (the title on the cross) has influenced the view that Jesus was crucified as a/the messiah.

Contrary to what was still assumed little more than a generation ago, however, there was no standard "Jewish expectation" of "the Messiah" that Jesus could have fulfilled. In Judean texts from late second-temple times the term "messiah" appears only rarely, and some of those occurrences, including in the Dead Sea Scrolls, refer to multiple "messiahs."[5] There are only a few texts that attest any expectation of "a/the messiah" among the literate elite. But several popular figures acclaimed as "kings" by their followers led regional revolts in 4 BCE and as part of the great revolt in 66–70, as discussed in chapter 2.[6] The question must thus be reformulated: might Jesus have been acclaimed by his followers as a popularly "anointed" king leading a revolt?

The earliest sources offer virtually no support for the idea that Jesus was crucified as a popularly acclaimed (or "anointed") king. Nothing in the Q speeches suggests that Jesus was understood as a popular king/messiah, much less executed as such. Like John the Baptist, he was killed as one in a long line of Israelite prophets (7:18–35; 11:47–51; 13:34).

The Gospel of Mark suggests that Jesus was understood by at least some followers, perhaps even some of the disciples, as a popular king. Jesus seems to step into the role of such a king in the entry to Jerusalem, riding on an ass, in allusion to the prophecy of Zechariah (9:9; Mark 11:1–10). But the followers' singing of a Passover psalm is at best only an indirect acclamation of Jesus as king. And in Mark's narrative this "demonstration" of a longing for liberation at the Passover celebration of the exodus is not what leads the high priests or the Roman governor to move against Jesus. In Mark's "subplot" of the disciples' misunderstanding of Jesus's mission, Peter acclaims Jesus as "the messiah." But when Peter protests Jesus's announcement of his imminent execution, Jesus sharply rebukes him, bluntly rejecting the role of a popular king leading a revolt (8:31–33). In his subsequent rejection of the request of James and John for prominent positions in Jesus's kingdom, he further rejects the whole idea of a kingship of power-holders (10:32–45).

The episodes in Mark's "passion" narrative are historically the least reliable parts of the Gospel, as noted earlier. It is not clear that there ever was a trial before the high priests, nor would it have been known what had been said. But even the trial of Jesus before the council as imagined in Mark (14:61–65) does not suggest that he was killed for claiming to be a/the messiah. The High Priest asks him, "Are you the messiah, the son of the Blessed One?" Jesus answers, "I am" but immediately adds, "and you will see the 'son of man' seated at the right hand of Power, and coming with the clouds of heaven" (author's trans.). At those words "the High Priest tore his clothes and said, 'You have heard his blasphemy!'" and the council condemned him as deserving death. Thus, in this episode, the offense for which the high priests condemn him is evidently his having blurted out the prophetic vision of "the son of man seated at the right hand of Power," not the threat to destroy and rebuild the temple or an admission that he is "the messiah." In the vision-and-intepretation in Daniel 7 "the one like a son of man" enthroned beside God was interpreted as a symbol for the restoration of Israel to sovereignty, as the oppressive imperial kings were condemned in the divine court of judgment (7:15–27). The specter of impending divine judgment would have been threatening to the high priests, collaborating as they were in Roman imperial rule. And of course it fits well with the mission of Jesus as portrayed in the earlier narrative in Mark, the renewal of Israel in opposition to the rulers.

When, in the Markan narrative, the council hands Jesus over to Pilate, the high priests "accused him of many things" but do not mention either the charge that he claims to be "a/the messiah" or the charge of "blasphemy." Pilate, however, immediately asks him, "Are you the king of the Judeans?" to which Jesus answers, "You say so." The form of Pilate's question is that of a Roman outsider. As in their appointment of Herod as "king of the Judeans," the Romans viewed the people in Israelite Palestine generally as "Judeans." It is at least conceivable that governors such as Pilate knew of the popularly acclaimed kings who had led revolts as "kings of the Judeans" thirty-some years earlier. But we can only speculate whether Pilate took Jesus as another one of those popular kings. The high priests would have known, as did the servant girl (Mark 14:66–69), that Jesus was a Galilean who had only just come up to Jerusalem at Passover. When they mock him from the foot of the cross, they call him "king of Israel." That the narrative presents this explicitly as mockery, however, suggests that Pilate is also contemptuously mocking Jesus with the term "king of the Judeans," which he also posts as the official charge on the cross. The soldiers' taunting Jesus by dressing and crowning him as a king and bowing down in homage only continue the mockery begun by Pilate in the previous episode. Even if Pilate and/or the high priests took Jesus as a popular king, the Gospel of Mark does not portray Jesus as a popular king leading a revolt. In fact, Mark represents Jesus as pointedly rejecting such a role.

Further indications that Jesus was not understood as the messiah when he was crucified are evident in the speeches supposedly delivered by Peter in the book of Acts. Although these speeches will have been "overwritten" in the composition of Acts, they include the early tradition that Jesus was understood as "(the) anointed" only after his crucifixion and his exaltation/vindication by God. In one speech he lacks the title "messiah" (Acts 5:30–31). In another Jesus is designated "the messiah appointed," but pointedly *after* he had been handed over, had suffered, and had been glorified (Acts 3:11–21). Yet another speech represents God as making him "both Lord and Messiah" only after he was raised up and exalted at the right hand of God (Acts 2.32–36). Moreover, this speech presents Jesus's actions that led up to his crucifixion as "deeds of power, wonders, and signs" (3:22–24), that is, those not of a messiah but of a prophet like Moses. The early sources thus provide little or no indication that Jesus was crucified as a sort of popularly acclaimed king.

Jesus was executed, according to the early Gospel sources, because of his prophetic actions as well as his pronouncements against the temple, the high priests, and the tribute to Rome. The sources portray a direct relation. In Jesus's prophetic statements included in the Q speeches, as discussed in chapter 2, Jesus pronounces God's judgment of the Jerusalem rulers for having killed the prophets (Q/Luke 11:49–51; 13:34–35). The pronouncements clearly imply that Jesus himself stands in the long line of Israelite prophets killed by the rulers in Jerusalem because of their pronouncements. Of course, if all Jesus had done was to make pronouncements against the temple from this or that village in Galilee, he would merely have been building up the "hidden transcript" of Israelite popular tradition. To have been crucified by the Roman governor of Judea, however, it was necessary for him to have journeyed to Jerusalem, where his disruption, whatever its scale, would have come to the attention of the high priests and the governor. As portrayed in the Gospel sources, however, his demonstration against the temple, like the pronouncements of judgment on the rulers, was integral to his agenda of the renewal of the people in opposition to the rulers, an agenda deeply rooted in Israelite prophetic tradition.

The Gospel of Mark presents the direct connection between Jesus's crucifixion and his demonstration and pronouncements against the ruling institutions, both in particular episodes and in the narrative sequence of episodes. Pronouncement of God's judgment of the temple is linked directly to his execution in both the trial before the council and the scene of the crucifixion itself. More important for Mark's portrayal of how Jesus's prophetic declarations and actions led to his crucifixion is the narrative sequence of episodes: the series of Jesus's confrontations with the Jerusalem rulers and their representatives led to their finally taking action to arrest him and hand him over to Pilate.

The Gospel of John, sometimes dismissed as a source because of its "spiritual" orientation and long discourses, makes the direct relation between Jesus's prophetic blockade of the temple and his pronouncements against the Jerusalem rulers even more prominent. As with Mark's story, we should not imagine that events happened as John narrates them. The point is that the Gospel sources portray a direct connection between Jesus's prophetic pronouncements and actions and his arrest and crucifixion.

Jesus's Confrontation and Crucifixion as a Breakthrough for His Movement

To understand the effect of Jesus's condemnation of the rulers and his crucifixion on the Jesus movement(s), one must appreciate the effects of coercive power and dehumanization on subjected peoples—and the creative forms of political resistance that people can muster. Historians have often assumed that if slaves, peasants, and other subjugated people were not in revolt, then they must have accepted the conditions of their domination. This is the impression usually given in written sources from antiquity, which, with the exception of the Gospels, almost always reflect the views of the ruling elite. Subtler and more realistic recent studies, however, have recognized the difference between what subjugated people say and do in public on the one hand and what they feel, think, and say to one another when out of earshot of their overlords on the other.

In order to extract tribute, taxes, and rents, the dominant practice violence, such as conquest and crucifixion, and the threat of violence (such as public crucifixion) against its subjects. In their relations with overlords, subjugated people are thus almost always acting and speaking under coercion, the threat of further violence. The indignities and dehumanization they suffer, however, do not eliminate and may even stimulate their desire for dignity. When they are safely "off-stage," back in their houses and villages among other subjugated people they trust, they share resentments and develop a discourse of dignity—and more than a discourse. The people's indignation about the indignities they suffer produces an oppositional emotion that can turn into a powerful motivation.[7]

Only rarely does a spokesperson become emboldened to step forward in defiance of domination and "speak truth to power." Depending on the circumstances, bold speech or an act of defiance can transform the collective indignation into an excitement and energy that inspire collective protest or resistance. Such a religious-political breakthrough can then escalate into a significant movement and/or energize a nascent movement into rapid expansion. Studies of movements in such circumstances in other societies find that a leader's public articulation of the people's indignation is often what energizes the coalescence and expansion of a movement.[8] The moment when a spokesperson suddenly declares the people's resentment and rejection on the public stage, directly in the face of the dominant group, becomes a politically charged occasion. The energy released by such a confrontation with domination flows from "the sense of personal release, satisfaction, pride, and elation" that indignant subjugated people feel when their spokesperson speaks truth instead of more submissive lies and equivocations.[9] Identifying with their leader's challenge to the dominant, the followers too finally talk back and resist rather than submit.

Jesus was just such a leader who spoke out the people's frustrated indignation in public in the face of the rulers and ruling institutions. In his prophetic pronouncements of God's judgment he built upon the popular memory of previous prophets who had pronounced God's condemnation of oppressive kings and their officers. In his symbolic prophetic demonstration in the temple, whatever its scope, at Passover time, he chose for his politically charged confrontation an already highly (religiously-politically) charged celebration of the people's foundational liberation to declare God's new judgment. His declaration of the people's indignation also brought a release of energy that had previously been used for self-control.

As might well have been expected, his declaration of his own and the people's intense indignation at their prolonged oppression directly in the face of the Roman imperial order drew down violent repression and his arrest and crucifixion as a dangerous agitator. His execution thus made him a martyr to his cause of the renewal of Israel in opposition to the rulers. The prophetic leader of the renewal boldly endured the torturous execution intended to prevent or suppress resistance. This evoked intensified indignation, now focused directly on Roman domination. The effect was to release all the more energy that the threat of crucifixion had previously helped contain. The crucifixion of Jesus inspired resistance, since crucifixion no longer had the power to intimidate them.

It was his prophetic pronouncements, his symbolic demonstration of God's judgment on the rulers, and his crucifixion-martyrdom (and not necessarily the resurrection by itself) that led to the *breakthrough* of the movement he had catalyzed in Galilean and other villages to rapid expansion and open resistance to the imperial order. This can be discerned precisely in the Gospel sources, especially in the way the followers of Jesus identify with his opposition to the rulers that led to his crucifixion and, in their rapid expansion of the renewal of Israel, their own resistance to Roman rule even though it might mean their own crucifixion.

The Q speeches are remarkable for how the death of Jesus as a climactic result of his opposition to rulers is embedded in the very identity of the people who make up the movement. Even though the speeches pay virtually no attention to the form of Jesus's execution, it is known that Jesus went to the cross.

The same might be required of his committed followers: "Whoever does not carry the cross and follow after me cannot be my disciple" (14:27). The Q community identified with Jesus's own prophetic opposition to the dominant order, symbolized by such violent repression. It is clear in the Q speeches that Jesus is speaking as the climactic prophet in the long line that God had sent to warn and condemn the ruling house in Jerusalem (13:34; 11:49–51). Like those of the prophets before him, his pronouncements evoked repressive violence. The communities that recited and heard these speeches understood themselves as collectively continuing the prophetic line, as indicated in the covenant renewal speech: "Blessed are you when they (exclude and) reproach you and speak evil of you on account of me/the 'son of man.' . . . For so their fathers did to the prophets" (6:22–23). As followers of Jesus proclaiming the kingdom of God and pressing for the renewal of Israel, they assumed the prophetic role themselves, prepared to undergo arrest, trial, and possible death. The speech in Q/ Luke 12:2–9 addresses just such treatment by the rulers. Jesus exhorts his followers to be steadfast in their commitment, even bold in their confession of loyalty, and not to worry about possible execution but rather to trust in God's providential care. The Q people are no longer content with staying in the sequestered sites of village communities but are themselves prepared to "speak truth to power," as indicated in the motivating sanction on their bold persistence (12:8–9). Hence they, like Jesus, may well be hauled before a court, where they must declare their loyalty in public and suffer the consequences.

The Gospel of Mark also represents Jesus's crucifixion, which resulted from his demonstration and pronouncement of God's judgment in Jerusalem, as the key event in the breakthrough that energized the expansion of the movement he had generated in Galilee. The arrest and crucifixion of Jesus by the rulers in response to his confrontations clearly form the climax of the story. The divine vindication of Jesus in the rending of the curtain of the temple just as Jesus dies reinforces this emphasis on the crucifixion, as does the centurion's recognition that Jesus was truly "a son of God."[10] Both events are clearly related to the crucifixion, not the resurrection. Finally, as noted earlier, the brief episode of the empty tomb serves primarily to send the disciples back to "Galilee" to continue the movement that has just climaxed in the crucifixion of Jesus as a martyr to his own mission of renewal of the people in opposition to the rulers.

The clearest and most important indication in Mark that Jesus's crucifixion became the empowering event for the dynamic expansion of the movement he had catalyzed is the last-supper episode, more particularly Jesus's word over the cup at this Passover meal that becomes also a covenant renewal meal.

Jesus reenacts the making of the Mosaic covenant on Sinai, his declaration "My blood of the covenant, which is poured out for many" invoking memory of the blood that symbolically bound God and the people who promised to observe the principles of social-economic justice (Exod 24:3–8). In Mark's story Jesus's crucifixion is thus indicated as the event that seals the renewal of the Mosaic covenant. And it is solemnly remembered in the empowering ceremony of the Lord's supper that anticipates full realization of the kingdom rule of God that Jesus had been proclaiming. The Roman governor and the Jerusalem high priests presumably hoped to check the movement with the terrorizing execution of its prophet-leader. Instead, the Romans' crucifixion of Jesus for his demonstration and pronouncement of God's judgment against the rulers became the climactic event and the symbol of resistance that empowered the solidarity and further expansion of his movement.

Like the Q speeches, Mark's story also indicates how this happened, as the followers both continued his program of renewal of the people and identified with his opposition to the rulers despite the risk of repressive action. The open ending of Mark's narrative suggests that the branch of the movement that produced the story had returned to "Galilee," where Jesus "met them" as they continued the renewal of the people (Mark 16:7; 14:28). The "Markan" branch of the Jesus movement, moreover, continued his program of renewal in intentional opposition to the imperial order. Precisely as he anticipated his arrest and execution, Jesus insisted that the leadership of the movement be an intentional alternative to hierarchical relations of power, sharply rejecting James's and John's request for positions of political power. In direct reference to the crucifixion, "the cup he drinks" and "the baptism with which he is baptized" are symbols of commitment to the common good of the movement of renewal even to the point of being crucified (Mark 10:35–45).

Mark also portrays Jesus's followers as expanding the renewal of the people in open opposition to the rulers. This becomes evident once we recognize that the composition and repeated performance of Mark's Gospel involved the active social memory of a community of the movement that was still resonating with Jesus's teachings—and not simply a recollection of isolated sayings and reminiscences. At the end of the dialogue focused on egalitarian covenantal economic relations (10:17–31), for example, Jesus reassures the disciples of the restoration of the families and lands that they have left temporarily while pursuing the mission. This is virtually the opposite of the individualistic construction of an itinerant individual vagabond "lifestyle." Nor is the envisaged restoration "apocalyptic" or "eschatological," as interpreters often claim. While the imagery of restoration includes considerable hyperbole ("a hundredfold"), it is to come "now in this age." And, far from being a panacea of peaceful rest, the restoration of household and fields is to involve continuing struggle, "with persecutions."

Two dramatic actions taken in a politically charged situation, Jesus's confrontation and crucifixion, brought the movement to the attention of the rulers, so that his followers had to contend with active opposition from the rulers. Rather than withdrawing into acquiescence, however, and inspired by and identifying with his martyrdom, they continued and rapidly expanded their movement in opposition to the imperial order, fully aware that they too might face crucifixion. Significantly in Mark's narrative sequence, the key admonition by Jesus follows directly upon his first announcement of the crucifixion and his rebuke of Peter's misunderstanding about "messiahship" (8:34–9:1). Jesus's followers may have to "take up their [own] cross," boldly facing their own condemnation—but will do so in the confidence that they will be vindicated in the divine judgment and that the direct rule of God will soon be "coming with power."

Crucifixion was a public display of dehumanizing violence intended to terrorize subjugated people into submission. Jesus's execution for his confrontation with the rulers in Jerusalem was transformed into a symbol of a movement of renewal and resistance. Jesus's crucifixion for his action in opposition to the imperial order broke through the power of crucifixion to utterly intimidate people into passive acquiescence in the steady disintegration of their families and communities. The communities of that expanding movement were still subject to the overwhelming power of Roman rule in various ways. But Jesus's bold confrontation of the rulers and his crucifixion by the Romans became the key events in the breakthrough that empowered his movement(s) to aggressively expand its renewal of the people in what was now a public opposition to the imperial order.

Notes

PREFACE

1. Critical deconstruction of the synthetic modern scholarly construct of apocalypticism in Horsley, *The Prophet Jesus*, chaps. 1–5; critical deconstruction of the scholarly concepts of ancient miracle and magic in Horsley, *Jesus and Magic*, parts I and II.

2. The many articles behind Horsley with Hanson, *Bandits, Prophets, and Messiahs*; and Horsley, *Jesus and the Spiral of Violence*.

3. It was particularly gratifying that John Dominic Crossan, perhaps the most influential scholar in the recent revival of interest in the historical Jesus (and one of the previous Hall lecturers), devoted Part II of *Historical Jesus* to the popular resistance movements that were rooted in the Israelite "little tradition" (see *Bandits, Prophets, Messiahs*)—even though he did not understand that texts from the intellectual elite were hardly expressions of the popular tradition.

4. See further Horsley, *Galilee*; and Horsley, *Archaeology, History, and Society*.

5. Keith and LeDonne, eds., *Jesus, Criteria, and the Demise of Authenticity*.

6. On the Markan Gospel as an historical story in historical context, see Horsley, *Hearing the Whole Story*; on the "Q" series of speeches, see Horsley with Draper, *Whoever Hears You Hears Me*.

7. The implications of oral communication and oral performance were included in Horsley with Draper, *Whoever Hears You Hears Me*; and Horsley, *Hearing the Whole Story*; Horsley, *Scribes, Visionaries* investigated the implications of several other, closely related lines of research as well, such as into different kinds of writing and their function, oral-written scribal training and practice, and their disorienting implication for biblical studies.

8. See esp. the articles of Joanna Dewey now collected in *Oral Ethos*; Horsley, *The Whole Story*, esp. chap. 3; Horsley with Draper, *Whoever Hears You Hears Me*; and the summary of recent lines of research in Horsley, "Oral Communication."

9. Beginning with the essays in Kirk and Thatcher, eds., *Memory*; implications explored in the articles collected in Horsley, *Jesus in Context*, chaps. 3–7; and Horsley, Draper, Foley, eds., *Performing the Gospel*.

10. Horsley with Draper, *Whoever Hears You Hears Me*; and Horsley, "Oral Com-

munication." On the lines of recent research into ancient communication see now ""Can Study of the Historical Jesus Escape its Typographical Captivity?"

11. Horsley, *Jesus and the Spiral of Violence*, 16–19, 30–31, 62–63, 68–71, 81–85, 181–80, 221–22.

12. Horsley, *Scribes, Visionaries.*

13. Wire, *Mark Composed*; and Horsley, "Imagining Mark's Story."

CHAPTER 1: GETTING THE WHOLE STORY

1. Presented most influentially, with extensive critical apparatus, by Crossan, *Historical Jesus*; more accessible but without the same critical discussion is Borg, *Jesus.*

2. Most carefully presented, with response to the liberals' criticism, by Allison, *Jesus of Nazareth*; more accessible but without such engagement is Ehrman, *Jesus.*

3. Sharply dismissive of the liberals' scholarship is Johnson, *Real Jesus*, who recognizes his complicity in the publisher's generation of controversy.

4. In attempting to figure out how to include dimensions of history that tend to be left out of consideration, I am discussing the standard assumptions, procedures, and concepts of historical Jesus studies as rooted in New Testament studies in general and not criticizing any books or articles in particular.

5. Eagleton, *Literary Theory*, 19–30, 43–50, 141, 205; Said, *Culture and Imperialism*, 12–14.

6. See especially Price, *Rituals and Power*; and Zanker, *Power of Images*; both excerpted, and other essays, in Horsley, ed., *Paul and Empire.*

7. On the modern Western construction of religions such as Buddhism, Hinduism, and Confucianism in India and China, see, for example, Lopez, ed., *Curators of the Buddha*; and King, *Orientalism and Religion*; the summary discussion in Horsley, "Religion and Other Products of Empire," 13–18; and Horsley, *Religion and Empire*, 13–18, 135–36, as well other books and articles cited there.

8. Particularly influential has been Sanders, *Judaism.*

9. For example, Neusner, Green, and Frerichs, eds., *Judaisms and Their Messiahs*; Schwartz, *Imperialism.*

10. The most influential treatment was Theissen, *Sociology*; the most influential Jesus book to have taken over this construction is Crossan, *Historical Jesus*. Criticism of the sociology and use of texts in Elliott, "Social-Scientific Criticism"; and Horsley, *Sociology and the Jesus Movement.*

11. Crossan, *Historical Jesus*, 287–91.

12. One might suspect that the individualistic liberal reading of Jesus's sayings is rooted in the individualistic Christian piety in Anglophone culture for which the older KJV translation of the saying "the kingdom of God is *within* you" has long been a key prooftext.

13. Crossan, *Historical Jesus*, after devoting part 2 to extensive discussion of the various types of agitators and leaders of movements in early Roman Palestine, constructs an abstract typology in which Jesus fills in the otherwise unattested quadrant

of popular and "sapiential." Jesus is thus a sui generis (Cynic-like) "Jewish peasant sage."

14. In Allison, *Jesus*, 78–94.

15. This is a contrast to the fully relational exploration by Gager, *Kingdom and Community*, not long after many of the studies of millenarian movements were published in the 1950s and 1960s.

16. See the fuller sketch of this relational and contextual approach in Horsley, *Jesus and Empire*, chap. 3.

17. It seems likely that the codification of the Gospel texts into chapter and verse and the appearance of each verse separately on the printed pages of the *Lutherbibel* and the KJV influenced this atomizing approach.

18. See Theissen, *Sociology*, followed by many liberal interpreters of Q and Jesus.

19. Allison, *Jesus*.

20. Crossan, *Historical Jesus*, 235.

21. Critical examination of how second-temple Judean "apocalyptic" texts do not attest the themes or events in the apocalyptic scenario articulated by Schweitzer, Bultmann, and others a century ago and still assumed by both liberals scholars and neo-Schweitzerians in Horsley, *The Prophet Jesus*, chaps. 1–5.

22. Of the growing body of literature, as steps into ever-fuller consideration of historical forms and context, see Kelber, *Mark's Story of Jesus*; Myers, *Binding the Strong Man*; Wills, *Historical Gospel*; and Horsley, *Hearing the Whole Story*.

23. Ideally we would all have access to a good translation of the Gospels without the intrusive chapter-and-verse numbers (and especially without the often misleading editorial headings for particular anecdotes). I encourage any reader who has not done so before to read straight through one or more of the Gospels (Mark is the shortest and the most lively). In order to encourage consideration of whole stories, I purposely do not give chapter-and-verse references to Mark, Matthew, and Luke. On the other hand, I find it difficult to give a sketch of John without them. And the only way to identify the (hypothetical) speeches in Q is by where they are used by Luke (and sometimes Matthew as well).

24. The following sketches of the Gospels, made specifically for this volume, are dependent on the treatments of others too numerous to mention. One of my motives in undertaking critical studies of Gospel texts in historical context was a desire to gain a much better sense of them as sources for the historical Jesus. These sketches and analysis of Gospel texts in the ensuing chapters are thus dependent on Horsley with Draper, *Whoever Hears You Hears Me*; Horsley, *Hearing the Whole Story*; and Horsley and Thatcher, *John, Jesus*.

25. Kloppenborg, *Formation of Q*; and Horsley with Draper, *Whoever Hears You Hears Me*, on which the following discussion of Q depends.

26. There is not even a hint of Jesus as a/the messiah in the Q speeches, where he is the final prophet in a long line of prophets killed by the rulers (Q/Luke 7:24–28; 11:49–51), and there is no mention of crucifixion.

27. In the context of Roman imperial rule, the Greek term *pistis*, like the Latin *fides*, meant political loyalty, as in being loyal to one's patron or to the imperial lord.

28. A fuller summary of recent research in various areas and its implication for

study of the Gospels and Jesus in Horsley, "Oral Communication, Oral Performance." See also Kelber, *Imprints, Voiceprints*.

29. Ulrich, *Dead Sea Scrolls*, esp. 11, 14, 40–41, 91–92, 102.

30. Parker, *Living Text*, 188.

31. Epp, "Multivalence of 'Original Text'"; Epp, "Oxyrhynchus New Testament Papyri," 10.

32. Print-cultural assumptions persist, however, in the work of Ehrman, *Orthodox Corruption* and *Misquoting Jesus*.

33. Gamble, *Books and Readers*, 79 n.132, reminds us that the newly converted Emperor Constantine sent instructions to the learned bishop Eusebius that he should "order fifty copies of the divine scriptures . . . for the instruction of the church, to be written on well-prepared parchment by copyists most skillful in the art of accurate and beautiful writing" (Eusebius, *Life of Constantine* 4.36).

34. See Harris, *Ancient Literacy*; Hezser, *Jewish Literacy*.

35. It has long been standard to refer to the Torah or the Law as the definitive and authoritative Scripture of "Judaism" in the late second temple times. The lines of research I am summarizing here, however, are concluding that the Dead Sea Scrolls show that there were texts of torah in the late second temple Judea other that those in the Pentateuch (that became known as the Torah, which along with the Prophets and the Writings constituted the Hebrew Bible), *and* that the text of the books of the Pentateuch was not yet stable. What the Pharisees were cultivating orally, moreover, was Mosaic torah. Hence I use the (lowercased) term *torah* in reference to the range of texts and teachings current at the time, and use the Torah or "the Torah" (uppercased) when referring to the statement of the standard view that is now being challenged.

36. Carr, *Writing on the Tablet of the Heart*, summarizes recent research on scribal practice in ancient Egyptian and Mesopotamian regimes and discusses the similar practice among the scribes in the monarchy of Judah and the Judean temple-state. On scribal practice in the Judean temple-state, see Horsley, *Scribes*, esp. chaps. 5–7.

37. Jaffee, *Torah in the Mouth*, presents an illuminating examination of scribal practice in the Qumran community and especially among successive generations of rabbinic circles.

38. Discussion of Pliny and others in composition in the ancient media context in Small, *Wax Tablets of the Mind*.

39. Fuller discussion in Horsley with Draper, *Whoever Hears You Hears Me*, esp. chaps. 5–6.

40. See, among other studies, especially Achtemeier, "*Omnes verbum somnat*."

41. See now Shiner, *Proclaiming the Gospel*.

42. Shiner, *Proclaiming the Gospel*, 26, 47.

43. See further Shiner, *Proclaiming the Gospel*, 45, 107.

44. The works most helpful for oral communication and New Testament interpretation are probably Foley, *Immanent Art*; *Singer of Tales in Performance*; *How to Read an Oral Poem*; and, more condensed, "Plenitude and Diversity." Foley's theoretical reflec-

tions are adapted for interpretation of the Q speeches in Horsley with Draper, *Whoever Hears You Hears Me*. On Mark see Dewey, "Oral Methods," "Mark as Interwoven Tapestry," and "Mark and Oral Hermeneutic"; and Horsley, "Oral Performance and Mark." On social memory in connection with oral performance, see the essays in Kirk and Thatcher, *Memory, Tradition, and Text*; Horsley, Draper, and Foley, eds., *Performing the Gospel*; and Horsley, *Jesus in Context*, chaps. 3–7.

CHAPTER 2: JESUS AND THE POLITICS OF ROMAN PALESTINE

1. I am discussing the standard assumptions, procedures, and concepts of historical Jesus studies as rooted in New Testament studies in general and not criticizing any books or articles in particular as I attempt to figure out how to include dimensions of history that tend to be left out of consideration.

2. Among the many accounts, see Chehabi, *Iranian Politics*, esp. 34.

3. See, for example, Guha, *Peasant Insurgency*; Chakrabarty, "Subaltern Studies."

4. See the criticism of structural-functional sociology in Gouldner, *Crisis*; and, as applied to New Testament materials, Elliott, "Social-Scientific Criticism"; Horsley, *Sociology and the Jesus Movement*; and the critical discussion of the applicability of the historical sociological model of Lenski to second-temple Judea in Horsley, *Scribes*, chap. 3.

5. A wide range of sources provides important information on the politics of Roman Palestine, including Judean texts such as "The Similitudes of Enoch" and the Psalms of Solomon, some of Philo's treatises, later rabbinic texts, and particularly the works of Flavius Josephus. The recent development of a far more critical reading of Josephus's histories in Mason, "Josephus and Historical Method"; Rodgers, ed., *Josephus and Historical Method*; and Edmonds, Mason, and Rivers, eds., *Josephus and Rome*, has demonstrated how we can work critically through (rather than try to strip away) Josephus's Flavian viewpoint.

6. Discussed further in Horsley, *Jesus Movement*, chap. 4; and more fully in Horsley, *Galilee*, chaps. 8–10.

7. Analysis and discussion of the social structure and social roles evident in ben Sira's instructional speeches in Horsley, *Scribes*, chaps. 3 and 7, esp. 62–70, 139–42.

8. Incisive analysis of Josephus's accounts of the Pharisees is Mason, *Josephus on the Pharisees*.

9. Fuller analysis of sources, with comparative material on protests, in Horsley, *Jesus and the Spiral of Violence*, 34–35.

10. Summary of extensive recent scholarly discussion in Horsley, *Scribes*, chap. 1.

11. See the discussion of the Hasmonean rule of the Galileans and why it is not appropriately reduced (anachronistically) to religious "conversion" in Horsley, *Galilee*, 37–52.

12. After the Hasmonean takeover of Galilee and continuing under Herodian rule there would thus have been a certain number of Judeans in Galilee as officers or repre-

sentatives of Jerusalem rule and, later, of the regime of Herod Antipas. Their residence in key sites in Galilee would account for the presence of Judean ritual jars and *miqvaoth* that archaeologists have found at those sites. As an alternative to the "forced conversion" of the Galileans to "Judaism" as a way of arguing that the Galileans at the time of Jesus were "Jews," some archaeologists and others have argued that there was a mass migration of Judeans to the "empty land" of Galilee following the Hasmonean takeover. But there are no textual references to such a migration. In his historical accounts Josephus consistently refers to the residents of Galilee as *hoi Galilaioi*, just as he refers to the inhabitants of (or from) Judea as *hoi Ioudaioi*. Further analysis and discussion in Horsley, *Galilee*, esp. 147–57.

13. See, for example, Mattern, *Rome and the Enemy*; Lendon, *Empire of Honour*.

14. Richardson, *Herod*, presents extensive discussion of most of these aspects of Herod's client kingship, which he views as relatively benign.

15. Jensen, "Antipas: Friend or Foe?" and *Herod Antipas*, reviews much of the plethora of recent research, particularly archaeological studies, on Galilee. Many of the findings would lead to different conclusions, however, if examined in the context of the political-economic-religious structure and conflicts evident though sources such as Josephus's histories—and not filtered through constructs such as "Judaism."

16. Analysis and discussion of Josephus's accounts in Horsley, "Power Vacuum and Power Struggle," 92–102.

17. See the earlier discussion in M. Goodman, *Ruling Class of Judaea*; and Horsley, "High Priests and Politics."

18. Schaper, "Jerusalem Temple."

19. See esp. the careful analysis by Gruen, "Hellenism and Persecution"; on the *gymnasion* in particular, Doran, "Jason's Gymnasion"; and the summary discussion with further references in Horsley, *Scribes*, 33–51.

20. Fuller discussion of the following texts and the conflicts they reflect in Horsley, *Scribes*, chaps. 8–9.

21. The previous claim that the "Ten-Week Apocalypse" in 1 Enoch 93:1–10, 91:11–17 mentions a new temple is based on a questionable translation of the Ethiopic text. The manuscripts of 91:7, 13 have "house (of glory and kingship/of the great king)." Considering that in another near-contemporary Enoch text, the Animal Vision, "house" refers to the people of God, with "tower" representing the temple, and that there is considerable continuity between Enoch texts otherwise, "house" in 91:7, 13 should also be taken as a reference to the people, not the temple. See the textual notes in Nickelsburg, *1 Enoch 1*, 436–37.

22. A now-standard construction of how allusions to historical figures in Qumran texts fit into historical context on the basis of information from other texts is in Vermes, *Dead Sea Scrolls*, 47–66.

23. Fuller discussion in Horsley, *Revolt of the Scribes*, chap. 8.

24. In this light it is suggestive that John the Baptist, who was evidently sharply critical of those (high priests?) who presumed on their lineage, is represented in

Lukan tradition (Luke 1:5–25) as of (ordinary) priestly descent. See further Webb, *John the Baptizer,* 60–62. His social location as an ordinary priest from the village of Anatoth was probably a factor in Jeremiah's prophecy against the established Jerusalem priests (e.g., Jer 7; 26).

25. I have treated the "fourth philosophy" at greater length both in Horsley with Hanson, *Bandits, Prophets, and Messiahs,* 190–99; and Horsley, *Jesus and the Spiral of Violence,* 77–89.

26. Further discussion of Josephus's accounts of the deepening opposition to the high priests in M. Goodman, *Ruling Class of Judaea;* Horsley, "High Priests and Politics"; and Horsley, *Jesus and the Spiral of Violence,* chaps. 3–4.

27. Analysis of the key texts and discussion in Horsley, "Sicarii."

28. Kautsky, *Aristocratic Empires.*

29. See, for example, Moore, *Social Origins;* Skocpol, *Social Revolution;* and Wolf, *Peasant Wars.*

30. Aviam, *Sites in Galilee;* Horsley, *Galilee,* 190–93.

31. Analysis and discussion of textual and archaeological evidence in Horsley, *Galilee,* chap. 10.

32. References, comparative material, and analysis in Horsley, "Josephus and the Bandits."

33. See further Horsley, "Power Struggle," 96–98.

34. Fuller analysis and documentation of the messianic movements in Horsley, "Messianic Movements"; and Horsley with Hanson, *Bandits, Prophets, and Messiahs,* chap. 3.

35. Fuller analysis and documentation in Horsley, "Two Types of Prophets" and "Prophetic Movements"; and Horsley with Hanson, *Bandits, Prophets, and Messiahs,* chap. 4.

36. The book of Acts mentions both of these movements but dates Theudas prior to the Fourth Philosophy (5:36) and then confuses the Egyptian prophet's movement with the *Sicarii* (21:38).

37. Scott, *Arts of Resistance.* In this highly suggestive theoretical reflection on the various forms of popular politics, Scott draws heavily on his earlier work in "Protest and Profanation" and *Weapons of the Weak.* Application to Jesus and the politics of Roman Palestine in several articles in Horsley, ed., *Hidden Transcripts.*

38. Scott, *Arts of Resistance,* 50–54.

39. Scott, *Arts of Resistance,* 67.

40. Scott, *Arts of Resistance,* 120–24.

41. Scott, *Arts of Resistance,* 18–19.

42. See especially the extensive research on the limited literacy in Hezser, *Jewish Literacy;* and the text-critical research on books later included in the Hebrew Bible by Ulrich, *Dead Sea Scrolls.*

43. Very illuminating for study of the Gospels and Jesus is the discussion and application of the concepts of "great" and "little" tradition in Scott, "Profanation and Pro-

test."

44. I have discussed these assertions and references more fully in Horsley with Draper, *Whoever Hears You Hears Me*, chap. 10; and Horsley, *Hearing the Whole Story*, 178–83.

45. The fundamental steps and textual basis for this analysis of the situation of the people and Jesus's response sketched in this and the next paragraphs were laid out initially in *Jesus and the Spiral of Violence*, 30–33, 181–90, 246–79, and further developed on the basis of further research in Horsley with Draper, *Whoever Hears You Hears Me*, chaps. 2, 9, 12; and Horsley, *Hearing the Whole Story*, chap. 8.

46. Further analysis and discussion in Horsley, *Hearing the Whole Story*, 183–95.

47. More extensive discussion in Horsley, *Hearing the Whole Story*, chap. 7; and Horsley with Draper, *Whoever Hears You Hears Me*, 285–91.

48. Further discussion, drawing on Scott, in Horsley, *Jesus in Context*, 193–95; cf. the incisive historical study by Lefebvre, *The Great Fear*.

49. For examples of the considerable variation in conceptualization, see for example: as a restoration of "Judaism," Sanders, *Jesus and Judaism*; as a restoration of Israel with emphasis on return of exiles (with a Christian twist), Wright, *Jesus*; as a renewal of Israel in its village communities in opposition to the rulers of Israel, Horsley, *Jesus and the Spiral of Violence*.

50. On the criticism or even rejection of the temple-state as well as the high priestly incumbents, see Horsley, *Revolt of the Scribes*.

51. See, most recently, Kinman, "Jesus' Royal Entry into Jerusalem."

52. See the incisive analysis in Chaney, "The Addressees of Isaiah 5:1–7."

53. Judging from what we know about patterns of land tenure, Galileans would have known about peasants forced into tenancy on the "royal lands" in the Great Plain to the south, and Judeans would have known of Judeans similarly forced into tenancy on developing large estates in the Judean hill country. See evidence and discussion in Horsley, *Galilee*, 207–21.

54. See further Reed, "Sign of Jonah," 134–36. While the *Vitae Prophetarum* may date from late antiquity, it reflects earlier popular traditions about the prophets; see Schwemer, *Studien*.

55. Another recent interpretation of this episode on the basis of Scott's insights into other forms of peasant politics, which includes Jesus's manipulating the Pharisees into showing their hand, is Herzog, "Onstage and Offstage."

56. See further the analysis based on comparative studies in Horsley, *Jesus and the Spiral of Violence*, 90–99.

CHAPTER 3: JESUS AND IMPERIAL VIOLENCE

1. To take just three illustrations from highly regarded colleagues: Crossan, *Historical Jesus*, while devoting a multichapter part 2 to Judean and Galilean resistance movements (building on my earlier work), treats the Roman imperial context primarily in terms of brokerage, and violence does not appear as a significant issue in discussion

of Jesus's sayings. Fredriksen, *Jesus of Nazareth*, e.g., 173–84, while acknowledging the imperial power relations, does not pick up on the imperial violence mentioned in the sources cited. Sanders, *Historical Figure*, who projects the modern concept of "government" onto Roman and Roman client rule over Palestine, does not discuss military violence.

2. Discussed in Horsley, *Jesus and the Spiral of Violence*, chaps. 1–2.

3. On Jesus's crucifixion, see Hengel, *Crucifixion*; Sanders, *Jesus and Judaism*, 294–322.

4. Cullmann, *Jesus and the Revolutionaries*; Hengel, *Was Jesus a Revolutionist?*; and Hengel, *Victory over Violence*.

5. E.g., Brandon, *Jesus and the Zealots*.

6. Especially important was Hengel, *Die Zeloten*.

7. Recent increasing awareness of how academic disciplines originated in Western imperial culture owes much to the work of Said, *Orientalism* and *Culture and Imperialism*. Asad, *Genealogies of Religion*, esp. chap. 1, offers a critique of the distinctive understanding of religion in the West. Among a number of fine recent analyses of modern Western constructions of others' religions are King, *Orientalism and Religion*; and van der Veer, *Imperial Encounters*.

8. Horsley with Hanson, *Bandits, Prophets, and Messiahs*, and the series of articles behind the book that gives fuller critical analysis and documentation.

9. As has happened in more recent times, the Romans thus, in effect, created the insurgents that they then struggled to defeat; see further Horsley, "Zealots."

10. This was one of the principal issues in my *Jesus and the Spiral of Violence*.

11. This was evident in the proliferation of discussions in program units of the Society of Biblical Literature at annual meetings from 2003 to 2008. Discussion prior to that upsurge of interest in Horsley, ed., *Paul and Empire* and *Jesus and Empire*; and Carter, *Matthew and Empire*.

12. Further discussion of structural violence and the "spiral" of violence in Roman Palestine in Horsley, *Jesus and the Spiral of Violence*, chaps. 1–4; and Horsley, *Sociology and the Jesus Movement*, 83–89.

13. Fuller discussion of the rise of Rome to domination in Italy and in the Western Mediterranean in Harris, *War and Imperialism*; and Rich and Shipley, ed., *War*.

14. Detailed treatment of Roman expansion into Greece and other areas of the East in Kallet-Marx, *Hegemony to Empire*.

15. Examples of critical studies are Mattern, *Rome and the Enemy*; Lendon, *Empire of Honour*; Nicolet, *Early Roman Empire*; Harris, *War*; and Hopkins, *Conquerors and Slaves*.

16. "The aim was to punish and to terrify . . . It was traditional; it was the Roman way." Mattern, *Rome and the Enemy*, 115–22. See also Wheeler, "Roman Strategy," 35–36.

17. Rome's expansion into the eastern Mediterranean is detailed in Kallet-Marx, *Hegemony to Empire*, 291–334; extensive discussion of Rome in the ancient Middle East

in Millar, *Roman Near East.*

18. Fuller discussion in Kallett-Marx, *Hegemony to Empire,* 315–23.

19. Fuller discussion and rich supply of references in Balsdon, *Romans and Aliens,* esp. 30–54, 60–70; and Mattern, *Rome and the Enemy,* esp. 66–80. Cf. the modern Western views of "Orientals" discussed by Said, *Orientalism.*

20. Fuller discussion with numerous references in Mattern, *Rome and the Enemy,* 168–70; Nicolet, *Early Roman Empire,* 29–47; Zanker, *Power of Images,* 185–92; Gruen, *Roman Policy,* 190–94; Wallace-Hadrill, "The Emperor," 322–23.

21. Fuller account of Herod's violent subjugation of his people and repressive rule in Horsley, *Liberation of Christmas,* 39–49; and Horsley, *Galilee,* 54–60.

22. Further references to Josephus's accounts in Horsley, *Liberation of Christmas,* 46–47; more general discussion of crucifixion in Hengel, *Crucifixion.*

23. Suggestive examination in Hengel, *Crucifixion.*

24. This seems to be what Paul is referring to in his letter to the Galatians, that "Christ was publicly exhibited before your eyes as crucified" (Gal 3:1).

25. Analysis of Josephus's accounts and discussion in Horsley, "Josephus and the Bandits"; and Horsley, "Ancient Jewish Banditry."

26. Discussion in Horsley, *Scribes,* chap. 8.

27. See especially Kramer, *Red Fez.*

28. Documentation and critical analysis in Horsley, "Messianic Movements."

29. Documentation and critical analysis in Horsley, "Two Types of Popular Prophets."

30. Fuller discussion in Horsley, *Jesus and the Spiral of Violence,* 100–104.

31. See further Horsley, *Jesus and the Spiral of Violence,* 110–16.

32. Further analysis of such scribal-retainer movements in *Jesus and the Spiral of Violence,* chap. 3.

33. Josephus's principal account of the "fourth philosophy," along with the Pharisees, Sadducees, and Essenes, begins and ends a lengthy passage in which he blames them for starting the "madness" that led to the great revolt sixty years later. Previous scholarship has often taken his account uncritically. For example, his term *apostasis* has been translated "revolt" or "rebellion," which it does mean in some contexts. But it can also mean "defection," which would be an appropriate term for this departure by scribes from their expected service of the temple-state. Since the Romans viewed refusal to pay the tribute as tantamount to revolt, *apostasis* as "revolt" would be an appropriate term for the Judean historian who had become a client of the Flavian emperors. From the rest of Josephus's account, however, it is clear that the refusal to pay the tribute was not a violent insurrection but nonviolent resistance.

34. See further Horsley, "Sicarii."

35. Critical analysis of the text and its stages of development in Nickelsburg, *Jewish Literature,* 74–77, 237–48; discussion of text in political context, Horsley, *Revolt of the Scribes,* 160–64.

36. Important introductory analysis in Nickelsburg, *Jewish Literature,* 248–56; analysis in political context in Horsley, *Revolt of the Scribes,* 164–75.

37. Introductory discussion of the Psalms of Solomon in Nickelsburg, *Jewish Literature,* 238–47; analyzed in political context in Horsley, *Revolt of the Scribes,* chap. 8.

38. Translation from Vermes, *Dead Sea Scrolls.*

39. More extensive analysis of 1QM and related texts in Horsley, *Revolt of the Scribes,* chap. 7. Since the community was destroyed by the Romans in the "mop-up" operations after their destruction of Jerusalem, some interpreters believe that the Qumranites may well have finally have fought against Roman troops in some way.

40. Critical review of some of the previous discussion and an alternative in Horsley, *Jesus and the Spiral of Violence,* 255–75. See also the wider discussion in the articles in Swartley, ed., *Love of Enemy,* especially the response by Wink ("Neither Passivity nor Violence") and the exchange between Horsley and Wink, 72–136.

41. Statement and exploration of this point in Horsley, *Jesus and the Spiral of Violence,* 265–75.

42. Discussed more fully in Horsley, *Covenant Economics,* chaps. 7 and 10.

43. Laid out in Horsley with Draper, *Whoever Hears You Hears Me.*

44. As laid out in Horsley, *Hearing the Whole Story,* chs 4–5.

45. Analysis of Mark's portrayal of Jesus as prophet and messiah in Horsley, *Hearing the Whole Story,* chap. 10.

46. Analysis of Josephus's account and discussion in Horsley, *Jesus and the Spiral of Violence,* 93–99.

47. These passages are more fully analyzed in Horsley with Draper, *Whoever Hears You Hears Me,* chap. 13.

48. I am not suggesting that we revert to trusting Mark's "passion narrative" as a reliable historical report. Episodes in the passion narrative are surely some of the least historically reliable parts of Mark's narrative. But we should make every effort to understand Mark's portrayal here, since the motif of "false testimony" in the trial episode is often claimed as good evidence that Jesus did not take a stance against the temple, hence was not opposed to the rulers and therefore politically innocuous. Far from portraying Jesus as politically innocent in the trial episode, Mark ends it with Jesus pointing the high priests and elders to their impending judgment, of which "the son of man coming with the clouds of heaven" was a standing image.

49. See, for example, Sanders, *Jesus and Judaism.*

50. Fuller discussion of the following in Horsley, *Jesus and the Spiral of Violence,* 286–92.

51. There is thus no warrant whatever in Mark's story for taking the tenants as "the Jews" and the "others" to whom the vineyard will be given as "the Gentiles." That reading imposes a later Christian theological scheme.

CHAPTER 4: ILLNESS AND POSESSION, HEALING AND EXORCISM

1. Meier, *Mentor, Message, and Miracles;* Funk, *Acts of Jesus.*

2. Bultmann, *Jesus,* 173.

3. Bultmann, *Jesus*, 174.

4. Meier, *Mentor, Message, and Miracles*, 648, 652, 726.

5. Again, Meier, *Mentor, Message, and Miracles*; and Funk, *Acts of Jesus*, are typical.

6. Smith, *Jesus the Magician*; Crossan, *Historical Jesus*.

7. Nock, "Paul and the *Magos*," 308–10; Horsley, *Liberation of Christmas*, 53–60.

8. Nock, "Paul and the *Magos*"; Aune, "Magic."

9. Smith, *Jesus the Magician*.

10. Horsley, "Social Role of the Accused"; and Horsley, "Reflections on Witchcraft."

11. An example of how long such schemes persisted among social scientists is Wilson, *Magic and the Millennium*, on which Crossan, *Historical Jesus*, is heavily dependent.

12. Smith, *Jesus the Magician*; Aune, "Magic."

13. Interested readers who do not have a command of Greek and/or Coptic can now "check on" the assertions of Smith, Aune, and others by using the English translations in Betz, ed., *Magical Papyri*—although the translations may at points be misleading insofar as the translators worked on the assumption that the concept of magic and associated terms are applicable to these eclectic materials from various cultural traditions.

14. See further the more extensive analysis in Craffert, *Life of a Galilean Shaman*, 253–60.

15. Kleinman, *Patients and Healers*, 72.

16. Crossan, *Historical Jesus*, understood them as different, resulting in the assertion that Jesus dealt only with illness and not with disease. See now the sharp criticism of the illness-disease distinction of cultural medical anthropologists by Craffert, "Medical Anthropology."

17. As done by Pilch, *Healing*.

18. Onoge, "Capitalism and Public Health"; Young, "Anthropology of Illness." See also the special issues of *Medical Anthropology Quarterly* 17 (1986) and *Social Science and Medicine* 30/2 (1990).

19. Singer, "Reinventing," 181.

20. Kleinman, *Social Origins*; McKinlay, "Political Economy of Illness."

21. Comaroff, *Body of Power*; Lock and Scheper-Hughes, "A Critical-Interpretive Approach."

22. Keesing, "Models."

23. Young, "Anthropology of Illness"; Taussig, "Reification"; Lock and Scheper-Hughes, "A Critical-Interpretive Approach."

24. Argued on certain Judean "apocalyptic" representations in Horsley, *Jesus and the Spiral of Violence*, 133–37.

25. Foucault, *History of Sexuality*, 95–96.

26. Scott, *Weapons of the Weak*; and Scott, *Arts of Resistance*.

27. Boddy, *Wombs and Spirits*; Comaroff, *Body of Power*.

28. Ong, *Spirits of Resistance*; and Ong, "The Production of Possession."

29. Scheper-Hughes, "Madness of Hunger"; Lock, "Politics of Identity Breaking." It is curious that the analysis of the effects of colonial domination by Frantz Fanon does not figure more prominently in "critical" medical anthropology. Fanon, a Paris-trained psychiatrist and director of a mental hospital in Algeria, found spirit possession rampant in French Algeria in the early 1960s. He found that overwhelming power generated efforts among the dominated that were both self-defensively creative and debilitatingly mystifying. Hollenbach, "Jesus, Demoniacs," pioneered the exploration of the social-psychological and ideological pertinence of Fanon's analysis for Jesus's exorcisms. Some first steps toward an analysis of the political-historical relevance of Fanon for Jesus's exorcism in Horsley, *Hearing the Whole Story,* chap. 6.

30. Kleinman, *Patients and Healers,* 26.

31. Davies, *Jesus the Healer.*

32. Kramer, *Red Fez,* chaps. 1–2, esp. 71–72.

33. Kramer, *Red Fez,* 74–75.

34. Kramer, *Red Fez,* 75–76.

35. Kramer, *Red Fez,* 77.

36. Kramer, *Red Fez,* 92.

37. Kramer, *Red Fez,* 97.

38. Kramer, *Red Fez,* 99.

39. Kramer, *Red Fez,* 100.

40. Boddy, *Wombs and Spirits,* 269–70.

41. Boddy, *Wombs and Spirits,* 280–83.

42. Boddy, *Wombs and Spirits,* 291–94.

43. Boddy, *Wombs and Spirits,* 289–90.

44. Kramer, *Red Fez,* 116–17.

45. Luig, "Spirit Possession."

46. Kramer, *Red Fez,* 118–22.

47. Kramer, *Red Fez,* 125.

48. Sundkler, *Bantu Prophets,* 247–49.

49. Kramer, *Red Fez,* 126.

50. Kramer, *Red Fez,* 134–35.

51. Horsley, *Scribes,* chaps. 8–9; Horsley, "Revolt against Rome"; and Horsley, *Prophet Jesus,* chap. 4.

52. Summary of the establishment of the temple-state, with references to the burgeoning critical studies, in Horsley, *Scribes,* chap. 1.

53. Discussed in Horsley, *Scribes,* chap. 3.

54. Analysis and discussion in Horsley, *Scribes,* 157–62.

55. See Horsley, "Popular Messianic Movements"; Horsley, "Two Types of Popular Prophets"; and Horsley, *Galilee,* 152–57.

56. Delineation of the "chains" in Achtemeier, "Origin and Function."

57. Horsley, "Q and Israelite Tradition."

58. More extensive analysis in Horsley, *Hearing the Whole Story,* 136–48.

59. See further Kee, "Mark's Exorcism Stories."

60. Translation from Vermes, *Dead Sea Scrolls*, 178.

61. Further discussion of the three interrelated "levels" on which decisive action is happening in Jesus's exorcisms in Horsley, *Jesus and the Spiral of Violence*, 172–80.

62. See further Horsley, *Hearing the Whole Story*, 140–41.

63. Fuller analysis in Horsley, *Hearing the Whole Story*, 208–12.

64. Levine, "Discharging Responsibility"; Kraemer, "Jewish Women"; Cohen, "Menstruants."

65. Brock, *Journeys by Heart*, 86.

CHAPTER 5: RENEWAL OF COVENANTAL COMMUNITY

1. See Hopkins, *Conquerors and Slaves*; and Alcock, *Graecia Capta*.

2. Virtually all of these matters (e.g., building, court, fortresses, beneficence) are covered by Richardson, *Herod*, but with little attention to the economic impact on the people except for mention of sabbatical (fallow) years and famine.

3. Fuller discussion of Antipas's rule in Galilee, with references, in Horsley, *Galilee*, 163–81.

4. See Broshi, "Temple in the Herodian Economy," 31–37; M. Goodman, "First Jewish Revolt," 422–34.

5. Collection of recently expanded evidence for large estates and discussion in Fiensy, *Social History*, 32–43.

6. Analysis of the fragmentary evidence, extrapolation from later rabbinic evidence, and discussion, in Horsley, *Galilee*, 210–14.

7. More extensive discussion of indebtedness and its circumstances, with references and other sources, in Horsley, *Sociology and the Jesus Movement*, 88–90; and esp. Horsley, *Galilee*, 215–21.

8. Further analysis and discussion of sources in Horsley, *Liberation of Christmas*, chap. 2, esp. 33–36.

9. The classic study is Veyne, *Bread and Circuses*; see also Garnsey, *Food Supply*, esp. 231.

10. See further Horsley, *Liberation of Christmas*, chap. 6, esp. 110–14.

11. Very influential on American interpreters of Jesus has been Theissen, *Sociology*, despite the serious criticism of its narrow focus on text fragments, its individualism, and its uncritical adoption of the conservative structural-functional sociology that had been largely abandoned in the field of sociology by the 1970s, in Elliott, "Social Science Criticism"; and Horsley, *Jesus Movement*.

12. Most influential has been Crossan, *Historical Jesus*, esp. 266–74, 287–91, and 72–88, 421–22. There have been several incisive criticism of the construction of Jesus as a (Jewish) Cynic sage.

13. Extensive comparative material and analysis in Scott, *Moral Economy*; applied to Israelite covenantal tradition and to Q in Horsley, *Covenant Economics*, chap. 3; and Horsley, *Jesus in Context*, chap. 10, respectively.

14. Episodes in Josephus analyzed and discussed in Horsley, *Galilee*, 152–55.

15. See especially Mendenhall, *Law and Covenant*; and Mendenhall, "Covenant."

16. The term is often translated as "judges," the role they assumed following their leadership as "liberators" in the book of Judges.

17. More extensive analysis in Horsley, *Covenant Economics*, chaps. 2–3, drawing upon the comparative anthropological and historical analysis of agrarian peasantries in Scott, *Moral Economy*.

18. Baltzer, *Covenant Formulary*.

19. More detailed analysis, including of the poetic form of the speech in Q/Luke 6:20–49 in performance, in Horsley with Draper, *Whoever Hears You Hears Me*, chap. 9.

20. More extensive discussion in Horsley, *Hearing the Whole Story*, chap. 8.

21. The following discussion indeed draws from the more extensive discussion in Horsley with Draper, *Whoever Hears You Hears Me*, 210–25. See also where the speech is laid out in poetic form appropriate to oral performance in Horsley with Draper, *Whoever Hears You Hears Me*. See also Horsley, *Covenant Economics*, chap. 7, and *Jesus and the Powers*, 136–41.

22. As first explained in Horsley, *Jesus and the Spiral of Violence*, 255–273, in which the many allusions to covenantal teaching that we know from Exodus 21–23, the Levitical code, and the Deuteronomic code are laid out.

23. The following discussion draws on the fuller treatment in Horsley, *Hearing the Whole Story*, 186–95; see also Horsley, *Covenant Economics*, chap. 8; and Horsley, *Jesus and the Powers*, 141–44.

CHAPTER 6: CONFLICT WITH THE SCRIBES AND PHARISEES

1. For example, Borg, *Jesus*; Wright, *Jesus*, chap. 9; Sanders, *Jesus and Judaism*, 260–64.

2. Neusner, *Rabbinic Traditions*; and Neusner, *Politics to Piety*.

3. Review of the evidence in Levine, "Jewish Patriarch"; Levine, *Rabbinic Class*, chap. 4; and Cohen, "Significance of Yavneh," 36–38.

4. Lenski, *Power and Privilege*. The discussion of "advanced agrarian societies" fuses studies of such diverse societies as those of feudal medieval Europe, ancient Greece and Rome, and the ancient Near East. Criticism of its application to ancient Judea in Horsley, *Scribes*, 58–62.

5. Analysis and discussion of the social structure and social roles evident in ben Sira's instructional speeches in Horsley, *Scribes*, chaps. 3 and 7, esp. 62–70, 139–42.

6. On scribal training in Judea, see the summary in Horsley, *Scribes*, 82–87, and the more extensive discussion of such training in the context of other ancient Near Eastern states in Carr, *Writing on the Tablet of the Heart*.

7. More extensive analysis of the key texts in historical context in Horsley, *Scribes*, chaps. 8 and 9, and *Revolt of the Scribes*, esp. chaps. 2–5, 7.

8. The most incisive critical analysis of Josephus's accounts of the Pharisees is Mason, *Josephus on the Pharisees*.

9. Confirmed by the pesher on Nahum from Qumran (4Q169 1:2–8).

10. Neusner, *Politics to Piety*, surely the most influential construction of the Pharisees based on critical analysis of the sources in the past four decades.

11. The older translation in the Loeb Classical Library by H. St. John Thackeray is misleading in a number of regards, including its translation of *to koinon ton Hierosolymiton* as "the national assembly of Jerusalem." It was rather a council more like what would today be called a "junta" in a revolutionary/counterrevolutionary situation.

12. For example, Wright, *The New Testament and the People of God*, 189–98. The effect is to make the Pharisees appear more like the old construct of "the Zealots" as a foil for interpreting Jesus.

13. This construction of the scribes and Pharisees and other scribal groups first outlined in Horsley, *Jesus and the Spiral of Violence*, 15–19; application of Lenski's model to scribes and Pharisees discussed at length in Saldarini, *Pharisees, Scribes*.

14. Neusner, *Rabbinic Traditions* and *Politics to Piety*.

15. See Mason, "Was Josephus a Pharisee?"

16. See now Harris, *Ancient Literacy*; Hezser, *Jewish Literacy*.

17. Analysis of scribal practice in Judah-Judea in the ancient Near Eastern context in Carr, *Writing on the Tablet of the Heart*; focus on Judean scribal practice in Horsley, *Scribes*, chaps. 4–6.

18. See especially Ulrich, *Dead Sea Scrolls*, esp. 11, 14, 40–41, 91–92, 102.

19. Summary and analysis of evidence in Horsley, *Scribes*, chap. 6.

20. Jaffee, *Torah in the Mouth*.

21. Again, the treatment of the "great tradition" and the "little tradition" most helpful for ancient Judean and Galilean society is Scott, "Protest and Profanation." More extensive discussion of Israelite popular tradition in Horsley with Draper, *Whoever Hears You Hears Me*, esp. chaps. 5–6.

22. Explanation that the most compelling reading of the fragmentary evidence from earlier centuries is that most Galileans in the second-temple times were descendants of northern Israelites left on the land by the Assyrians when they deported the ruling elite of Samaria in Horsley, *Galilee*, 25–33.

23. See Miller, *Studies in the History and Traditions of Sepphoris*, 62–88, 120–27.

24. Explanation and presentation of a more appropriate and comprehensive approach in Horsley, *Galilee*, 39–56.

25. Baumgarten, "*Korban* and the Pharisaic *Paradosis*."

26. Versus Mack, *Myth of Innocence*, 94–96, 192–98; and Meier, *Companions and Competitors*, respectively.

27. See the helpful survey of scribal-rabbinic discussions of Sabbath observance in Sanders, *Jewish Law*, 6–23. Insofar as Sanders's agenda is to explain away seeming conflict between Jesus and the Pharisees, his discussion sheds little light on the controversy story in Mark 2.

28. It can be stated even more strongly than does Cohn-Sherbok, "Plucking Grain on the Sabbath," that Jesus does not conform to rules of rabbinic argumentation from scripture.

29. For example, a manuscript of 1 Samuel found among the Dead Sea Scrolls, 4QSam[b], has words missing from the Hebrew text of 21:4 (as we know it from the modern reconstructed text): ". . . from women, you [pl] may eat of it"—that is, Ahimelech is permitting David and his men to eat the bread. This does not justify the claim, based on the assumption (now recognized as problematic) of widespread literacy and possession of scrolls, that "Jesus will have known a text of Samuel similar to that preserved in 4QSam[b]," as Casey suggests in "Culture and Historicity," 8–9.

30. Neusner, *Judaic Law*.

31. Sanders, *Judaism*; see also Sanders, *Jewish Law*, 31, 35, 39, 229–30.

32. See further Baumgarten, "The Pharisaic *Paradosis*."

33. Discussion of the textual variations in Gundry, *Mark*, 350–51, who seeks a textual explanation rooted in the assumption of widespread literacy and availability of scrolls and codices.

34. See further Baumgarten, "*Korban* and the Pharisaic *Paradosis*," 6. The later Christian theologian Origen cites a Jewish informant who mentioned that in revenge against debtors who could not or would not repay their loans, creditors would declare that what was owed was *qorban*—thus forgoing repayment themselves but leaving the debtors still obligated to pay their debts (Baumgarten, "*Korban* and the Pharisaic *Paradosis*," 16).

35. Previous readings that took the whole controversy to be a dispute about purity laws understood Jesus's ensuing discussion with the crowd and the disciples (7:14–15, 17–23) as an extension of the controversy. The Pharisees and scribes are indeed still in the background as the "straw men" of purity practices. But Jesus has moved on to a discussion of eating food. Again this has previously been taken as addressed to "Gentile Christians" to relieve them of being subject to Jewish food laws. Jesus's discussion here sounds more like earthy peasant wisdom with more than a touch of humor. His statement in 7:15 about "what comes out the other end" is almost scatological. And his humor becomes earthier yet when he enters the house to instruct the ever-dense (Markan) disciples, as if the audience did not yet "get it." What one eats "enters not the heart but the stomach and comes out into the shithole—decontaminating all foods" (7:19). The concluding participle is the term for "catharsis"; the person has just been "purged." This reading follows one of the later manuscript traditions. Another manuscript tradition has provided the somewhat flimsy basis for the usual modern (Christian theological) reading: "Thus [Jesus] declared all foods clean." That reading, however, has serious problems, not the least of which is its obvious relevance to a later stage in the history of the movement when "Gentile Christians" supposedly wanted to be relieved of any residual Jewish food laws (see Räisänen, "Jesus and the Food Laws"). The term for "food" in this reading, moreover, does not occur elsewhere in Mark, and the whole phrase is missing in Matt 15:1–20, which otherwise reproduces the whole Markan episode(s) (see Guelich, *Mark*, vol. 1, 378–79).

36. For example, Kloppenborg, *Formation of Q,* 167.

37. Tuckett, *Q and the History of Early Christianity,* 404–24.

38. Wild, "Pharisees and Christian Judaism," 105–24.

39. Kloppenborg, "Nomos and Ethos."

40. The discussion here builds upon previous analyses and discussion in Horsley, "Q and Jesus," esp. 191–94; Horsley with Draper, *Whoever Hears You Hears Me,* 285–91; and Horsley, "Pharisees and Jesus."

41. Analysis and discussion of the woes in the prophets and in the Epistle of Enoch in Horsley, "Social Relations and Social Conflict."

42. As documented and explained by Neusner, "First Cleanse the Inside."

43. See further Satran, *Lives of the Prophets,* who argues that the *Lives of the Prophets* as we have it is a later, largely Christian document; and Schwemer, *Studien,* esp. 1.65–71, who makes compelling arguments that most material in the *Lives* stems from prior to 70 CE.

44. Schwemer, *Studien,* vol. 2, 283–321.

45. Still useful is Jeremias, *Heiligengräber;* much more up-to-date is Roller, *Building Program of Herod;* cf. Richardson, *Herod,* chap. 8.

46. So Kloppenborg, *Q Parallels.*

47. See further Horsley, "Social Conflict in the Synoptic Sayings in Q," 49.

CHAPTER 7: THE CRUCIFIXION AS BREAKTHROUGH

1. Further discussion of crucifixion in Fitzmyer, "Crucifixion."

2. The Psalms, often understood as prophecy, exerted a strong influence on the embellishment of the passion narratives. Many of the images and allusions come from Psalm 22 in particular (for example, the soldiers casting lots for his garments, Mark 15:24; John 19:23–25; Gospel of Peter 4:12; Ep. Barn. 6:6; cf. Ps 22:18; the passers-by shaking their heads at him and the others crucified with him taunting him, Mark 15:29, 32, cf. Ps 22:6–8).

3. Extended close analysis of the Gospels' passion narratives in Brown, *Death of the Messiah;* sharply critical response by Crossan, *Who Killed Jesus;* theological analysis in Carroll and Green, *Death of Jesus.*

4. This interpretation has been argued again recently by Fredriksen, *Jesus of Nazareth,* esp. chap. 5.

5. An early discussion of the lack of evidence for a standard expectation of "the Messiah" and the diverse representation of future leadership was the survey by de Jonge, "Use of 'Anointed,'" 132–48. For more extensive discussion, see the many particular studies in Neusner, Green, and Frerichs, *Judaisms and Their Messiahs,* and Charlesworth, ed., *The Messiah.* Collins, *Scepter and Star,* attempts to rehabilitate the synthetic scholarly concept of the Messiah. On the Psalms of Solomon and the Dead Sea Scrolls as products of circles of dissident scribes, see further Horsley, *Revolt of the Scribes,* chaps. 7, 8.

6. Analysis and discussion of popular "messianic" movements in Horsley, "Messianic Movements," and "'Messianic' Figures and Movements."

7. Political scientist James C. Scott's reflections on his own extensive field work among peasants and the extensive comparative material on which he draws in *Arts of Resistance* go far to illuminate the dynamics of power relations between the dominant and the subordinated. For application of Scott's reflections to Jesus's mission see Horsley, ed., *Hidden Transcript*; and Horsley, ed., *Oral Performance*. My own articles in those volumes are reprinted in revised form in Horsley, *Jesus in Context*, chaps. 8–10.

8. Scott, *Arts of Resistance*, draws upon many previous historical and anthropological studies as well as on his own field research.

9. Scott, *Arts of Resistance*, 207–8.

10. Note: not the "messianic" title "*The* Son of God."

Bibliography

Achtemeier, Paul J. "The Origin and Function of the Pre-Markan Miracle Catenae." *Journal of Biblical Literature* 91 (1972) 198–221.

———. "*Omnes verbum somnat*: The New Testament and the Oral Environment of Late Western Antiquity." *Journal of Biblical Literature* 109 (1990) 3–27.

Alcock, Susan E. *Graecia Capta: The Landscapes of Roman Greece*. Cambridge: Cambridge University Press, 1994.

Allison, Dale C. *Jesus of Nazareth: Millenarian Prophet*. Minneapolis: Fortress, 1998.

Asad, Talal. *Genealogies of Religion: Disciplines and Reasons of Power in Christianity and Islam*. Baltimore: Johns Hopkins University Press, 1993.

Aune, David. "Magic in Early Christianity." In *Aufstieg und Niedergang der römischen Welt* II.23.2 (1980) 1507–57.

Aviam, Mordechai. *Survey of Sites in the Galilee*. Jerusalem, 1995.

Balsdon, J. P. V. D. *Romans and Aliens*. Chapel Hill: University of North Carolina Press, 1979.

Baltzer, Klaus. *The Covenant Formulary: In Old Testament, Jewish, and Early Christian Writings*. Translated by David E. Green. Philadelphia: Fortress, 1971.

Baumgarten, Albert I. "*Korban* and the Pharisaic *Paradosis*." *Journal of the American Near Eastern Society* 16–17 (1984–85) 2–19.

———. "The Pharisaic *Paradosis*." *Harvard Theological Review* 80 (1987) 63–77.

Betz, Hans Dieter, ed. *The Greek Magical Papyri in Translation*. Chicago: University of Chicago Press, 1986.

Boddy, Janice. *Wombs and Alien Spirits: Women, Men, and the Zar Cult in Northern Sudan*. New Directions in Anthropological Writing. Madison: University of Wisconsin Press, 1989.

Borg, Marcus. *Jesus: A New Vision*. San Francisco: Harper & Row, 1987.

Brandon, S. G. F. *Jesus and the Zealots: A Study of the Political Factor in Primitive Christianity*. Manchester: Manchester University Press, 1967.

Brock, Rita Nakashima. *Journeys by Heart: A Christology of Erotic Power*. New York: Crossroad, 1988.

Broshi, Magen. "The Role of the Temple in the Herodian Economy." *Journal of Jewish Studies* 38 (1987) 31–37.

Brown, Raymond E. *The Death of the Messiah: From Gethsemane to the Grave: A Commentary on the Passion Narratives in the Four Gospels*. 2 vols. New York: Doubleday, 1987.

Bultmann, Rudolf. *Jesus and the Word*. Translated by Louise Pettibone Smith and Erminie Huntress. New York: Scribners, 1934. [German orig., 1926].

Carr, David M. *Writing on the Tablet of the Heart: Origins of Scripture and Literature*. New York: Oxford University Press, 2005.

Carroll, John T., and Joel B. Green. *The Death of Jesus in Early Christianity*. Peabody, MA: Hendickson, 1995.

Carter, Warren. *Matthew and Empire: Initial Explorations*. Harrisburg, PA: Trinity, 2001.

Casey, Maurice. "Culture and Historicity: Plucking of the Grain (Mark 2:23–28)." *New Testament Studies* 34 (1988) 1–23.

Chakrabarty, Dipesh. "Subaltern Studies and Postcolonial Historiography." In *Handbook of Historical Sociology*, edited by Gerard Delanty and Engin F. Isin, 367–69. London: Sage, 2003.

Chaney, Marvin L. "Whose Sour Grapes? The Addressees of Isaiah 5:1–7 in the Light of Political Economy." *Semeia* 87 (1999) 105–22. Reprinted in Chaney, *Peasants, Prophets, and Political Economy: The Hebrew Bible and Social Analysis*, 160–74. Eugene, OR: Cascade Books, 2017.

Charlesworth, James H., ed. *The Messiah: Developments in Earliest Judaism and Christianity*. Minneapolis: Fortress, 1992.

Chehabi, H. E. *Iranian Politics and Religious Modernism: The Liberation Movement of Iran under the Shah and Khomeini*. Ithaca, NY: Cornell University Press, 1990.

Cohen, Shaye. "The Significance of Yavneh: Pharisees, Rabbis, and the End of Jewish Sectarianism." *Hebrew Union College Annual* 55 (1984) 27–53.

————. "Menstruants and the Sacred." In *Women's History and Ancient History*, edited by Sarah Pomeroy, 271–99. Chapel Hill: University of North Carolina Press, 1991.

Collins, John J. *The Scepter and the Star: The Messiahs of the Dead Sea Scrolls and Other Ancient Literature*. Anchor Bible Reference Library. New York: Doubleday, 1995.

Comaroff, Jean. *Body of Power, Spirit of Resistance: The Culture and History of a South African People*. Chicago: University of Chicago Press, 1985.

Cohn-Sherbok, D. M. "An Analysis of Jesus' Arguments Concerning the Plucking of Grain on the Sabbath." *Journal for the Study of the New Testament* 2 (1979) 31–41.

Craffert, Pieter. *The Life of a Galilean Shaman: Jesus of Nazareth in Anthropological-Historical Perspective*. Matrix 3. Eugene, OR: Cascade Books, 2008.

————. "Medical Anthropology as an Antidote for Ethnocentrism in Jesus Research? Pulling the Illness-Disease Distinction into Perspective." *Teologiese Studies* 67 (2011) 1–14.

Crapanzano, Vincent, and Vivian Garrison, eds. *Case Studies in Spirit Possession*. Contemporary Religious Movements. New York: Wiley, 1977.

Crossan, John Dominic. *The Historical Jesus: The Life of a Mediterranean Jewish Peasant*.

San Francisco: HarperSanFrancisco, 1991.

———. *Jesus: A Revolutionary Biography*. San Francisco: HarperSanFrancisco, 1994.

———. *Who Killed Jesus? Exposing the Roots of Anti-Semitism in the Gospel Story of the Death of Jesus*. San Francisco: HarperSanFrancisco, 1995.

Cullmann, Oscar. *Jesus and the Revolutionaries*. Translated by Gareth Putnam. New York: Harper & Row, 1970.

Davies, Stephan L. *Jesus the Healer: Possession, Trance, and the Origins of Christianity*. New York: Continuum, 1995.

Dewey, Joanna. "The Gospel of Mark as Oral Hermeneutic." In *Jesus, the Voice and the Text: Beyond the Oral and Written Gospel*, edited by Tom Thatcher, 71–87. Waco: Baylor University Press, 2008.

———. "Mark as Interwoven Tapestry: Forecasts and Echoes for a Listening Audience." *Catholic Biblical Quarterly* 52 (1991) 221–36.

———. "Oral Methods of Structuring Narrative in Mark." *Interpretation* 53 (1989) 332–44.

Doran, Robert. "Jason's Gymnasion." In *Of Scribes and Scrolls: Studies on the Hebrew Bible, Intertestamental Judaism, and Christian Origins Presented to John Strugnell*, edited by Harold Attridge et al., 99–109. Resources in Religion 5. Lanham, MD: University Press of America, 1990.

Dunn, James D. G. *Jesus Remembered*. Grand Rapids: Eerdmans, 2003.

Eagleton, Terry. *Literary Theory: An Introduction*. Minneapolis: University of Minnesota Press, 1983.

Edmonds, Jonathan, Steve Mason, and James Rivers, eds. *Flavius Josephus and Flavian Rome*. Oxford: Oxford University Press, 2005.

Ehrman, Bart D. *Jesus: Apocalyptic Prophet of the New Millennium*. New York: Oxford, 1999.

———. *The Orthodox Corruption of Scripture: The Effect of Early Christological Controversies on the Text of the New Testament*. New York: Oxford University Press, 1993.

———. *Misquoting Jesus: The Story Behind Who Changed the Bible and Why*. San Francisco: HarperSanFrancisco, 2005.

Elliott, John H. "Social-Scientific Criticism of the New Testament and Its Social World." *Semeia* 35 (1986) 1–33.

Epp, Eldon J. "The Multivalence of the Term 'Original Text' in New Testament Text Criticism." *Harvard Theological Review* 92 (1999) 245–81.

———. "The Oxyrhynchus New Testament Papyri: 'Not without Honor except in Their Own Hometown'?" *Journal of Biblical Literature* 123 (2004) 5–55.

Fiensy, David. *The Social History of Palestine in the Herodian Period: The Land Is Mine*. Studies in the Bible and Early Christianity 20. Lewiston, NY: Mellen: 1991.

Fitzmyer, Joseph A., S.J. "Crucifixion in Ancient Palestine, Qumran Literature, and the New Testament." *Catholic Biblical Quarterly* 40 (1978) 493–513.

Foley, John Miles. *How to Read an Oral Poem*. Chicago: University of Illinois Press, 2002.

————. *Immanent Art: From Structure to Meaning in Traditional Oral Epic*. Bloomington: Indiana University Press, 1991.

————. "Plenitude and Diversity: Interactions between Orality and Writing." In *The Interface of Orality and Writing*, edited by Annette Weissenrieder and Robert B. Coote, 103–18. 2010. Reprint, Biblical Performance Criticism Series 11. Eugene, OR: Cascade Books, 2015.

————. *The Singer of Tales in Performance*. Bloomington: Indiana University Press, 1995.

Foucault, Michel. *The History of Sexuality*. Translated by Robert Hurley. Social Theory. New York: Pantheon, 1978.

Fredriksen, Paula. *Jesus of Nazareth, King of the Jews*. New York: Vintage, 1999.

Funk, Robert W. *The Acts of Jesus: The Search for the Authentic Deeds of Jesus*. San Francisco: HarperCollins, 1998.

Gager, John G. *Kingdom and Community: The Social World of Early Christianity*. Prentice-Hall Studies in Religion Series. Englewood Cliffs, NJ: Prentice-Hall, 1975.

Gamble, Harry Y. *Books and Readers in the Early Church: A History of Early Christian Texts*. New Haven: Yale University Press, 1995.

Garnsey, Peter. *Famine and Food Supply in the Graeco-Roman World*. Cambridge: Cambridge University Press, 1988.

Good, Byron. *Medicine, Rationality, and Experience: An Anthropological Perspective*. Cambridge: Cambridge University Press, 1994.

Goodman, Felicitas D. *How about Demons? Possession and Exorcism in the Modern World*. Bloomington: Indiana University Press, 1988.

Goodman, Martin. "The First Jewish Revolt: Social Conflict and the Problem of Debt." *Journal of Jewish Studies* 33 (1982) 422–34.

————. *The Ruling Class of Judaea: The Origins of the Jewish Revolt against Rome A.D. 66–70*. Cambridge: Cambridge University Press, 1987.

Gouldner, Alvin. *The Coming Crisis of Western Sociology*. New York: Basic Books, 1970.

Gruen, Erich S. *Studies in Greek Culture and Roman Policy*. Berkeley: University of California Press, 1996.

————. "Hellenism and Persecution: Antiochus IV and the Jews." In *Hellenistic History and Culture*, edited by Peter Green. Berkeley: University of California Press, 1998.

Guelich, Robert A. *Mark*. 2 vols. World Bible Commentary 34A. Dallas: Word, 1989.

Guha, Ranajit. *Elementary Aspects of Peasant Insurgency in Colonial India*. Delhi: Oxford University Press, 1983.

Gundry, Robert H. *Mark: A Commentary on His Apology for the Cross*. Grand Rapids: Eerdmans, 1993.

Harris, William V. *War and Imperialism in Republican Rome, 327–70 B.C.* Oxford: Oxford University Press, 1979.

————. *Ancient Literacy*. Cambridge: Harvard University Press, 1989.

Hengel, Martin. *Crucifixion in the Ancient World and the Folly of the Message of the Cross.* Translated by John Bowden. Philadelphia: Fortress, 1977.

———. *Judaism and Hellenism: Studies in Their Encounter in Palestine during the Early Hellenistic Period.* 2 vols. Translated by John Bowden. Philadelphia: Fortress, 1974.

———. *Victory over Violence.* Translated by David E. Green. Philadelphia: Fortress, 1973.

———. *Was Jesus a Revolutionist?* Translated by William Klassen. Facet Books: Biblical Series 28. Philadelphia: Fortress, 1971.

———. *Die Zeloten: Untersuchungen zur jüdischen Freiheitsbewegung in der Zeit von Herodes I. bis 70 n. Chr. Arbeiten zur Geschichte des Spätjudentums und Urchristentums 1.* Leiden: Brill, 1961.

———. *The Zealots: Investigations into the Jewish Freedom Movement in the Period from Herod I until 70 A.D.* Translated by David Smith. Edinburgh: T. & T. Clark, 1989.

Herzog, William B., II. "Onstage and Offstage with Jesus of Nazareth: Public Transcripts, Hidden Transcripts and Gospel Texts." In *Hidden Transcripts and the Arts of Resistance,* edited by Richard A. Horsley, 41–60. Semeia Studies 48. Atlanta: Society of Biblical Literature, 2004.

Hezser, Catherine. *Jewish Literacy in Roman Palestine.* Tübingen: Mohr/Siebeck, 2001.

Hollenbach, Paul. "Jesus, Demoniacs, and Public Authorities: A Socio-Historical Study." *Journal of the American Academy of Religion* 49 (1981) 567–88.

Hopkins, Keith. *Conquerors and Slaves: Sociological Studies in Roman History.* Sociological Studies in Roman History 1. Cambridge: Cambridge University Press, 1978.

Horsley, Richard A. "Ancient Jewish Banditry and the Revolt against Rome." *Catholic Biblical Quarterly* 43 (1981) 409–32.

———. *Archaeology, History, and Society in Galilee: The Social Context of Jesus and the Rabbis.* Harrisburg, PA: Trinity, 1996.

———. "Can Study of the Historical Jesus Escape its Typographical Captivity?" *Journal for the Study of the Historical Jesus* 19.1 (2021) 1-65.

———. *Covenant Economics: A Biblical Vision of Justice for All.* Louisville: Westminster John Knox, 2009.

———. "Further Reflections on Witchcraft and European Folk Religion." *History of Religion* 19 (1979) 71–95.

———. *Galilee: History, Politics, People.* Valley Forge, PA: Trinity, 1995.

———. *Hearing the Whole Story: The Politics of Plot in Mark's Gospel.* Louisville: Westminster John Knox, 2001.

———, ed. *Hidden Transcripts and the Arts of Resistance: Applying the Work of James C. Scott to Jesus and Paul.* Semeia Studies 48. Atlanta: Society of Biblical Literature, 2004.

———. "High Priests and the Politics of Roman Palestine." *Journal for the Study of Judaism* 17 (1986) 23–55.

———. "Imagining Mark's Story Composed in Oral Performance." In *Text and Tradition in Performance and Writing,* 246–78. Biblical Performance Criticism Series 9. Eugene, OR: Cascade Books, 2013.

————. *Jesus and Empire: The Kingdom of God and the New World Disorder.* Minneapolis: Fortress, 2003.

————. *Jesus and the Powers: Conflict, Covenant, and the Hope of the Poor.* Minneapolis: Fortress, 2011.

————. *Jesus and the Spiral of Violence: Popular Jewish Resistance in Roman Palestine.* 1987. Reprint, Minneapolis: Fortress, 1993.

————. *Jesus in Context: Power, People, and Performance.* Minneapolis: Fortress, 2008.

————. "Josephus and the Bandits." *Journal for the Study of Judaism* 10 (1979) 37–63.

————. *The Liberation of Christmas: The Infancy Narratives in Social Context.* New York: Crossroad, 1989.

————. "'Like One of the Prophets of Old': Two Types of Popular Prophets at the Time of Jesus." *Catholic Biblical Quarterly* 47 (1985) 435–63.

————. "'Messianic' Figures and Movements in First Century Palestine." In *The Messiah: Developments in Earliest Judaism and Christianity,* edited by James H. Charlestworth, 276–95. Minneapolis: Fortress, 1992.

————. "Oral Communication, Oral Performance, and New Testament Interpretation." In *Method and Meaning: Essays on New Testament Interpretation in Honor of Harold W. Attridge,* edited by Andrew B. McGowan and Kent Harold Richards, 125–55. Resources for Biblical Studies 67. Atlanta: Society of Biblical Literature, 2011.

————. "Oral Performance and Mark." In *Jesus, the Voice and the Text: Beyond the Oral and Written Gospel,* edited by Tom Thatcher, 45–70. Waco: Baylor University Press, 2008.

————. ed. *Oral Performance, Popular Tradition, and Hidden Transcript in Q.* Semeia Studies 60. Atlanta: Society of Biblical Literature, 2006.

————, ed. *Paul and Empire: Religion and Power in Roman Imperial Society.* Harrisburg, PA: Trinity, 1997.

————. "The Pharisees and Jesus in Galilee and Q." In *When Judaism and Christianity Began: Essays in Memory of Anthony J. Saldarini,* edited by Alan J. Avery-Peck, Daniel Harrington, and Jacob Neusner, 117–45. Journal for the Study of Judaism Supplements 85. Leiden: Brill, 2004.

————. "Popular Messianic Movements around the Time of Jesus." *Catholic Biblical Quarterly* 46 (1984) 471–93.

————. "Popular Prophetic Movements at the Time of Jesus: Their Principal Features and Social Origins." *Journal for the Study of the New Testament* 26 (1986) 3–27.

————. "Power Vacuum and Power Struggle in 66–67 C.E." In *The First Jewish Revolt: Archaeology, History, and Ideology,* edited by Andrea M. Berlin and J. Andrew Overman, 87–109. London: Routledge, 2002.

————. *The Prophet Jesus and the Renewal of Israel: Moving beyond a Diversionary Debate.* Grand Rapids: Eerdmans, 2012.

————. "Q and Jesus: Assumptions, Approaches, and Analyses." *Semeia* 55 (1991) 175–209.

————. *Religion and Empire: People, Power, and the Life of the Spirit.* Minneapolis: Fortress, 2003.

———. "Religion and Other Products of Empire." *Journal of the American Academy of Religion* 71 (2003) 13–44.

———. *Revolt of the Scribes: Resistance and Apocalyptic Origins.* Minneapolis: Fortress, 2010.

———. *Scribes, Visionaries, and the Politics of Second Temple Judea.* Louisville: Westminster John Knox, 2007.

———. "The *Sicarii*: Ancient Jewish Terrorists." *Journal of Religion* 59 (1979) 159–92.

———. "Social Conflict in the Synoptic Sayings Source Q." In *Conflict and Invention*, edited by John S. Kloppenborg, 37–52. Valley Forge, PA: Trinity, 1995.

———. "Social Relations and Social Conflict in the Epistle of Enoch." In *For a Later Generation: The Transformation of Tradition in Israel, Early Judaism, and Early Christianity*, edited by Randall Argall et al., 100–15. Harrisburg, PA: Trinity, 2000.

———. *Sociology and the Jesus Movement.* New York: Crossroad, 1989.

———. "The Speeches in Q and Israelite Tradition." In *Text and Tradition in Performance and Writing.* Biblical Performance Criticism Series 9. Eugene, OR: Cascade Books, 2013.

———. *Text and Tradition in Performance and Writing.* Biblical Performance Criticism Series 9. Eugene, OR: Cascade Books, 2013.

———. "Who Were the Witches? The Social Role of the Accused in the European Witch Trials." *Journal of Interdisciplinary History* 9 (1979) 689–715.

———. "The Zealots: Their Origins, Relationships, and Importance in the Jewish Revolt." *Novum Testamentum* 28 (1986) 159–92.

Horsley, Richard A., with Jonathan Draper. *Whoever Hears You Hears Me: Prophecy, Performance, and Tradition in Q.* Harrisburg, PA: Trinity, 1999.

Horsley, Richard A., Jonathan Draper, and John Miles Foley, eds. *Performing the Gospel: Orality, Memory, and Mark.* Minneapolis: Fortress, 2006.

Horsley, Richard A., with John S. Hanson. *Bandits, Prophets, and Messiahs: Popular Movements at the Time of Jesus.* 1985. Reprint, Minneapolis: Fortress, 1993.

Horsley, Richard A., and Tom Thatcher. *John, Jesus, and the Renewal of Israel.* Grand Rapids: Eerdmans, 2013.

Horsley, Richard A., and Patrick Tiller. *After Apocalyptic and Wisdom.* Eugene, OR: Cascade Books, 2012.

Jaffee, Martin S. *Torah in the Mouth: Writing and Oral Tradition in Palestinian Judaism, 200 BCE—400 CE.* Oxford: Oxford University Press, 2001.

Jensen, Morten Horning. *Herod Antipas in Galilee.* Wissenschaftliche Untersuchungen zum Neuen Testament 2/215. Tübingen: Mohr/Siebeck, 2006.

———. "Herod Antipas in Galilee: Friend or Foe of the Historical Jesus?" *Journal for the Study of the Historical Jesus* 5 (2007) 3–19.

Jeremias, Joachim. *Heiligengraeber in Jesu Umwelt (Mt. 23, 29; Lk. 11, 47): Eine Untersuchung zur Volksreligion der Zeit Jesu.* Göttingen: Vandenhoeck & Ruprecht, 1958.

Johnson, Luke Timothy. *The Real Jesus: The Misguided Quest for the Historical Jesus and the Truth of the Traditional Gospels.* San Francisco: HarperSanFrancisco, 1996.

Jonge, M. de. "The Use of the Word 'Anointed' in the Time of Jesus." *Novum Testamentum* 8 (1966) 132–48.

Kallet-Marx, Robert M. *Hegemony to Empire: The Development of the Roman Imperium in the East from 148–62 B.C.* Berkeley: University of California Press, 1995.

Kautsky, John H. *The Politics of Aristocratic Empires.* Chapel Hill: University of North Car-olina Press, 1982.

Kee, Howard Clark. *Miracle in the Early Christian World: A Study in Sociohistorical Method.* New Haven: Yale University Press, 1983.

———. "The Terminology of Mark's Exorcism Stories." *New Testament Studies* 14 (1968) 232–46.

Keesing, Roger M. "Models, 'Folk and Cultural.'" In *Cultural Models in Language and Thought,* edited by Dorothy Holland and Naomi Quinn, 369–95. Cambridge: Cambridge University Press, 1987.

Keith, Chris, and Anthony LeDonne, eds. *Jesus, Criteria, and the Demise of Authenticity.* London: T. & T. Clark, 2012.

Kelber, Werner. *Imprints, Voiceprints, and Footprints of Memory: Collected Essays of Werner H. Kelber.* Resources for Biblical Studies 74. Atlanta: Society of Biblical Literature, 2013.

———. *Mark's Story of Jesus.* Philadelphia: Fortress, 1979.

King, Richard. *Orientalism and Religion: Postcolonial Theory, India, and 'the Mystic East'.* London: Routledge, 1999.

Kinman, Brent. "Jesus's Royal Entry into Jerusalem." In *Key Events in the Life of the Historical Jesus: A Collaborative Exploration of Coherence and Context,* edited by Darrel L. Bock and Robert L. Webb, 383–427. Wissenschaftliche Untersuchungen zum Neuen Testament 247. Tübingen: Mohr/Siebeck, 2009.

Kirk, Alan, and Tom Thatcher, eds. *Memory, Tradition, and Text: Uses of the Past in Early Christianity.* Semeia Studies 52. Atlanta: Society of Biblical Literature, 2005.

Kleinman, Arthur. *Patients and Healers in the Context of Culture.* Berkeley: University of California Press, 1980.

———. *Social Origins of Distress and Disease: Depression, Neurasthenia, and Pain in Modern China.* New Haven: Yale University Press, 1986.

Kloppenborg, John S. *The Formation of Q: Trajectories in Ancient Wisdom Collections.* Studies in Antiquity and Christianity. Philadelphia: Fortress, 1987.

———. "Nomos and Ethos in Q." In *Gospel Origins and Christian Beginnings: In Honor of James M. Robinson,* edited by James E. Goehring et al., 35–48. Forum Fascicles 1. Sonoma, CA: Polebridge, 1990.

———. *Q Parallels: Synopsis, Critical Notes, and Concordance.* Foundations & Facets: Reference Series. Sonoma, CA: Polebridge, 1988.

Kramer, Fritz W. *The Red Fez: Art and Spirit Possession in Africa.* Translated by Malcolm Green. New York: Verso, 1993. [German orig., 1987].

Kraemer, Ross Shepard. "Jewish Women and Women's Judaism(s) at the Beginning of Christianity." In *Women and Christian Origins,* edited by Ross Shepard Kraemer and

Mary Rose D'Angelo, 50–79. Oxford: Oxford University Press, 1999.

Lefebvre, Georges. *The Great Fear of 1789: Rural Panic in Revolutionary France.* Translated by Joan White. New York: Pantheon, 1973.

Lendon, J. E. *Empire of Honour: The Art of Government in the Roman World.* Oxford: Clarendon, 1997.

Lenski, Gerhard. *Power and Privilege: A Theory of Social Stratification.* New York: McGraw-Hill, 1966.

Levine, Amy-Jill. "Discharging Responsibility: Matthean Jesus, Biblical Law, and Hemorrhaging Woman." In *Treasures Old and New: Recent Contributions in Matthean Studies,* edited by David R. Bauer and Mark Allan Powell, 383–95. SBL Symposium Series 1. Atlanta: Scholars, 1996.

Levine, Lee I. "The Jewish Patriarch (Nasi) in Third Century Palestine." In *Aufstieg und Niedergang der Römischen Welt* II.19.2 (1979) 649–88.

———. *The Rabbinic Class of Roman Palestine in Late Antiquity.* New York: Jewish Theological Seminary of America, 1989.

Lewis, I. M. *Ecstatic Religion: An Anthropological Study of Spirit Possession and Shamanism.* Pelican Anthropology Library. Harmandsworth, UK: Penguin, 1971.

Lock, Margaret. "On Being Ethnic: The Politics of Identity Breaking and Making in Canada, or Nevra on Sunday." *Culture, Medicine, and Psychiatry* 14 (1990) 237–54.

Lock, Margaret, and Nancy Scheper-Hughes. "A Critical-Interpretive Approach in Medical Anthropology: Rituals and Routines of Discipline and Dissent." In *Medical Anthropology: A Handbook of Theory and Method,* edited by Thomas M. Johnson and Carolyn F. Sargent, 47–72. London: Praeger, 1996.

Lopez, Donald S. *Curators of the Buddha: The Study of Buddhism under Colonialism.* Chicago: University of Chicago Press, 1995.

Luig, Ute. "Constructing Local Worlds: Spirit Possession in the Gwembe Valley, Zambia." In *Spirit Possession, Modernity & Power in Africa,* edited by Heike Behrend and Uta Luig, 124–41. Madison: University of Wisconsin Press, 1999.

Mack, Burton L. *A Myth of Innocence: Mark and Christian Origins.* Philadelphia: Fortress, 1988.

Mason, Steve. "Contradiction or Counterpoint? Josephus and Historical Method." *Review of Rabbinic Judaism* 6 (2003) 145–88.

———. *Flavius Josephus on the Pharisees: A Composition-Critical Study.* Studia Postbiblica 39. Leiden: Brill, 1991.

———. "Was Josephus a Pharisee? A Re-examination of *Life* 10–12." *Journal of Jewish Studies* 40 (1989) 31–45.

Mattern, Susan P. *Rome and the Enemy: Imperial Strategy in the Principate.* Berkeley: University of California Press, 1999.

McKinlay, John B. "A Case for Refocusing Upstream: The Political Economy of Illness." In *The Sociology of Health and Illness: Critical Perspectives,* edited by Peter Conrad and Rochelle Kern, 484–98. New York: St. Martin's, 1986.

Meier, John P. *A Marginal Jew: Rethinking the Historical Jesus.* Vol. 2: *Mentor, Message, and Miracles.* Anchor Bible Reference Library. New York: Doubleday, 1994.

———. *A Marginal Jew: Rethinking the Historical Jesus.* Vol. 3: *Companions and Competitors.* Anchor Bible Reference Library. New York: Doubleday, 2001.

Mendenhall, George H. *Law and Covenant in the Israel and the Ancient Near East.* Pittsburgh: Presbyterian Board of Colportage of Western Pennsylvania, 1955.

———. "Covenant." In *Interpreters' Dictionary of the Bible*, 1:714–23. Nashville: Abingdon, 1962.

Millar, Fergus. *The Roman Near East 31 B.C.–A.D. 337.* Cambridge: Harvard University Press, 1993.

Miller, Stewart S. *Studies in the History and Traditions of Sepphoris.* Studies in Judaism in Late Antiquity 37. Leiden: Brill, 1984.

Moore, Barrington, Jr. *The Social Origins of Dictatorship and Democracy: Lord and Peasant in the Making of the Modern World.* Boston: Beacon, 1966.

Moran, William L. "Law and Covenant in the Israel and the Ancient Near East." *Biblica* 41 (1960) 297–99.

Myers, Ched. *Binding the Strong Man: A Political Reading of Mark's Story of Jesus.* Maryknoll, NY: Orbis, 1988.

Neusner, Jacob. "'First Cleanse the Inside': The Halakic Background of a Controversy Saying." *New Testament Studies* 22 (1976) 486–95.

———. *From Politics to Piety: The Emergence of Pharisaic Judaism.* 2nd ed. 1979. Reprint, Eugene, OR: Wipf & Stock, 2003.

———. *Judaic Law from Jesus to the Mishnah: A Systematic Reply to Professor E. P. Sanders.* South Florida Studies in the History of Judaism 84. Atlanta: Scholars, 1993.

———. *The Rabbinic Traditions about the Pharisees before 70.* 3 vols. Leiden: Brill, 1971.

Neusner, Jacob, William S. Green, and Ernest Frerichs, eds. *Judaisms and Their Messiahs at the Turn of the Christian Era.* Cambridge: Cambridge University Press, 1987.

Nickelsburg, George W. E. *1 Enoch 1.* Hermeneia. Minneapolis: Fortress, 2001.

———. *Jewish Literature between the Bible and the Mishnah.* 2nd ed. Minneapolis: Fortress, 2005.

Nicolet, Claude. *Space, Geography, and Politics in the Early Roman Empire.* Jerome Lectures, 19th Series. Ann Arbor: University of Michigan Press, 1991.

Nock, Arthur Darby. "Paul and the *Magos.*" In *Essays on Religion and the Ancient World*, edited by Zeph Stewart, 308–10. Cambridge: Harvard University Press, 1972.

Ong, Aihwa. "The Production of Possession: Spirits and the Multinational Corporation in Malaysia." *American Ethnologist* 15 (1988) 28–42.

———. *Spirits of Resistance and Capitalist Discipline: Factory Women in Malaysia.* SUNY Series in the Anthropology of Work. Albany: State University of New York Press, 1987.

Onoge, Omafume. "Capitalism and Public Health: A Neglected Theme in the Medical Anthropology of Africa." In *Topias and Utopias in Health*, edited by Stanley R. Ingman and Anthony E. Thomas, 219–32. World Anthropology. The Hague: Mouton, 1975.

Parker, D. C. *The Living Text of the Gospels*. Cambridge: Cambridge University Press, 1997.

Pilch, John J. *Healing in the New Testament: Insights from Medical and Mediterranean Anthropology*. Minneapolis: Fortress, 2000.

Price, Simon R. F. *Rituals and Power: The Roman Imperial Cult in Asia Minor*. Cambridge: Cambridge University Press, 1984.

Räisänen, Heikki. "Jesus and the Food Laws: Reflections on Mark 7:15." *Journal for the Study of the New Testament* 16 (1982) 79–100.

Reed, Jonathan L. "The Sign of Jonah and Other Epic Traditions in Q." In *Re-imagining Christian Origins: Essays in Honor of Burton L. Mack*, edited by Elizabeth Castelli and Hal Taussig, 134–36. Valley Forge, PA: Trinity.

Rich, John, and Graham Shipley, ed. *War and Society in the Roman World*. Leicester-Nottingham Studies in Ancient Society 5. London: Routledge, 1993.

Richardson, Peter. *Herod: King of the Jews and Friend of the Romans*. Studies on Personalities of the New Testament. 1996. Reprint, Minneapolis: Fortress, 1999.

Rodgers, Zuleika, ed. *Making History: Josephus and Historical Method*. Journal for the Study of Judaism Supplements 110. Leiden: Brill, 2006.

Roller, Duane W. *The Building Program of Herod the Great*. Berkeley: University of California Press, 1998.

Rostovtzeff, M. *The Social and Economic History of the Hellenistic World*. 3 vols. Oxford: Oxford University Press, 1941.

Said, Edward W. *Orientalism*. New York: Random House, 1978.

———. *Culture and Imperialism*. New York: Random House, 1993.

Saldarini, Anthony J. *Pharisees, Scribes, and Sadducees in Palestinian Society: A Sociological Approach*. Wilmington, DE: Glazier, 1988.

Sanders, E. P. *Jesus and Judaism*. Minneapolis: Fortress, 1985.

———. *Jewish Law from Jesus to the Mishnah*. Philadelphia: Trinity, 1990.

———. *Judaism: Practice and Belief, 63 B.C.E.–66 C.E.* Philadelphia: Trinity, 1992.

———. *The Historical Figure of Jesus*. London: Penguin, 1993.

Satran, David. *Biblical Prophets in Byzantine Palestine: Reassessing the Lives of the Prophets*. Studia in Veteris Testamenti Pseudepigrapha 11. Leiden: Brill, 1995.

Schaper, Joachim. "The Jerusalem Temple as an Instrument of the Achaemenid Fiscal Administration." *Vetus Testamentum* 45 (1995) 528–39.

Scheper-Hughes, Nancy. "The Madness of Hunger: Sickness, Delirium, and Human Needs." *Culture, Medicine, and Psychiatry* 12 (1988) 189–97.

Schwartz, Seth. *Imperialism and Jewish Society: 200 B.C.E. to 640 C.E.* Princeton: Princeton University Press, 2001.

Schwemer, Anna Maria. *Studien zu den frühjüdischen Prophetenlegenden* Vitae Prophetarum. 2 vols. Texte und Studien zum Antiken Judentum 49, 50. Tübingen: Mohr/Siebeck, 1995.

Scott, James C. *Domination and the Arts of Resistance: Hidden Transcripts*. New Haven: Yale University Press, 1990.

———. *The Moral Economy of the Peasant: Rebellion and Subsistence in Southeast Asia.* New Haven: Yale University Press, 1976.

———. "Protest and Profanation: Agrarian Revolt and the Little Tradition." *Theory and Society* 4/1–2 (1977) 1–38, 211–46.

———. *Weapons of the Weak: Everyday Forms of Peasant Resistance.* New Haven: Yale University Press, 1985.

Shiner, Whitney. *Proclaiming the Gospel: First-Century Performance of Mark.* Harrisburg, PA: Trinity, 2003.

Singer, Merrill. "Reinventing Medical Anthropology: Toward a Critical Realignment." *Social Science and Medicine* 30 (1990) 179–87.

Skocpol, Theda. *States and Social Revolution: A Comparative Analysis of France, Russia, and China.* Cambridge: Cambridge University Press, 1979.

Small, Jocelyn Penny. *Wax Tablets of the Mind: Cognitive Studies of Memory and Literacy in Classical Antiquity.* New York: Routledge, 1997.

Smith, Morton. *Jesus the Magician.* San Francisco: Harper & Row, 1978.

Sundkler, Bengdt G. M. *Bantu Prophets in South Africa.* 1948. Reprint, Oxford: Oxford University Press, 1961.

Swartley, Willard M., ed. *The Love of Enemy and Nonretaliation in the New Testament.* Louisville: Westminster John Knox, 1992.

Taussig, Michael. "Reification and the Consciousness of the Patient." *Social Science and Medicine* 14B (1980) 3–13.

Tcherikover, Victor. *Hellenistic Civilization and the Jews.* Philadelphia: Jewish Publication Society of America, 1959.

Theissen, Gerd. *Sociology of Early Palestinian Christianity.* Translated by John Bowden. Philadelphia: Fortress, 1978.

Tuckett, Christopher M. *Q and the History of Early Christianity.* Peabody, MA: Hendrickson, 1996.

Ulrich, Eugene. *The Dead Sea Scrolls and the Origins of the Bible.* Studies in the Dead Sea Scrolls and Related Literature. Grand Rapids: Eerdmans, 1999.

Veer, Peter van der. *Imperial Encounters: Religion and Modernity in India and Britain.* Princeton: Princeton University Press, 2001.

Vermes, Geza. *The Complete Dead Sea Scrolls in English.* London: Penguin, 1997.

Veyne, Paul. *Bread and Circuses: Historical Sociology and Political Pluralism.* Translated by Brian Pearce. London: Penguin, 1990.

Wallace-Hadrill, Andrew. "The Emperor and His Virtues." *Historia* 30 (1981) 322–23.

Webb, Robert L. *John the Baptizer and Prophet: A Socio-historical Study.* 1991. Reprint, Eugene, OR: Wipf & Stock, 2006.

Wheeler, E. L. "Methodological Limits and the Mirage of Roman Strategy." *Journal of Military History* 57 (1993) 35–36.

Wild, Robert A. "The Encounter between Pharisees and Christian Judaism: Some Early Gospel Evidence." *Novum Testamentum* 27 (1985) 105–24.

Wills, Lawrence M. *The Quest of the Historical Gospel: Mark, John, and the Origins of the Gospel Genre*. London: Routledge, 1997.

Wilson, Bryan. *Magic and the Millennium: A Sociological Study of Religious Movements of Protest among Tribal and Third-World Peoples*. New York: Harper & Row, 1973.

Wire, Antoinette Clark. *The Case for Mark Composed in Oral Performance*. Biblical Performance Criticism Series 3. Eugene, OR: Cascade, 2011.

Wolf, Eric. *Peasant Wars of the Twentieth Century*. New York: Harper & Row, 1969.

Wright, N. T. *Jesus and the Victory of God*. Christian Origins and the Question of God 2. Minneapolis: Fortress, 1996.

———. *The New Testament and the People of God*. Christian Origins and the Question of God 1. Minneapolis: Fortress, 1992.

Young, Allan. "The Anthropology of Illness and Sickness." *Annual Review of Anthropology* 11 (1982) 257–85.

Zanker, Paul. *The Power of Images in the Age of Augustus*. Translated by Alan Shapiro. Jerome Lectures, 16th Series. Ann Arbor: University of Michigan Press, 1988.

Index of Ancient Documents

∾ ∾ ∾

New Testament
Matthew

∾ ∾ ∾

❦ ❦ ❦

Dead Sea Scrolls

1QapGen (Genesis Apocryphon)

1QpHab (Habakkuk Commentary)

1QS (Community Rule)

ꙍ ꙍ ꙍ

Rabbinic Writings

Babylonian Talmud

Mishnah

Mekilta

Index of Subjects

CPSIA information can be obtained
at www.ICGtesting.com
Printed in the USA
LVHW111908140722
723438LV00002B/195